EXPLORING THE
LAKELAND FELLS

EXPLORING
— THE —
LAKELAND FELLS

Tom Lawton

Photographs by the author

Diagrams in collaboration with Dr. William Rouse

WARD LOCK

This book is dedicated to my wife Bridget,
and my two daughters Katrina and Helen, with whom
I have made many pleasurable excursions into
the Lakeland Fells from our base in the Langdales.

I will lift up mine eyes unto the hills:
from whence cometh my strength . . .
121st Psalm

First published in Great Britain in 1993
by Ward Lock Limited, Villiers House, 41/47 Strand,
London WC2N 5JE, England
A Cassell Imprint

Text filmset by August Filmsetting, Haydock, St Helens.

Printed and bound in Slovenia
by printing house
DELO Tiskarna by arrangement with Korotan Italiana

British Library Cataloguing in Publication Data
A catalogue record for this book is available from the British Library

ISBN 0–7063–7064–3

Contents

Preface 7

Author's Acknowledgements 7

1 USING THE BOOK 9

2 THE NORTHERN FELLS Part 1 13
Route 1 Skiddaw 13
Route 2 Bleaberry Fell and High Seat 19

3 THE NORTHERN FELLS Part 2 25
Route 3 Blencathra 25
Route 4 High Rigg and St John's 33

4 THE NORTH-WEST AND WESTERLY FELLS Part 1 37
Route 5 Grasmoor and Grisedale Pike 37
Route 6 Thornthwaite Forest and Lord's Seat 43

5 THE NORTH-WEST AND WESTERLY FELLS Part 2 49
Route 7 Dale Head, Hindscarth and Robinson 49
Route 8 Hause Gate and Grange Crags 55

6 THE NORTH-WEST AND WESTERLY FELLS Part 3 59
Route 9 Hay Stacks and High Stile Group 59
Route 10 Mosedale and Crummock Water 65

7 THE NORTH-WEST AND WESTERLY FELLS Part 4 69
Route 11 Pillar and Red Pike 69
Route 12 Ennerdale 75

8 THE CENTRAL FELLS Part 1 79
Route 13 Burnmoor Tarn and Sca Fell 79
Route 14 Eskdale and Harter Fell 83

9 THE CENTRAL FELLS Part 2 89
Route 15 Scafell Pike and Bow Fell 89
Route 16 Pike of Blisco and Blea Tarn 95

10 THE CENTRAL FELLS Part 3   99
   Route 17   Great Gable and Glaramara   99
   Route 18   Watendlath and Lodore   105

11 THE CENTRAL FELLS Part 4   111
   Route 19   Crinkle Crags and Bow Fell   111
   Route 20   Lingmoor Fell and Side Pike   117

12 THE CENTRAL FELLS Part 5   121
   Route 21   Sergeant Man and the Langdale Pikes   121
   Route 22   Silver How and Rydal   127

13 THE CENTRAL FELLS Part 6   131
   Route 23   Helvellyn   131
   Route 24   Ullscarf and Dead Pike   137

14 THE CENTRAL FELLS Part 7   143
   Route 25   Fairfield Horseshoe   143
   Route 26 Wansfell Pike and Troutbeck   149

15 THE EASTERLY FELLS Part 1   153
   Route 27   High Street and Red Screes   153
   Route 28   Boredale and Ullswater   159

16 THE EASTERLY FELLS Part 2   163
   Route 29   Kentmere Horseshoe   163
   Route 30   Lower Kentmere   169

17 THE CONISTON FELLS   175
   Route 31   Dow Crag, Coniston Old Man and Wetherlam 175
   Route 32   Tarn Hows and Tilberthwaite   181

   Appendix 1: Relevant Addresses   186
   Appendix 2: Statistical Summary   188

   Publisher's Acknowledgements   189

   Index   190

Preface

I have always been an impatient reader of introductions and so this one will be short.

It was John Ruskin who said 'Mountains are the beginning and the end of all natural scenery'. This book is about mountains, exploring them on foot, and it begins and ends with this. The area covered by these explorations is the English Lake District, where the mountains are called fells. The Lakeland Fells have for ages been a source of pleasure, relaxation, challenge and inspiration to many, ranging from world-famous writers and poets to lesser mortals like you and I.

All of us, however, share a common bond based on the ecological concept that the mountains of the Lake District are a community. The distinguished American ecologist Aldo Leopold wrote, 'when we see the land as a community to which we belong, we may begin to use it with love and respect'. All serious fell-walkers, may I suggest, identify with this poignant concept.

My selected explorations of the Lakeland Fells are described by a detailed text and illustrated with colour photographs and innovative diagrams that have been generated by computer techniques. My hopes are that this presentation will give further purpose to seasoned fell-walkers, and provide encouragement to those who have yet to venture on foot into these mountains. Should either of these aspirations become fulfilled to any significant extent, my efforts will have been well rewarded.

T. L.

Author's Acknowledgements

I am indebted to a vast number of kind people for their generous contributions to this book. Without their help and encouragement the book, in its published form, would never have seen the light of day. To all these people may I place on record my warm appreciation of their efforts, together with my grateful thanks.

There are some contributors who deserve a more specific mention. Heading this list must be, collectively, the walking companions who accompanied me on researching the routes; we shared some great times together on the fells and my memories are of the good things that happened to us up there. It has been only a constraint on space that has prevented this valuable contribution from being more deservedly recorded.

My special thanks are due to Bill Rouse, a friend of long standing and a fellow walking enthusiast. His collaboration on the computer diagrams has been invaluable. We spent many a long evening together before he was satisfied with the outcome!

I am grateful to Eddie Fidler and Bernard McLoughlin for checking through the text and diagrams, to Heather Green for arranging the duplication of the manuscript and to David Sellors and Ian Morris for their help with the computer output.

The text has been read by several experts including Dr Fred Broadhurst, now teaching geology at the Department of Extra Mural Studies, University of Manchester, and the Rangers from both the Lake District National Park and the Forestry Commission. I thank these knowledgeable people for their guidance, and for their helpful, constructive suggestions.

I talked to many fellow walking enthusiasts while on the fells and these pleasant exchanges of views provided additional stimulation for my writings.

My final acknowledgement must record my debt of gratitude to my wife and two daughters who put up with seeing so little of me while I was either roaming the fells or sitting glued to my computer.

1
USING THE BOOK

The main objective of this book is to provide a collection of interesting walking routes in the Lakeland Fells that comprehensively cover the higher mountains, and also a selection of the lower ones. The walks are presented clearly and concisely, with diagrams and photographs to provide an authoritative and appealing collection of routes. The text describes the routes in some detail, and points out other fells and mountain features of interest as these are observed, given favourable weather, along each walk.

Arrangement

Thirty-two walking routes are covered and these have been arranged into 16 sections of 2 walks each. Each section is comprised of a high-level route and an associated lower-level route. Wherever possible, starting locations from a car-park convenient for both routes have been chosen. The route directions commence from these car-parks.

Nearly half the routes are located in the Central Fells, with the remainder dispersed among the more peripheral mountains, i.e.:

WALKING AREA	ROUTES
The Northern Fells	4
The NW and Westerly Fells	8
The Central Fells	14
The Easterly Fells	4
The Coniston Fells	2
Total	32

In total the 32 walking routes cover over 500 km (300 miles), which is about the same distance as from London to Keswick. The cumulative height climbed is approaching 30,000 m (over 90,000 ft), which is more than three times higher than Mount Everest!

The characteristics of the high level and lower level of walks are summarized in the following table:

CHARACTERISTIC	HIGH LEVEL ROUTES		LOWER LEVEL ROUTES	
	From	To	From	To
Walking time hours	5.5	9.0	4.5	7.0
Walking distance (excluding height) kilometres	12.9	21.1	10.2	18.0
miles	8.0	13.1	6.3	11.2
Total height gained metres	900	1650	240	750
feet	2953	5413	787	2461
Highest peak metres	736	978	270	726
feet	2414	3210	885	2370

Diagrams

There is a diagram for each route giving a plan, a cross-sectional relief and pertinent statistics for the walk. These diagrams have been computer-generated and are based upon grid reference points down-loaded from Ordnance Survey maps – the Outdoor Leisure Series 1 : 25000 – 4 cm to 1 km ($2\frac{1}{2}$ in to 1 mile).

The relief cross-section is mathematically integral with the plan. This relief is wrapped out from the starting location and accurately follows the exact line of the route so that if the same fell is climbed twice, e.g., Helvellyn on Route 23, the summit is also displayed twice in the correct approach sequence.

Camera symbols locate the position and direction of each photograph. These have been allocated a distinctive number identical to that referenced beneath each photograph as part of its caption. The first part of the number indicates the route, while the second part refers to the sequence of the photographs within each route. Photographs taken along the route are indicated by the camera symbol pointing either along or away from the line of the walk, whereas photographs taken of the route from other locations are identified by the camera symbol pointing inwards from the edge of the plan.

Estimates of walking time have been provided, and these include allowances for all stops, including lunch. The estimates have been calculated by allowing 1 hour to walk each 4 km (2½ miles), plus an allowance of a further 1 hour for each 600 m (2,000 ft) climbed, plus 1 hour for lunch and all other stops, and a final adjustment of plus or minus up to ½ hour per walk, depending upon additional factors, such as the degree of difficulty of route finding, state of the paths, type of terrain and so on. You can adjust these basic estimates to suit your own capabilities.

In the statistics it will be observed that in some of the routes where the walk is essentially one long up and down, sometimes the total height gained is less than the height of the principal peak. This is due to the height of the starting position, which needs to be subtracted from the highest peak when making valid comparisons between these two heights.

Photographs

On average each section of two walks is illustrated by three colour photographs, usually two photographs of the high level route and one of the lower route. The photographs have been taken with a Canon EOS 650 camera using a standard 50 mm lens and a 35–135 mm zoom lens, in each case with polarizing filters. Fujichrome 100 colour-slide film has been used exclusively.

Abbreviations

The minimum number of abbreviations has been used, and only to avoid constant repetition. These are listed below, starting with the familiar directional signals and compass bearings.

L	left	NNW	north-north-west
R	right	cm	centimetre(s)
N	north	CMS	Cumberland
NNE	north-north-east		Motor Services
NE	north-east	cp	car-park
ENE	east-north-east	ft	feet
E	east	k-gate	kissing-gate
ESE	east-south-east	km	kilometre
SE	south-east	l-stile	ladder-stile
SSE	south-south-east	m	metre(s)
S	south	mm	millimetre(s)
SSW	south-south-west	MR	map reference
SW	south-west	OLM	Outdoor Leisure
WSW	west-south-west		Map
W	west	OS	Ordnance Survey
WNW	west-north-west	p-stile	post-stile
NW	north-west	yd	yard(s)

Miscellaneous

MAPS AND COMPASS
No guide book is an adequate substitute for maps and a compass. Use the Ordnance Survey Outdoor Leisure maps previously referred to and a reliable compass at all times when you are walking in the Lakeland Fells. Be sure that you know how to use this combination correctly.

COMPASS BEARINGS
All compass bearings have been given to the nearest $22\frac{1}{2}°$ point, e.g., N, NNE, NE, etc. This is considered to be sufficiently accurate over the relatively small distances travelled between the taking of successive readings. Note that some Lakeland rocks contain minerals with magnetic properties and therefore certain compass bearings will not be true; this is particularly prevalent in the vicinity of Bow Fell. Therefore take frequent bearings, particularly when visibility is poor.

DYNAMICS

The human features of Lakeland are constantly changing, fences appear and disappear, k-gates replace l-stiles and vice-versa, additional way-marker signs appear, some signs get removed and so on. Therefore should you locate isolated differences along the route from those described, presume that these have occurred since the book went to press, and proceed with confidence to the next feature mentioned.

RECORDED HEIGHTS OF FELLS

The heights of the major fells have been given in both metric and imperial measurements extracted from relevant Ordnance Survey maps. There are some minor anomalies between the two sets of

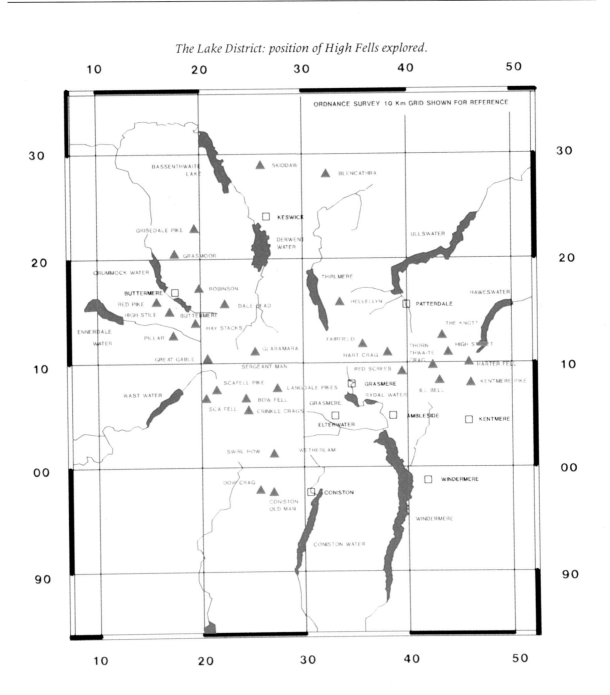

The Lake District: position of High Fells explored.

measurements that are not explained by rounding off differences.

SPELLING

Sometimes there is more than one version of the spelling of place names. In such instances the spelling that appears on the OS OLM's has been used, unless otherwise indicated.

ORDNANCE SURVEY MAPS

The Ordnance Survey maps are excellent but not infallible! On the rare occasions where there are differences between the route descriptions and the paths shown, or not shown, as the case may be, on the OS maps, rely on the route descriptions.

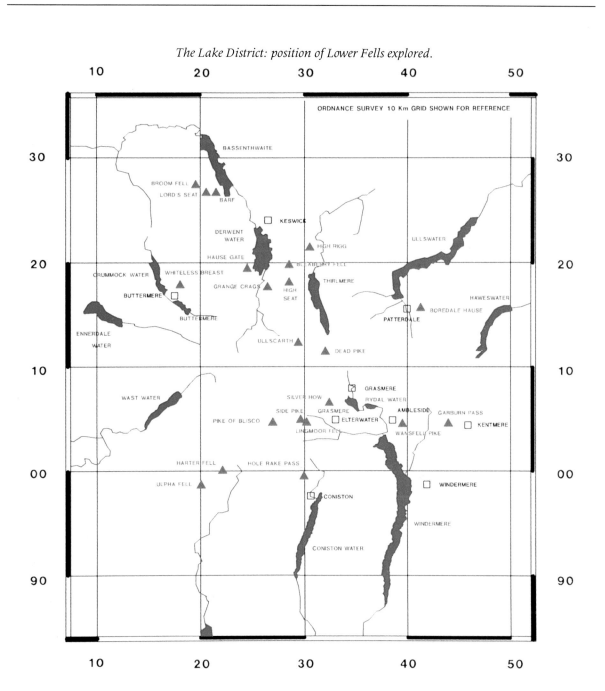

The Lake District: position of Lower Fells explored.

SKIDDAW

High Level Route 1

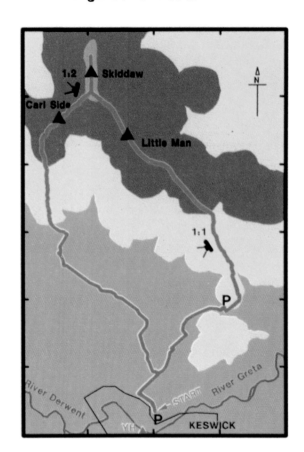

SOUTH–NORTH (Km)

WEST–EAST (Km)

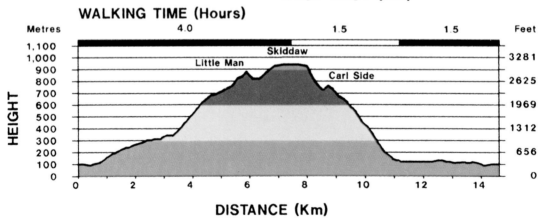

WALKING TIME (Hours)

DISTANCE (Km)

STATISTICS

START and FINISH
- Keswick Old Station CP - OLM 4 / MR 270237

WALKING DISTANCE	Km	Miles
- Excluding Height	14.5	9.0
- Including Height	14.8	9.2

TOTAL WALKING TIME : 7.0 Hours

TOTAL HEIGHT GAINED
- 980 Metres 3215 Feet

PRINCIPAL HEIGHTS	Metres	Feet
- Little Man	865	2837
- Skiddaw	931	3053
- Carl Side	746	2448

OTHER FEATURES OF INTEREST
- Fine views across Derwent Water into Borrowdale, Newlands Valley & NW Fells.

2
THE NORTHERN FELLS
Part 1

Route 1 · Skiddaw

Allow 7 hours

STARTING LOCATION
Car-park at Keswick old railway station.
OLM 4/MR 270237.
Large car-park.
CMS bus routes 34/35, 58, 79, 104, 555, and 720.
Motor launch Derwent Water.

OVERVIEW/INTEREST
Long gruelling initial climb.
Superb views down over Derwent Water.
Exhilarating fast descent.
Return through delightful meadows and villages.
Strenuous rewarding route.

FOOTPATHS
Good and certain for most of the way.
Top section of the descent requires care.

SW	Glaramara and Allen Crags. Great End and Scafell Pike on the distant horizon. Cat Bells, Maiden Moor, and High Spy Ridge, leading to Dale Head, Hindscarth and Robinson. Pillar and High Stile Ridge peeping out, with Derwent Water and Keswick nestling below.
WSW	Causey Pike, Scar Crags and Sail Ridge, climbing to Crag Hill and Grasmoor beyond.
W	Grisedale Pike and Sand Hill.
NW	Lord's Seat and Barf.
NNW	Bassenthwaite Lake.
N	Skiddaw.

The way to Skiddaw
Allow 4 hours

Leave the car park to the N and cross the round-about. Continue up the lane leading to Briar Rigg, which you veer L along, passing a junction to your R signed 'Windebrowe Brundholme'. There is a footpath on the R along here for part of the way. Then turn R along Spoony Green Lane, which is signed 'Public Bridleway Skiddaw'. The lane crosses the main A66 road and a wide gravel path leads uphill into the Skiddaw foothills.

At the second k-gate move to the wire fence on your L, and then turn around to enjoy the superb panorama spread out below to the S. The main features in it are:

The bridleway then winds up the folds of the grassy fellside and crosses small culverts, which have nicked V shapes in the otherwise rounded slopes. Plantings of conifers are skirted to your L, and following this, the path reaches the end of a road at which point a car-park is located.

Turn R through this car-park, exit via the stile or k-gate at the far end, and select the path signed 'Public Bridleway Skiddaw Bassenthwaite Mosedale' NE. Way over on your R Clough Head and The Dodds appear to the SE with the vast slopes of Helvellyn to their R (SSE). The lower, pointed hills of Little and Great Mell Fells are also visible to the E. Two k-gates now have to be negotiated

13

before you continue by way of the L fork alongside a wire fence.

Your route veers NNW and soon an impressive monumental cross is reached. This is in memory of several shepherds, two of whom were breeders of prize Herdwick sheep. The monument bears a poignant inscription:

Great Shepherd of thy Heavenly Flock
These men have left our hill
Their feet were on the living rock
Oh guide and bless them still.

Cross the brow ahead and then you have a short downwards respite before the climb begins with tackling the steep gradient ahead. Take the path to the R of the eroded ground, which is indicated with short, wooden marker posts, following the route nearest to Whit Beck on your R. When you have gained some height, you will be rewarded by new sightings to your rear:

SW   Low and High Rigg positioned beneath Helvellyn.
S   Bleaberry Fell, High Raise and Langdale Pikes.
SSW   Bow Fell and Esk Pike.
SW   Newlands Valley.

A gate and stiles are reached. Afterwards grit your teeth and climb the steep, relentless slopes up the wide pathways that ascend the heather-clad fell. Your direction is generally N. Eventually the demanding gradient slackens off as the way up swings more to the NW. To give you encouragement here the tops of the peaks leading to Little Man pop up to the NNW. At this point the W slopes of Blencathra appear on your R, to the E.

Your way now curves round the fellside at a shallow rate of ascent. When you again reach steeper ground to your L, a fence crosses the bridleway with an access stile positioned in it. This is Jenkin Hill. Here take the narrower path that climbs up the slope on your L to the NW to attain the rocky crag higher up, marked by a distinctive cairn of rocks and tangled, rusty, iron railings. From this cairn continue climbing NNW to reach the summit of Little Man, a short distance higher up. From the top of this conical fell the broad

rounded summit of Skiddaw, higher still to the NNW, beckons you on.

Descend to the NNW, keeping to the higher ground of the connecting ridge. In inclement weather locate the fence to your R, and follow this until, some distance further on, it turns abruptly away to the R from your direction of travel. A hause is reached and then the ground rises once more to the N, and your narrow path, after scaling this, rejoins the main route up Skiddaw. You turn L along this broad path to reach the extensive summit area.

Continue along the summit ridge, which passes numerous cairns and rounded shelters before the summit cairn, large shelter, trig. point and rounded commemoration configuration are reached. These features lie at 931 m (3,053 ft). Before absorbing the breathtaking panorama from here, descend just a little further N, to the end shelter, for a view down from this furthermost point of your route across the flat plain that lies to the N of the Lake District. Then retrace your steps to the trig. point and enjoy the vast competing views all around you, weather permitting.

You will already be aware of most of these, but in very clear weather try to spot the Isle of Man, which may be visible to the WSW, and the Solway Firth in the NNW. Nearer to the superb ridge below you to the WSW is Longside Edge leading to Ullock Pike, which you will see closer to hand during your adventurous descent route.

The way to Millbeck   *Allow 1½ hours*

Start your descent by retracing your approach steps, this time southwards, along the summit ridge. Just before the main path veers to the L (SE), there are two aligned cairns pointing to a narrower path that descends to the SW and this is your route down. The narrow path, a little indistinct in places, zigzags down the loose, leaden, grey slates at a frightening rate of descent. Be careful here because the broken slate is slippery. Pause from

1:1 Looking down Borrowdale from the lower slopes of Skiddaw.

time to time going down, not just to arrest your momentum, but also to take in the stupendous view below you. This is of the broad green rounded hause below Carl Side, the tiny blue tarn nestling in its bosom, and the slaty spurs leading from the hause in several directions. Of all these outcrops the serrated top of Longside Edge is the most riveting.

The steep path will lead you quite quickly down to the hause. From here head off uphill to your L, which is sw, along a diagonal traverse to reach the top of Carl Side, on which a large cairn stands. Veer to the L from the top and descend ssw down a good, gravel and clay path on a long traverse to the R. The broad dark spur of Carsleddam appears to your L as you surrender more height. Your unwavering straight path brings you to an unusual grouping of quartz rocks, named White Stones. This is a favourite perch for walkers, and a good place to pause.

Thread your way downwards through the outcrop of rocks and descend s down the good gravel path that leads through the heather-laden fellside. A gap is used to breach a stone wall, and then you are faced with further very steep lines of descent over grassy slopes, crossing a fence part of the way down. Continue downhill over the final grassy sward to reach the hamlet of Millbeck. Turn R at the bottom with the dwelling of Ben-Y-Craig on your L, and a short distance further on turn L into the more distinct country lane.

The way back to Keswick   *Allow 1½ hours*

The lane crosses Mill Beck and then leads slightly uphill towards the village of Applethwaite. It is possible to descend to a footpath here, running below and parallel to your route, but you are advised to continue along the quiet lane as the footpath can be like a quagmire at times and the higher elevation provides better views.

A war memorial is passed on your L situated near the Underskiddaw Church Room. After this, take the next turning downhill on your R, passing a small line of dwellings bordering the L side of the lane. Opposite a detached house named Toftgarth

turn R down the bridleway. This bends to the L, passes Croft Head Farm, and then meets up again with the lane ahead. Veer L here onto the lane and then turn immediately off it to the R, down the footpath by the side and to the R of the establishment recently renamed Field View.

Cross the stream by the elevated stone surround, and further on ignore the path through the gate, continuing along a more discrete path signed 'Public footpath Underscar' to the L of a second gate. Proceed up the wooden steps here, pass over two p-stiles that provide access through a holly hedge. There is now a small stream running to your L as further on you encounter another k-gate before you cross a field on a diagonal line to your R, walking sse. Pass through a gate, bearing a 'footpath' sign, in the far corner of the parkland, having first crossed a stream, and continue by the side of a castellated beech hedge that delineates the boundary of the grounds of Ormathwaite Hall to your L.

At the track ahead, turn L through iron gates on to a surfaced road, then R to follow the lane past the Hall and farm buildings on your L. After another gate turn R down the more pronounced road ahead. Some distance along this road locate a path off on your L, signed 'Public Footpath', and turn down this by passing through the k-gate. Next follow the elevated cart track, pass through a further k-gate, and then, still on the cart track, pass under the spreading branches of a large oak tree through which smaller ash trees are growing. Continue across the field until you approach a hedge with an iron gate in it. Then find a p-stile some 15 or so paces above and to the L of the gate, and proceed over this to cross a wire fence. This is a critical manoeuvre.

Over the wire fence, cross a small culvert by means of a wooden beam and then walk up the brow of the field at a diagonal to the s to reach a fence coming in on your R. Follow the line of this to pass above the buildings ahead. The way then leads to a k-gate a short distance further on. This provides entry to the lane along which you walked some hours earlier. Turn R here and follow your departure route back to the car-park a short distance away.

Alternative routes

1:2 Ullock Pike and Longside Edge from the upper slopes of Skiddaw.

ESCAPES

If you decide to give up anywhere before you reach the top of Skiddaw, simply turn around and retrace your approach steps to lower ground, where you can select from a variety of alternative paths to walk back to the car-park at Keswick.

Not climbing Little Man saves marginal time and effort at the expense of sticking to the relatively boring alternative main path below this peak.

To return along your ascent route from the top of Skiddaw, as many other walkers will do, is less adventurous but also less demanding than the described round.

EXTENSIONS

From the higher slopes of Skiddaw it is feasible to return by way of Blencathra by travelling fast across the intervening slopes to the N of Longscale and Blease Fells. If you decide to have a go at this, come off Blencathra down the spur of Blease Fell along the path that descends to near the Blencathra Centre. From here there are paths leading you back to the higher car-park that you passed through on your outward route, situated at MR 281254.

Another shorter extension is a traverse along Longside Edge to Ullock Pike and back as part of your descent route.

17

BLEABERRY FELL and HIGH SEAT

Lower Level Route 2

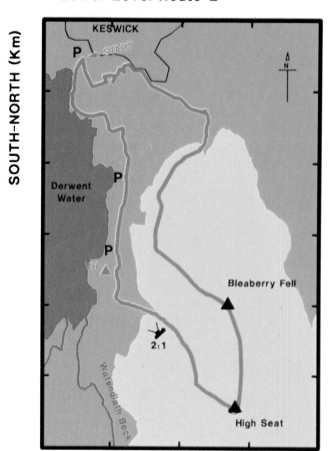

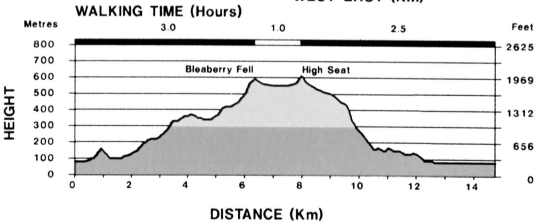

STATISTICS

START and FINISH
- Keswick (Nr. Lake) - OLM 4 / MR 265228

WALKING DISTANCE	Km	Miles
- Excluding Height	14.7	9.2
- Including Height	14.9	9.3

TOTAL WALKING TIME : 6.5 Hours

TOTAL HEIGHT GAINED
- 700 Metres   2300 Feet

PRINCIPAL HEIGHTS	Metres	Feet
- Bleaberry Fell	590	1932
- High Seat	608	1995

OTHER FEATURES OF INTEREST
- Fine views of Derwent Water and Skiddaw; climbers on Falcon Crag.

Route 2 · Bleaberry Fell and High Seat

Allow 6½ hours

The way to Bleaberry Fell   *Allow 3 hours*

Depart from the car-park through the gap in the stone wall near to the Century Theatre. Once on the path through here fork L. You are now in a fine, mature deciduous woodland, passing through glades of mainly beech trees. Your direction of travel is SSE. At a crossing of paths just before reaching a large sycamore tree, turn L down a hawthorn-edged path leading to the B5289 road. Along here there is a good view of Skiddaw rearing up to your L in the N.

Cross the road, pass through a gap in the wall, and climb the steps. Follow the path uphill, initially to your L, and then immediately fork to the R and proceed further uphill on a wide gravel path NE. Veer round to the R and climb the slope to reach the rocky promontory of Castlehead Crag. This outcrop provides excellent views overlooking Derwent Water to the W, and the following can be identified from here:

SSE	Walla Crag.
SSW	Borrowdale and Scafell Pike beyond.
SW	Maiden Moor and Cat Bells.
WSW	Robinson and the Newlands Valley.
	Causey Pike and Crag Hill.
W	Grisedale Pike.
NNW	Barf and The Bishop Rock.
	Bassenthwaite Lake.
N	Skiddaw.

To return to the main path below, retrace your final approach steps leading to the crag, and then turn R along this heading SSW. Follow the path down through the densely packed deciduous wood of mainly beech, oak and sycamore trees. You then take a L fork, and pass through a k-gate leading to a second edged pathway, which you proceed along. This leads to Springs Lane. Turn R along it, walking slightly uphill. A beck is then crossed by a stone bridge. Continue through Springs Farm, passing gates and reassuring signs, one of which reads 'Rakefoot Stone Circle'.

The stony path leads uphill into Springs Wood with its less mature trees, as a beck appears down below on your L. The way then bends to your R, from ESE to SSE, and is signed 'Rakefoot Farm Walla Crag Castlerigg Stone Circle'. Then you veer R away from a path on your L that descends to the beck. Your way continues to climb, now squeezed between trees and a fence and lane. The lane provides access up to a communication pylon.

After coming to a stile and k-gate continue ahead ignoring a path off to your R to 'Great Wood'. You then walk SE up a path with a wire fence to your R and a steep-sided wooded gully on your L through which a beck flows. Another k-gate follows and then a yellow arrowhead waymarker confirms your direction of travel. Continue through a pleasant dell before reaching a wider path, along which you turn. You then cross the stream at a narrow footbridge, climb the steps on the far side and pass through a gate to reach a lane. Turn R here and walk towards Rakefoot.

The lane bends to the R in the direction signed 'Walla Crag' and a farm is passed to your L. Next

19

cross the beck to your R by the wooden footbridge, turn immediately L and take the stony footpath leading uphill alongside a stone wall SW. Further up look around for a fine unobstructed view of Skiddaw NNW, Blencathra NNE and down to Keswick with Bassenthwaite Lake beyond to the NW. A p-stile is reached and here there is a National Trust sign indicating 'Castlerigg'. Your good path continues up the wide grassy band veering to the R and heading S to SW as it follows the line of the dry-stone wall. Then the rounded heights of Bleaberry Fell, your first major target, come into view over on your L, to the S.

After passing through another k-gate the stony path leads round the more revealing edge of the fellside. Just beyond, some magnificent views open up across Derwent Water, right into the heart of the folded, high north-westerly fells. To the SW are Hindscarth and Robinson towering above Cat Bells, the Causey Pike ridge rising to the dominating mass of Crag Hill W and further to the R the separate, distinctive peak of Grisedale Pike rises in the NW; and these are only a selection of the highlights! You may also have the thrill of seeing falcons along here.

Advance along the well-used path close to the edge of the cliff-face of Walla Crag, which drops very steeply on your R through densely wooded slopes with intermittent rocky promontories jutting out. When you reach the next cairned, craggy outcrop of rocks at Lady's Rake you will be able to view the mighty Helvellyn range of mountains. These stand out on the SE skyline over to your L. From here descend slightly along the grassy path leading down SSW. Near the stile ahead, which you cross, the shapely, far-off peak of Bow Fell can be made out on a clear day on compass bearing SSW. Turn R over the wall and when you reach the cairn below, fork L to the SSE, and continue through the high moorland opening out to your L. Just past two further cairns, locate a less distinct track that branches L away from the main path, and this will lead you SE towards Bleaberry Fell. The landscape now changes quite abruptly, and soon you are walking through an open terrain of bracken, heathers and scrubland above the tree-line, save for one solitary ash tree.

2:1 Looking westward across Derwent Water to Grisedale Pike.

The ground underfoot becomes boggy in parts here, and this, unfortunately, is a taste of what is to come further on. You then cross a small beck above a miniature waterfall, and following more soggy patches, a firm grassy path becomes clearly established. Make for the rocky plug ahead to the S under the lee of which the remains of a dilapidated sheepfold still stand. Your path bends to the L of this structure, and then ascends further in a broad sweep to the L across more boggy ground to reach the final, severe slopes of Bleaberry Fell away to the ESE. The worst parts of these hags demand careful and wide detours, particularly after prolonged heavy rain. This area is, however, a site of

special scientific interest and therefore merits minimum disturbance.

Next comes the ascent of the rocky mound of Bleaberry Fell. A large marker cairn is passed at the top of the steepest part of the climb, after which a wide stony path leads s over moderately rising ground to bring you to another equally impressive cairn at the summit. Bleaberry Fell rises to 590 m (1,932 ft), and its isolated summit commands open views in all directions. You will already be familiar with most of these, but one further revelation is the relatively low-lying, but nevertheless, very interesting separated ridge of Low and High Rigg to be seen to the NE.

The way to High Seat   *Allow 1 hour*

Continue along the path s from the summit of Bleaberry Fell towards the craggy promontory of High Seat some 2 km (1¼ miles) away. The way undulates through less distinctive terrain, which in the hollows becomes somewhat featureless. Small narrow tarns are passed tucked away in the many folds of the fells you are walking over. Keep to the highest ground whenever you can, always tracking between s and ssw towards the approaching outline of High Seat.

There is one particularly frustrating spot along here. Eventually your path will lead you to a newly

21

constructed taut wire fence that runs across your way forward. A minimal low stile has been provided for you to get across. The problem is on the other side. The land is quite boggy, especially along the line of the fence to your L, which appears to be the way the interfered-with path is intended to lead you. There are alternative ways forward, either directly ahead, or by circumventing the nasty wet area on the rising ground to the R. None of these alternatives is entirely satisfactory, and in wet conditions you will have done well if you manage to keep your boots dry here.

Through the worst of the boggy area take a diagonal line to your L to reach a well-defined path ahead bordered by defunct fenceposts. Turn R along this sanctuary and climb to the summit of High Seat at 608 m (1,995 ft). There are magnificent 360° views from this interesting craggy top. From the direction of the new view of Thirlmere reservoir SE the following extensive summarized panorama, locked into main compass bearings, is revealed in fine weather:

SE   Catstye Cam, Helvellyn and Fairfield.
S   Steel Fell, Ullscarf, High Raise and Pike of Stickle.
SW   Crinkle Crags, Bow Fell, Esk Pike, Glaramara, Great End and The Scafells, Borrowdale and The Gables.
W   Pillar, Dale Head, Hindscarth and Robinson.
NW   Whiteless Pike, Grasmoor, Crag Hill, Hopegill Head and Grisedale Pike.
N   Derwent Water, Bassenthwaite Lake, Skiddaw and Bleaberry Fell.
NE   Blencathra and The Dodds.

The way back to Keswick   *Allow 2½ hours*

Descend from High Seat through heathers along a grassy path leading NW. At the division of the ways veer to your L. Continue towards the rocky promontories and hillocks ahead on which cairns have been positioned. You will have to contend with more wet, soggy patches before you reach firmer ground ahead. This is attained after crossing the remains of a dry-stone wall at rising ground

further on. Veer R here along the distinct path before continuing NW and making for a cairn on the near horizon. In this area there are several variants possible, and your exact route will depend upon how many of the rocky crags you wish to visit along the edge of the high ground overlooking Derwent Water. Whatever else you do in this area, do not yet surrender significant height to the W, and quickly abandon any paths, including cairned ones, leading steeply down in that direction.

Continue to work your way along the tops between N and NW, forging your own route among the mounds with the aid of paths that start and finish with bewildering complexity. Your next goal is a prominent fell above Ashness Gill, which is a meeting point of the ways. From this confluence of minor and indistinct tracks, a definite, narrow, stony path leads down, initially in the direction of Bleaberry Fell ENE. The descent becomes steeper as the path bends northwards to transport you quickly to the stream below. The final section is quite difficult, down a packed earth shoot, where secure footholds are not easy to maintain.

The stream at the bottom compensates for the exacting descent. Continue down round the spur of the fellside along the clearly marked pathway, with Ashness Gill below in the rocky gully to your R. Your path then rounds a pleasant terraced traverse, and the way continues through heathers and bracken. The path drops to a l-stile, and then you continue downhill to reach the road near Ashness Bridge. Turn R and cross the famous Ashness Bridge.

Take the footpath immediately to your R snaking up the fellside to a crooked l-stile ahead. There is a sign here that reads 'Footpath to Great Wood and Keswick'. Select the lower path, which descends gradually to the N. The stony way traverses along the fellside, undulating through sparse hawthorn trees, gorse bushes and the inevitable bracken. Falcon Crag is passed on your R with its great sheer rock buttresses and steep scree and rock-shattered slopes below. You may be able to watch the athletic endeavours of climbing parties testing their skills on the rock pitches along here.

The path continues N, and at the fork ahead keep to the higher path on the R. Your way then enters

Great Wood and rises alongside a stone wall to the L before you cross a stream. Walk downhill from here to your L. At the next junction keep straight on, avoiding a path off to the R leading to Walla Crag via Rakefoot. Proceed along the forest trail and keep to this wide track as a car-park is passed on your L. The track leads to a gate and a p-stile on your L about 50 paces from the entrance to Great Wood car-park. Turn L over the stile and walk down the car-park entrance lane. Cross the busy B5289 and veer R down the path through the woods, crossing a wooden footbridge before the way bends back to the R, alongside the road. An excellent path then leads N beneath a shading canopy of mainly coniferous trees. Some distance along here turn L down a surfaced lane signed 'Public Footpath' and pointing WSW.

Pass through a gate at a cattle grid ahead. Turn R through a further gate and walk along the path into another wooded area alongside a tiny watercourse on your R. After a footbridge and gate, your way leads down to the attractive shoreline of Derwent Water. The path continues across a footbridge, round a sweeping shingle bay and on towards Keswick through another gate. Turn L along here for a short detour to the well-regarded viewing point of Friar's Crag on your L. Then continue along the wide gravel path, which will bring you past the boat moorings back again to the car-park situated beyond the Century Theatre.

Alternative routes

ESCAPES

The most satisfactory way of shortening the described route is at Lady's Rake MR 276212 by keeping to the R-hand main path and not climbing Bleaberry Fell. Select the path which leads SSW above Falcon Crag and which will take you down towards Ashness Bridge, where you may rejoin the main route previously described. This certainly will provide you with more time to observe the manoeuvres of climbers on the rock faces around Falcon Crag and perhaps to linger along the shoreline of Derwent Water.

EXTENSIONS

For a lower-level route most walkers will find the combination of crossing boggy ground, route-finding in areas where the paths are indistinct, and the options of exploring a variety of adjacent fells along the way, sufficient to satisfy a healthy walking appetite.

If this is not sufficient, it is feasible to make your way pioneering along the soggy ridge further S to High Tove. From here there is a marked footpath down to Watendlath, after which you can follow the further footpaths alongside Watendlath Beck, and by making use of the road, reach Ashness Bridge. This demanding extension is only considered suitable for strong walkers.

BLENCATHRA

High Level Route 3

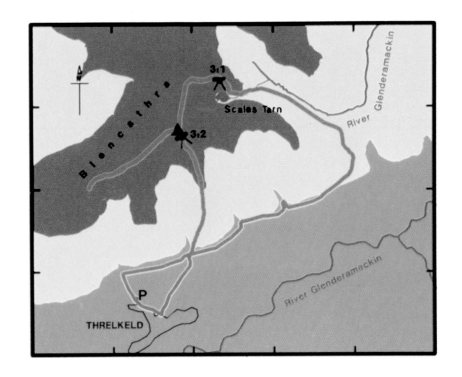

SOUTH-NORTH (Km)

WEST-EAST (Km)

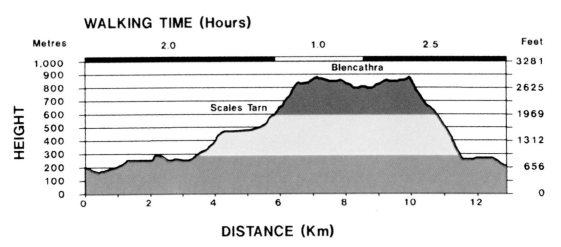

WALKING TIME (Hours)

HEIGHT

DISTANCE (Km)

STATISTICS			
START and FINISH		**TOTAL HEIGHT GAINED**	
- Threlkeld - OLM 5 / MR 318257		- 900 Metres 2953 Feet	

WALKING DISTANCE	Km	Miles		PRINCIPAL HEIGHTS	Metres	Feet
- Excluding Height	12.9	8.0		- Scales Tarn	600	1970
- Including Height	13.1	8.1		- Blencathra	868	2847

TOTAL WALKING TIME :   5.5 Hours

OTHER FEATURES OF INTEREST
- Superb knife-edge aretes of Sharp Edge and Hall's Fell Ridge.

3
THE NORTHERN FELLS
Part 2

Route 3 · Blencathra

Allow 5¼ hours

STARTING LOCATION
Car-park NW of Threlkeld.
OLM 5/MR 318257.
Small car-park – holds between 10 and 15 cars.
CMS bus route 104.

OVERVIEW/INTEREST
Two of the finest arêtes in the Lake District.
Sharp Edge and Hall's Fell Ridge.
Scales Tarn – high-level combe.
Extensive views over Derwent Water.
Route challenging but exhilarating.

FOOTPATHS/RIDGES
Good and firm footpaths with minimum erosion.
Ridges exposed – a head for heights required.
Moderate scrambling necessary.

The way to Scales Tarn   *Allow 2 hours*

Leave the car-park by the lower L-hand exit nearest to the village. Pass through a k-gate and proceed down the way signed 'Public Footpath' and indicated by yellow waymarkers. There is a stream to your L, which is crossed by a wooden footbridge. Another k-gate and footbridge have to be negotiated before you make an important turn to your L over a further footbridge, as the main path continues to descend into Threlkeld. Go through the enormous waymarked k-gate ahead.

At the top of the grassy brow an extensive view of the long S edges of Blencathra appears with a series of sharp ridges leading impressively up to the heights above. The pointed Hall's Fell Ridge, down which you will descend later in the day, is clearly in view as it majestically snakes up to the top rim of the mountain. Over to your R, across the dividing valley, the rounded shapes of Clough Head and White Pike block more distant views to the SE.

Cross the field diagonally, moving NNE, and continue on this line over marked stiles towards Gategill Farm. A few mature oak trees break the rolling landscape of meadows abundant with soft rush and sorrel. You pass a farm outbuilding to your R, and more stiles and gates follow in quick succession as you make your way through the main farm buildings. In one of the more open aspects here, turn around for a pleasant view to your rear of High Rigg Ridge SSW in the middle distance, overshadowed by Bleaberry Fell to the SW.

Some of the higher NW fells are also visible and panning from L to R, in clear weather, you should be able to make out the Maiden Moor spur leading to the heights of Dale Head, Hindscarth and Robinson, and on the far horizon Red Pike WSW. Further to the R is the distinctive helmet of Causey Pike and the rocky band leading from it to the dominating bulk of Crag Hill W. Ahead lies the relatively small, rounded hillock of Great Mell Fell, with the lower peak of Little Mell Fell

Overleaf:
3:1 Scales Tarn from Sharp Edge – Blencathra.

popping up over its shoulder. Turn to the L within the enclaves of the farm and continue through more gates up the narrow path alongside a gully on your R. This leads to the un-walled open fellside. Turn sharp R here and cross Gate Gill at the site of a disused lead mine. Select the lower R path ENE to Scales Fell. There are now views of the Pennines ahead in the far-off distance.

Soon another impressive ridge of Blencathra is observed to your L – this is Doddick Fell – as you reach and pass further gates. Crossing the two gullies either side of this spur provides interesting interludes along this part of the walk, and the minor scrambling necessary to cross the far one below Goat Crags gives a taste of things to come. Just before Scales is reached, take the narrower path off to your L, which diverges uphill as the other path descends to the R. Your path now climbs at a moderate gradient NE up through the gorse-covered slopes on a long, diagonal traverse. The N end of the Helvellyn Range comes into view in the shape of Great Dodd and Watson's Dodd over to your R SSW, and nearer to, gorse is displaced by bracken as your path ascends higher.

The path bends progressively to the L, for a brief spell heading NNW up a steep slope, before it again veers to the R resuming its previous direction of travel at a more moderate rate of climb. Over to your R there is a good example of a hanging valley above the steep slopes of Mousthwaite Comb. Round the next bend on your L suddenly it is there! The impressive arête of Sharp Edge seen to the NW, its serrated, rocky outline rising up over needle pinnacles to merge with the higher, vast, crumbling, precipitously rocky east face of Atkinson Pike. This is the most northerly blip on the broad summit of Blencathra. Your continuation path can be seen for some distance ahead, snaking invitingly towards the ridge.

Proceed along this path, and at Scales Beck veer to the left and climb up the moraine deposits, through the gully that the stream flows down, to reach the delightful trapped corrie waters of Scales Tarn. This is a beautifully wild spot, and on warm summer days it is very pleasant to linger here by the side of the still waters, relax for a time and anticipate the challenge that is in view high above.

In such conditions, a leisurely stroll round the tarn is very agreeable. By contrast in the rawness of winter's cold, with the tarn frozen over, and snow and ice on the fells, a quick appreciative glance around will suffice, before the walk is quickly resumed in order to conserve body heat.

The way to Blencathra   *Allow 1 hour*

A good, clear path leads up from the tarn to the N to reach the starting position for scaling Sharp Edge. Before you begin to climb assert your confidence over what lies ahead, make your mind up that you will be in charge, and that you are here to enjoy the thrill of treading along the exposed edge of what is probably close to the ultimate sensible challenge for walkers who do not possess knowledge of rock climbing technqiues. There are several different ways along the edge. These vary from the extreme of walking, standing up, along the very top and of scaling every separate pinnacle, to treading along a relatively sheltered path to the R some way below the jagged top. Most walkers choose an intermediate route where they can experience the thrill of walking along some of the top sections but where they can use hand holds as well.

The separate ridge is quite short, certainly by comparison with Striding Edge on Helvellyn, and you will soon find yourself standing before the rocky buttresses that rise up to the summit. Some parts of these are technically more demanding than scrambling along the edge, but they are less exposed and you can concentrate on finding good footholds and handholds, some of which you will need to stretch for. Avoid going too far to either L or R here and keep to the clefts in the firm rock. These will lead you securely to the rim of the summit where a good path becomes established as the rocky buff surrenders to a more rounded stone and grassy slope. Turn L and walk SW along the edge of the mountain to explore the delights that lie ahead.

The summit area of Blencathra is huge, and it consists of several separate peaks joined together by bands of slightly lower rock that fall and rise along its undulating top. The appearance of these are like saddles, hence its alternative name of Saddleback. Your entry to these features from along Sharp Edge is towards the N end of the summit area at one of its lower points. Therefore walk between S and SW along the SE edge of the mountain in order to visit the other peaks along the rim. The views to your L as you do this are superb. First you pass the way up from Scales Fell, then the long spur of Doddick Fell comes into sight with its sections of serrated rocks more spaced out than those of Sharp Edge. Scales Tarn is directly below, deep down, tucked into the fellside in its gouged-out basin. In contrast, far away to the SE the faint outlines of the more easterly fells come into prominence with the High Street Range dominating. Further up the slope, the summits of the Skiddaw group appear over to your R, on the skyline in the WNW. Then Thirlmere comes into view ahead to your L (SSW).

Soon, to your rear, you will be looking down on part of the summit area and its general shape will be revealed, including the positions of a large white cross and several summit cairns. A solitary, well-sited cairn marks the start of your descent route down Hall's Fell Ridge, and it also indicates the highest point of the summit of Blencathra at Hallsfell Top. This stands at 868 m (2,847 ft). Do not start your descent just yet, however, but continue along the ridge path SW to Knowe Crags, the SW tip of the mountain. Along here the distant vista includes:

SSE	The Dodds and Helvellyn Range.
SSW	St John's in the Vale.
	Tewet Tarn.
	Low and High Rigg.
SW	Bleaberry Fell.
WSW	Derwent Water and the high westerly fells beyond.
WNW	Little Man and Skiddaw.

On very clear days part of the Solway Firth may also be observed through a gap in the nearer fells to the NW. Make your way back eastwards along the spur to the cairn at Hallsfell Top, for the start of your descent route down Hall's Fell Ridge.

The way back to Threlkeld   *Allow 2¼ hours*

By comparison with Sharp Edge, Hall's Fell Ridge is much longer, not as exposed and has only sections where you will need to scramble and to use protective handholds. Nevertheless, it is a formidable descent and going down over steep rock is usually more demanding than climbing up and you will be more tired than at the outset. Therefore take the descent seriously, again assert your mastery, and enjoy your walk down.

As on Sharp Edge, there are several alternative routes down, varying both in degree of difficulty and extent of exposure. Choose the combination that best suits your skills, and with which you are most comfortable. There is just one tricky section. About halfway down there is a rocky buff impeding your direct progress. This can be circumnavigated to either L or R, but there is some exposure. To the L down a narrow, interesting funnel you will have to stretch for footholds. At the bottom of this turn R, when facing out, and cautiously make your way round the rock-face using footholds and handholds on the exposed section until you once more regain the security of the path ahead.

A large cairn marks the end of the rocky section, and the rest of the way down is along pathways. Part of these are steep and quite severely eroded into wide, firmly packed, sandy-coloured gravel tracks. These thread their way down through the colourful adjacent heathers and wiry green bilberries. The descent path will lead you down to the disused lead mine that you passed on your outward travels.

Turn R, cross the stream and pass through the gate at the top of the brow ahead. Then avoid the L-hand path that you used some hours previously, and instead continue along the path that leads SW round the fell slopes at a more or less constant height. You are now back in the land of crossing stiles and passing through gates until you arrive at a gate on your L, with a nearby sign positioned on the wall, which reads 'Threlkeld'. This is immediately before Blease Gill, and you turn L here and follow the stream down to the village and the carpark on the L.

Alternative routes

ESCAPES

Anywhere along the first part of the route up to and including Scales Tarn, the best escape is simply to turn round and go back along the way you have come. From above the tarn onwards, there are few possibilities for shortening the prescribed route. You can, however, avoid climbing Sharp Edge and/or descending down Hall's Fell Ridge if the weather conditions are not favourable. Sharp Edge is avoided by walking up the slopes of Scales Fell, and there is a connecting path from the tarn that will take you to the main path up. To avoid coming down Hall's Fell Ridge, descend by Blease Fell, and make your way back to above Threlkeld by using the footpaths to your L leading E.

EXTENSIONS

The walk described is intended as a short, sharp ridge walk and it can be completed in half a day. You can therefore go round the other way in the afternoon!

It is feasible also to get to the summit of Skiddaw, by crossing the high intervening moorland of Skiddaw Forest. If you decide to have a go at this you will find the jog down the rounded westerly slopes of Blencathra very exhilarating. When you reach the top of Skiddaw you will have another decision to make. Only walkers with the stamina of long-distance runners should attempt to get back to the top of Blencathra and then climb down by the described route of Hall's Fell Ridge. Others should be content with having reached the summits of these two high peaks on the same day, and should descend from Skiddaw along Jenkin Hill to the small car-park situated at MR 282254. From here there is a maze of paths, tracks and lanes that will lead you E, back to the car-park at Threlkeld.

3:2
Hall's Fell Ridge in evening sunlight – Blencathra.

HIGH RIGG and ST. JOHN'S
Lower Level Route 4

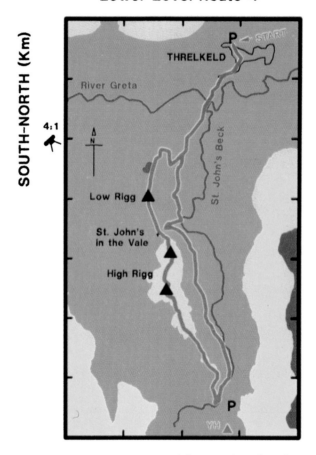

SOUTH-NORTH (Km)

THRELKELD

River Greta

4:1

Low Rigg

St. John's
in the Vale

High Rigg

St. John's Beck

P ← START

N

P

YH

WEST-EAST (Km)

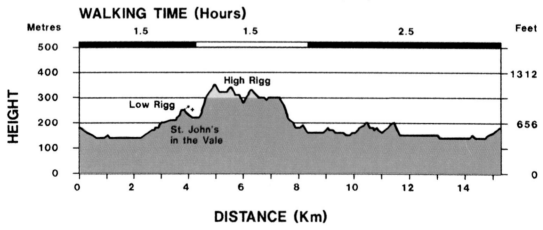

WALKING TIME (Hours)

Metres	1.5	1.5	2.5	Feet

500

400 — 1312

High Rigg

300

Low Rigg

200 — 656

St. John's
in the Vale

100

0 — 0

HEIGHT

0 2 4 6 8 10 12 14

DISTANCE (Km)

STATISTICS

START and FINISH
- Threlkeld - OLM 5 / MR 318257

WALKING DISTANCE	Km	Miles
- Excluding Height	15.3	9.5
- Including Height	15.4	9.6

TOTAL WALKING TIME : 5.5 Hours

TOTAL HEIGHT GAINED
- 510 Metres   1673 Feet

PRINCIPAL HEIGHTS	Metres	Feet
- High Rigg	357	1163

OTHER FEATURES OF INTEREST
- St. John's in the Vale Church.

Route 4 · High Rigg and St John's

Allow 5½ hours

STARTING LOCATION

Car-park NW of Threlkeld.
OLM 5/MR 318257.
Small car-park – holds between 10 and 15 cars.
CMS bus route 104.

OVERVIEW/INTEREST

Pleasant meadows and farmland at start and finish.
Modest undulating ridge with trapped tarns.
St John's in the Vale church.
Splendid shorter route ideal for families.

FOOTPATHS

Good and for the most part clear – no erosion.
In places a sheer delight to walk along.
Dry and comfortable except after prolonged heavy rain.

The way to the Southern Tip of the Ridge

Allow 3 hours

Turn L from the car-park and walk down Blease Road into Threlkeld, turning R at the T-junction. Pass the village store and post office on your L. Follow the village road down to the main A66 (T) artery, cross this diagonally and turn L down the minor road. A short distance along here you cross a bridge under which the waters of St John's Beck and the River Glenderamackin flow, to re-appear on the other side as the single River Greta!

Take the next footpath off to your L just past a bungalow. This way is signed 'Public Footpath'. Cross the sloping field, making for the k-gate ahead as the outline of Low Rigg shows up beyond. Good views open up to your L of Threlkeld Knotts and the slopes of Clough Head to the SE. To the rear there is a revealing view back across the low-lying fields to the massive slopes of Blencathra rising majestically to the N. Cross several fields with the aid of four further, helpfully positioned, k-gates, before reaching a gate in a stone wall. Your path then bends L, and following this goes through another gateway, at the end of the next stone wall.

Maintain your SSW direction of travel, and follow first a wire fence and then a broken stone wall to your L, where you will observe a further footpath sign and waymarker arrowheads. Continue to the R of the wall towards the farm buildings ahead to the SW. Cross the next wall by the wooden l-stile and walk along the permitted way to the farm, once more signed 'Footpath'. A gate in the wall ahead gives entry to a lane at Shundraw Farm. Turn sharp R along this lane, walk uphill and take the next path off to your L through a gate, and reassuringly signed 'Public Footpath St John's in the Vale Church via Tewit Tarn' (Note: spelled Tewet Tarn on OS map). Hereabouts the formidable slopes of Skiddaw appear to the NNW. Follow the grassy cart track uphill as it bends to the L. You next pass through a gate in a wall and then continue by forking R along the path nearest to the stone wall and signed footpath. Tewet Tarn can now be seen ahead, and beyond this nearer landmark, the distant slopes of Causey Pike and Grisedale Pike come into view to the W. Your path leads to the L of the tarn.

Go round the tarn, with it on your R, heading up the grassy slope SSW. Your way leads through soft rush (otherwise known as juncus grass) to a gate and stile. Use the gate, which has an interesting innovative clasp, as the stile is wobbly! Follow the grassy path, and at the division of the ways veer L to the col ahead (S). At the top of here a closer view of the High Rigg ridge is seen. Proceed down the grassy track, which descends to a gap/stile in the stone wall that crosses your path at right angles.

Follow the path down to St John's Church, ahead to the SSE, ignoring all side diversions, both up and more acutely down the fellside. The views along here are mellow, with the rounded fells ahead leading the eyes towards the dark green clump of trees surrounding the church, and the higher fells, including the Helvellyn group, which rise steeply beyond the attractively located buildings.

4:1 High Rigg and Helvellyn from the Castlerigg Stone Circle.

Gain access to the church lane at a stile, near a large sycamore tree, in the stone wall that runs alongside it. The church is well worth a visit and there are informative leaflets inside that record its colourful history and detail its rebuilding in 1845. There is also information on the associated Carlisle Diocesan Youth Centre. Outside again, turn up the lane passing the Youth Centre on your L. Immediately past the building turn L up the gravel path, climb the small rocky outcrop above, and then continue uphill on a diagonal to your L to pass through a k-gate in a stone wall. The track to the L that winds steeply up the craggy fell is your way from here. A good, distinct path follows, which bends to the R before it reaches two cairns on the horizon ahead to the S, and the highest point of the ridge. Thirlmere reservoir snaking southwards is visible. The height at the cairns is 357 m (1,163 ft).

From the top, descend S along the path to your L. This follows the E edge of the ridge for some distance, and then gradually slopes down to the R of a stone wall below in the direction of Thirlmere. The well-established path undulates over small humps, and a L fork needs to be taken to maintain the correct line of travel. When the path forks again just before reaching a rock-face, veer to the L alongside the wall, and soon you will pass a small tarn to your L. The grassy path descends to a wall

and a l-stile ahead. You are now treading over springy, grassy ground where a solitary, fine ash tree is passed to your R. The main path then winds uphill to your L (SSE). Further on there is a rocky crag to your L, which is worth climbing. To do this veer round to the L and climb up the grassy col before turning R and scrambling up the steep rock and grass slope to reach the top. Another small tarn appears below to your L as you walk along the rocky ridge, making for the pointed cairn to the S.

Continue southwards along the now wide grassy band, keeping to the crests of the hillocks, until you reach a further rocky crag. Veer L here towards a fence and follow the path to the R of this down to the stile below. Cross this and select the path on the L, which maintains its elevation along the top of the ridge, where a wooden waymarker is in place on your R. Your direction here is SE. Before you stretches the fine ridge section named Long Band. Further on, you pass a large symmetrical cairn to your L.

The higher ground of the rocky ridge ends abruptly, and at this spot locate and descend down a narrow path to the R. This leads to a wider grassy path below, which bends round the rocks to the L and drops to a wall further down still. Proceed through a gap in the wall, where your path continues on the far side. (There are alternative routes down to this gap in the wall, which is an important landmark.) The path climbs for a short distance along a resumption of the ridge, as the start of an area of mature Scots pines appears on the R. Your path now winds pleasantly down through the sweet-smelling pines, which become interspersed with a sprinkling of oak trees. At the T-junction of paths ahead turn to your L at a position that marks the southernmost tip of your route.

The way back to Threlkeld   *Allow 2¼ hours*

A good, compacted earth and gravel path traverses round the steep slopes of the fell. Along here there is a particularly steep fall to St John's Beck below, and it will be necessary to keep a tight hold on younger children until the worst of this short section is safely completed. The path winds through tall larch trees before it descends to the beck below. You are now back among gates and stiles as a lush grassy path continues northwards along the W side of the flat, U-shaped valley. Continue along the obvious well-signed path and soon you will approach Low Bridge End Farm, which you pass above to the L.

A sign which reads 'Low Bridge End St John's Church' confirms that you are on the correct way as you continue N, with more gates and stiles to be negotiated. The path then rises steadily to the L, and following a long diagonal straight stretch it ends at the church lane just below the building. Climb over the stile and turn R down the lane. Within 50 paces veer off R and pass through a gate in the wall signed 'Footpath'. Continue along the delightful, broad, grassy path that winds steeply downhill. The buildings of Bridge House are reached at the bottom. Walk between the farmhouse and the outbuildings and then turn L along a broad track by the side of St John's Beck.

Cross a stile, but do not cross the beck by the imposing footbridge on your R. Do, however, turn off to the L just beyond the house by mounting the stile and continuing N across the fields ahead, making for a large sycamore tree. This way leads alongside walls and over a stile to a narrow, single-track lane, into which you turn L after climbing

another stile. Within 30 paces turn off to your R through a gate and down a track signed 'Public Footpath'. At this point Yew Tree Farm is just along the lane on the L.

Follow the obvious footpath, well indicated by yellow arrowhead waymarkers, as it brings you to further stiles and leads you across a watercourse. Another stile gives you entry to a second metalled road along this section. Turn R here and then almost immediately L, following the public footpath sign directing you through a gate. Continue alongside a fence to your L, pass through a gate and immediately turn L through a gap in a stone wall, followed by a sharp turn to the R to reach a point along your earlier departure route. Retrace your outward steps along this route back to the car-park at Threlkeld.

Alternative routes

ESCAPES
This is an ideal walk for splitting into halves if you wish, breaking the route in two at St John's Church.

The northern part from Threlkeld may be terminated at the church, where you turn down the lane and take the footpath off to your R below the church. Follow the described route from here back to your starting point in the village.

To walk the more interesting High Rigg part, take your car to St John's Church, have a look round the church and pick up the described route from this point.

EXTENSIONS
High Rigg is a separate ridge and there are no really satisfactory extensions to the route at a lower level.

It is feasible to include a visit to the Stone Circle at Castlerigg to the W, but this involves walking along roads and lanes for most of the extension. If you decide to do this, the best departure point from the main route is just beyond Shundraw Farm by continuing along the lane at MR 307238 instead of turning L up the footpath. Return to this point after visiting the Circle to resume the main route.

35

GRASMOOR and GRISEDALE PIKE

High Level Route 5

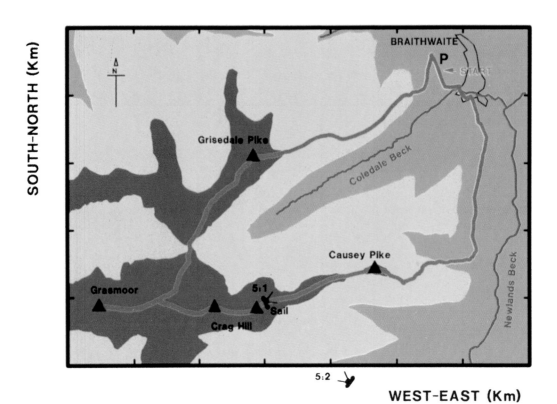

WEST-EAST (Km)

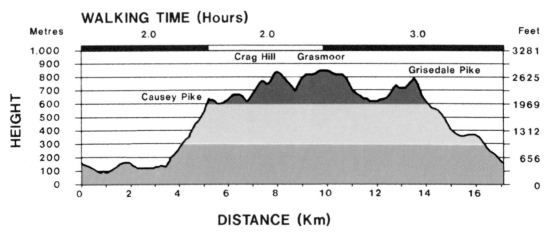

DISTANCE (Km)

STATISTICS

START and FINISH
- North of Braithwaite - OLM 4 / MR 227237

WALKING DISTANCE	Km	Miles
- Excluding Height	17.1	10.6
- Including Height	17.4	10.8

TOTAL WALKING TIME : 7.0 Hours

TOTAL HEIGHT GAINED
- 1270 Metres   4167 Feet

PRINCIPAL HEIGHTS	Metres	Feet
- Causey Pike	637	2090
- Crag Hill	839	2749
- Grasmoor	852	2791
- Grisedale Pike	791	2593

OTHER FEATURES OF INTEREST
- Views of Derwent Water, Borrowdale and Buttermere.

4

The North-west and Westerly Fells

Part 1

Route 5 · Grasmoor and Grisedale Pike

Allow 7 hours

STARTING LOCATION
Car-park off Whinlatter Pass Road above
Braithwaite.
OLM 4/MR 227237.
Tiny car-park – holds less than 10 cars!
(Alternative parking along Newlands Road).
Not on a bus route!

OVERVIEW/INTEREST
Pleasant and enjoyable ridge walk.
Relatively undemanding with climbs well spaced
out.
Extensive views from open, high-level terrain.
Ideal route for developing the stamina of growing
teenagers.

FOOTPATHS
Rank amongst the best, well-used, high-level paths
anywhere in the Lake District.
Minimum erosion and wet, boggy areas.
A most enjoyable walking route underfoot.

The way to Causey Pike

Allow 2 hours

Turn R out of the car-park and proceed downhill
along the road back into Braithwaite. At the
approach to the village fork R, and pass the Ivy
House Hotel to your R. Turn R again and cross Coledale Beck before selecting the minor road signposted 'Newlands Buttermere 6½'. Continue along this
road to a sharp L-hand bend, and here take the
track off to the R signed 'Public Bridleway' at an
iron gateway and cattle grid. Follow the wide track
uphill to Braithwaite Lodge, passing the farm
buildings to your L. After gaining only modest
height, good views immediately appear; on your L
is Skiddaw NE and Blencathra ENE, ahead of you is
Causey Pike SSW, while to your R you can glimpse
your return route in the shape of Grisedale Pike
SSW.

At the lodge observe the path signs by passing
through a wooden gateway to reach a bridleway on
the R of the buildings. A public footpath is crossed
and your way continues uphill SSE over a stile to
the R of a gate. Cross the field ahead, keeping on
the R edge alongside a wire fence. You then come
to a wooden wicket gate, and on the other side veer
immediately to your L over the brow of the hill
towards a tree-fringed skyline. Primeval ferns
grow in this area. Now peer round to your L for a
sighting of the S tip of Bassenthwaite Lake to the N.
Keep to the lower L-hand path signed to 'Newlands', and proceed along the way through the
bracken, alongside a copse of mixed trees including spruce, larch and birch. Further on, a grouping
of Scots pines is passed. The path then descends
back to the narrow Newlands Road. Continue
along this road, where you soon have an extensive
view down the Newlands Valley stretching away to
the S, flanked on the far side by Cat Bells SSE and

5:1 A dusting of snow on the approach to Sail.

then the band of high mountains leading up from here and terminating in Dale Head. The isolated, attractively wooded plug of Swinside appears next over on your L (ESE). After reaching the dwelling of Stoneycroft on your L, the road bridges a stream, and immediately after this select the path off on your R and climb up this to reach a wooden seat above the road.

From these surrounds, a view up to the higher slopes of Causey Pike can be observed to the WSW. Continue up the path, which soon strikes an upward diagonal leading SW towards Causey Pike. Avoid routes off down into the valley on your R, and at an intersection ahead bear R off the severe gradient that climbs steeply up to Rowling End. Proceed along a more comfortable line of ascent,

keeping to the continuing long diagonal path across the fellside. This climbs eventually to reach the main ridge below the upper craggy slopes of Causey Pike WSW.

When you have gained further height, look around from time to time to record the progressively more revealing views opening up to your rear, across Derwent Water, to the northerly fells in the mighty Helvellyn Group ESE, and to Blencathra in the NE. These two massive mountain areas are divided by a wide, flat, glaciated valley through which the rivers Greta and Glenderamackin now meander. Once you have turned abruptly to the L and climbed up the scree-like, more severe slope, over which the path twists between SSW and W, you will reach the broad band where your route joins the alternative way up to Causey Pike via Rowling End.

At this vantage point pause for a few moments to admire the views down into the Newlands Valley and across Derwent Water, and consolidate your recognition of the vast array of surrounding high mountain peaks. The positions of these have been previously disclosed, apart from Maiden Moor and Eel Crags SSE, Dale Head S, Hindscarth SSW and Robinson SW. On the very distant horizon to the S the peaks of Bow Fell and Esk Pike are just visible, while to the R of the nearer Robinson the tips of the High Stile range can be made out to the SW.

Then turn R along the broad ridge path, which soon commences to climb zigzagging to the top of Causey Pike ENE. The path leads up the spur of the fell to a rocky outcrop; take the narrow path off to the L here and then traverse up a cleft to your R, after which it is an easy, obvious, short scramble to the summit.

Causey Pike at a height of 637 m (2,090 ft) is by no means one of the giants of the Lake District Fells, but it does have a presence, its summit is rocky but accommodating, and the views in all directions are fascinating. The highlights to be observed in the diffuse panorama visible from here, starting by looking westwards and then turning round clockwise, are:

WSW	Crag Hill.
NW	Grisedale Pike.
N	Bassenthwaite Lake.
NE	Skiddaw and Blencathra.
E	Derwent Water.
SE	Maiden Moor and in the distance the Helvellyn Range.
SSE	Eel Crags with the peaks of the Langdales, Glaramara and Bow Fell beyond.
S to SSW	Dale Head, Hindscarth and Robinson, with the tips of the Scafells, Great Gable, High Crag and High Stile just appearing on the distant skyline.
SW	Red Pike with Pillar beyond.

The way to Grasmoor   *Allow 2 hours*

Continue along the ridge path leading W. The route is easy to follow and there are cairns to assist you in misty conditions. Keep to the higher ground, and when you reach a division of the path veer L. The main features of this part of the route are the climb up the broad gravel path to attain the summit of Sail, and from here passing through The Scar by scrambling up the craggy outcrops, to gain the summit of Crag Hill. Along this section in fine weather you will obtain fleeting views down to your L to Buttermere, where part of the lake is visible with the High Stile range towering above it SSW to SW.

The summit of Crag Hill standing at 839 m (2,749 ft) is gracefully rounded off. Make for the summit cairn on your R (NW), where there are also some sheltering rock formations. At the cairn your ultimate westerly goal of the massive outline of Grasmoor comes into view to the WNW. The path that snakes to its summit is clearly visible, rising up from the grassy hause between these two imposing crags.

Descend down the rounded, sparsely-grassed, westerly slopes of Crag Hill following a line of cairns to the col below. Your direction is SW down from the summit, and then W along the path, which will lead you away from the edge to your L. At the wide depression ahead cross another clear path at right angles. This path, in its northerly direction, leads to Coledale Hause, and will be used as part of the return route. However, first you must climb up the moderate slope ahead to the summit of Grasmoor to the W. After another steepish incline, the terrain once again levels off as the broad top of Grasmoor is approached, and the wide gravel path snakes round to bring you to the large, flat summit area to your R. Before you arrive there, providing the views are clear, you will have seen Crummock Water stretched out below on your L to the SW.

There is a large, welcoming stone shelter on the top of Grasmoor and the path leads to this. There are also cairns, and other sheltered spots at different vantage points just below the very highest ground, and these are worth the effort of a visit,.

The summit is 852 m (2,791 ft) high, and marks the apex of your excursion, although it is not all downhill from here! If you make an extensive exploration of all the viewing positions lining the summit edge you will have the pleasure of seeing from the most westerly point a fine view of Buttermere Lake SSE, Crummock Water SW, and the smaller lake of Loweswater WNW, and from the northerly rim, the splendid ridge to the N of Gasgale Crags, which are really quite spectacular when viewed from this angle. This spur leads E to Hopegill Head and Sand Hill, NE from your viewing position. The remaining extensive mountain panorama to be observed from this lofty summit has already been positioned. However, in exceptionally clear weather, the Isle of Man and Scotland are also visible from here.

The way back to Braithwaite   *Allow 3 hours*

It is usual to start the return by retracing your steps, this time eastwards, to the hause between Grasmoor and Crag Hill, and then turning L, to the N, along the path previously mentioned, to reach Coledale Hause. In good weather you could take a more ambitious route by trekking further to the N along the summit rim of Grasmoor and descending NE to join the path down from the hause between Grasmoor and Crag Hill, further to the N than on the main route down. If you do decide to do this, be particularly vigilant because the N edge of Grasmoor at Dove Crags is precipitously steep, the path is intermittent, and there is some rough ground to cross on the slopes during your final diagonal descent to the secure path below. The rewards for this more adventurous descent are stupendous views into the dark upper recesses of the gouged-out combes and shattered rock formations that line the northerly face of Grasmoor, particularly in the vicinity of Dove Crags. There is also, literally, a bird's eye view, of the large, flat, triangular, hanging valley below, which then drops abruptly into Gasgale Gill.

Having arrived at the targeted path from either of the two different directions of approach, continue northwards along it, as the path shelves gradually downhill to the R round the contours of the fellside. Soon you will once again see the summit of Grisedale Pike rising across the lower ground to your R in the NW, and this is the final mountain to be climbed.

Cut off to the L across the fellside to the N at Coledale Hause, where the more pronounced path veers off further R down the valley. At the next confluence take the R fork, and avoiding the worst of the boggy ground hereabouts, make for the distinct narrow path leading diagonally uphill to the NE.

This converges with another path along the ridge from Hopegill Head to Grisedale Pike. Veer to your R along this merged way, adjacent to the remains of a dilapidated wall on your L. The path undulates in a NW direction along the rocky spur, and a pool is crossed.

Next, climb through a rocky outcrop and relocate the cairned path, which will lead you to the summit of Grisedale Pike. The height of Grisedale Pike is 791 m (2,593 ft), and from this summit the only significant new views are those to the N where an extensive area of rolling fellside covered in coniferous forests is exposed below. The dominant shapes in this lower terrain are Lord's Seat and Barf NNE.

Leave Grisedale Pike by the rocky path that descends in twists and turns to the E and then to the SE, and in misty conditions look out for a large cairn ahead. The deep valley to your R is now occupied by Coledale Beck, which is relentlessly adding a V-nick in the wider U-shape, originally formed by glacier activity. Follow the rough stony path down ENE as it convulses over the tangled mass of irregular, shattered rock, until you reach a broad rounded spur with its flanks partially grassed. This is Sleet How. From here continue along the crest of the ridge as the rocky path gives way to more stable ground, and your rate of descent slackens. The way continues down ENE to a fork in the path. Here select the L-hand route signed 'Footpath', cross the stile and proceed along the descending diagonal that veers to the L, and then bends R along a narrowing track. This leads to a flight of steps down to the car-park below.

Alternative routes

5:2 A long range shot of Grasmoor, Crag Hill, Sail and Grisedale Pike from Maiden Moor.

ESCAPES

The hause between Crag Hill and Grasmoor is the decision point for shortening this route. From here you can decide not to venture up Grasmoor on the route out, and coming back you can continue round Eel Crag and down by the side of Coledale Beck instead of climbing Grisedale Pike.

EXTENSIONS

A very rewarding extension during the return is possible when you reach Coledale Hause. Climb up Sand Hill to Hopegill Head beyond. From here you may walk w along the ridge above Gasgale Crags to Whiteside before turning back to climb Grisedale Pike.

41

THORNTHWAITE FOREST and LORD'S SEAT
Lower Level Route 6

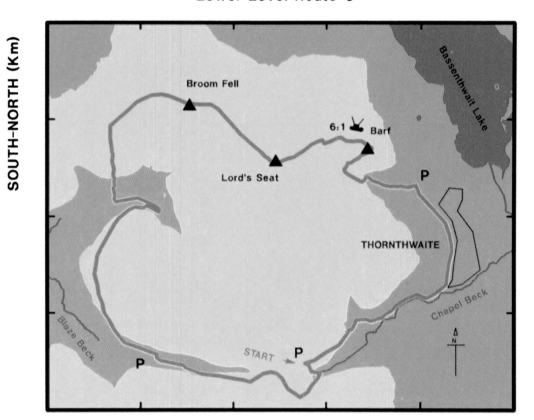

SOUTH-NORTH (Km)

Broom Fell

6:1 Barf

Lord's Seat

Bassenthwait Lake

P

THORNTHWAITE

P

Blaze Beck

P

START →

Chapel Beck

N

WEST-EAST (Km)

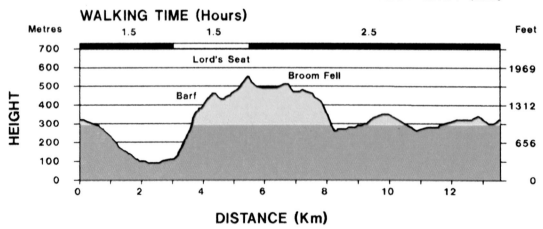

WALKING TIME (Hours)

| Metres | 1.5 | 1.5 | 2.5 | Feet |

Lord's Seat

Broom Fell

Barf

HEIGHT

700 — 1969
600
500
400 — 1312
300
200 — 656
100
0 — 0

0   2   4   6   8   10   12

DISTANCE (Km)

STATISTICS

START and FINISH		
- Forest Visitor Centre - OLM 4 / MR 208245		

WALKING DISTANCE	Km	Miles
- Excluding Height	13.5	8.4
- Including Height	13.7	8.5

TOTAL WALKING TIME : 5.5 Hours

TOTAL HEIGHT GAINED
- 700 Metres   2297 Feet

PRINCIPAL HEIGHTS	Metres	Feet
- Barf	468	1536
- Lord's Seat	552	1811
- Broom Fell	511	1670

OTHER FEATURES OF INTEREST
- Forest Visitor Centre and views of Bassenthwaite Lake; Bishop Rock, Barf.

Route 6 · Thornthwaite Forest and Lord's Seat

Allow 5½ hours

STARTING LOCATION

Forest Visitor Centre – Whinlatter Pass.
OLM 4/MR 208245.
Extensive and superbly laid-out facilities.
Not on a bus route!

OVERVIEW/INTEREST

Enjoyable walk through coniferous forests and over rounded fells.
Plenty of interest, including the Bishop of Barf Rock, and the Forest Visitor Centre.
Spectacular views over Bassenthwaite Lake and of Skiddaw.
Route suitable for older children in fine weather.

FOOTPATHS

For the most part very good.
On the tops, paths somewhat indistinct, with one steep descent.
Forest Guide Map available.

The way to Beckstones   *Allow 1¼ hours*

From the car-park make your way past the Forest Visitor Centre, and walk down the forest road. Continue NE, passing Marker Post 15 on your L, and then select the lower road, which shortly ahead passes a cottage to your R. The track enters the coniferous forest. To your rear on the R is a sighting through the trees of Grisedale Pike SW. At the road junction near Marker Post 14 veer R along the road leading downhill, and a short way further on, at Marker Post 13, turn L heading northwards. Then look out for a forest trail on the R heading more steeply downhill. Turn along this trail, which winds steeply down the fellside between the conifers. The path crosses a small beck, and then a forestry road on a diagonal, as it continues to descend steeply NE.

Keep to the trail and soon a gully forms below to your R, through which a larger stream, Comb Beck, gushes. Then you pass some abandoned mine workings on your L signed 'Danger Mineworkings Keep out'. After going through a gate you reach an attractive dwelling that appears to have two names, 'Woodford House' and 'Oak Lea'! Skiddaw mountain is now visible ahead NE across the flat, silted up plain separating Bassenthwaite Lake from Derwent Water. The path then leads over a rocky buff down to a lane. This lane descends to the charming and peaceful village of Thornthwaite.

Turn L on entering the village, past Thwaite Hill Cottage on your L, and then 'Seldom Seen' dwellings to your R. Continue L along the lanes heading NNE. Clough Head, White Pike, Great Dodd and the other huge, rounded, grassy fells composing the northern part of the massive Helvellyn group can soon be seen rising to your R (SE). Descend to the road ahead, and turn along this to your L, passing a vehicle repair workshop on your L. Immediately after, take the surfaced lane to the L signed 'Public Footpath', which leads uphill NNW. Through the nearer trees you will see a large, distinctive, white-painted rock on the fellside ahead. This has been named the 'Bishop of Barf' after a Bishop who fell to his death at this spot while undertaking a wager. Continue along the lane to Beckstones.

The way to Lord's Seat   *Allow 1¼ hours*

Be careful now to cross the first stile on your L on the southern side of Beckstones Gill. This provides access to a narrow path leading up the fell within the Forestry Commision's boundary fence. The path backtracks momentarily on your direction of approach, but soon bends to the R, climbing the increasingly steep slope to the WNW. The vegetation on this fellside is a compact mixture of larch and silver birch trees, gorse and bracken.

Eventually you come to a pronounced bluff of exposed rock. Veer to the L, following the path that

Overleaf   *6:1 Looking down on Bassenthwaite Lake from Barf.*

twists and turns up the outcrop. Do not be tempted along the inviting grassy path that leads off to the R at a lower level just before the rocks are encountered. At the top of this section the path swings to the L, and there is a view of the N tip of Derwent Water and Keswick down below on the L (SE), with the Helvellyn group beyond. The path continues to climb steeply through the coniferous forest, under predominantly tall Scots pines, and this leads to Marker Posts 20 and 21. The latter post is situated at the junction of a welcoming, almost level way along which you turn R (NW).

At the next division of the paths, turn R, down the lower gravel trail. Cross the stile, and then the beck, before continuing to climb along the path to the R, winding up the fellside. More sightings follow, including Causey Pike SSW, and the complete length of Bassenthwaite Lake below on your R, as the path curves NW to reach the summit cairn of Barf Fell at 468 m (1,536 ft). There are excellent, contrasting views from this peak, down over Bassenthwaite Lake to the steep slopes of Skiddaw beyond, and then in the opposite direction the expanse of high, grassy moorland undulating to reach the top of Lord's Seat in the W. Other landmarks that can be seen from here include the Langdales S, the tips of Bow Fell and the Scafells SSW, and the top of Grisedale Pike SW.

Leave by the path to the NW, which crosses the heather and bilberry-clad moorland of peaty, acidic soil, snaking in a wide semi-circle up the higher ground over some boggy patches. The path then swings towards the SW as you come to elevated terrain, and the way is up this to reach, after a further moderate climb, the top of Lord's Seat. This fell is 552 m (1,811 ft) high, and the summit marks the crest of your route. The mountain scenery in view from this position covers:

S	Grisedale Pike.
SSW	Hopegill Head.
WSW	Lorton Vale.
W	Greystones.
NW	Broom Fell.
ENE	Barf, Skiddaw and Little Man.

The way back to Thornthwaite Forest Visitor Centre

Allow 2½ hours

From the summit of Lord's Seat, descend along the broad band leading NW over grassy moorland to Todd Fell and then rising again to Broom Fell. In places the path is somewhat indistinct, but if you always keep to a NW line of travel you will find a clearer path as the ground shapes into a more definitive ridge. Follow this, climbing a stile over a fence *en route*. Keep to the higher ground that swings to your L, veering towards W, and climb steadily to reach the top of Broom Fell at 511 m (1,670 ft). The coastline can be sighted from here to the NW on a clear day.

Descend along the high band NNW and then WSW, towards the most easterly upper corner of Darling How Plantation down below, to reach a crumbling stone wall and wire fence running alongside the tree-line. Turn L along the path here, walking due S with the obstacles on your R. The delightful, flat Vale of Lorton is visible down below to your R (SW). When the path starts to bend away from the line of the wall, abandon it, and descend in a series of sharp zigzags through the bracken down the steep fellside S to the small stream below, keeping close to the forest to your R.

At the bottom of this steep descent you will find yourself in a remote, barren, high-level valley through which a modest beck meanders. This out-of-the-way spot is hemmed in by higher ground, up which extensive forest areas have been planted. Cross the beck, avoiding the worst of the swampy ground in this vicinity, climb up the opposite bank, and then cross the fence on your R by the stile provided. On reaching the broad, slate-surfaced forestry road turn L (E) along it.

Before you arrive at Marker Post 27 on the L, turn sharply to your R up the signed cycle route. This initially heads W, but it bends progressively to the L as it rounds Brown How in the form of a broad grass and gravel track that rises gradually through densely planted larch, pine and spruce trees. After a gateway the path starts to descend to the L, at this point veering S. Here there is a restricted view of Hopegill Head rising ahead between the funnel of trees.

The way continues to bend to the L, and as this takes place Grisedale Pike comes into sight again, to the L of Hopegill Head. Hobcarton Gill, an attractive high-level watercourse, runs down between these two imposing peaks. Your path now descends, as you continue along it, avoiding a track leading off uphill on the L. The ground falls to the narrow Whinlatter Pass Road (B5292) near the top of the cleft, and still within the forested area. Duck under the traffic-control barrier, and turn to your L up this road. Within a short distance turn R off the road, at the fellwalkers car-park, and then turn immediately L, following the green bicycle signs and passing in succession Marker Posts 32 and 33. The wide forest road winds marginally uphill to the SE. Another forest road is joined, and the route continues L along this ESE as it runs parallel to the public road below to the L.

The path undulates, always tracking to the E, and along here avoid taking a side path downhill to the L. At Marker Post 41 turn L down the forest road that crosses at a T-junction. The wide forest road you have just turned onto leads downhill NE. Cross the stream by the bridge, and then at Marker Post 43 turn L down a final forestry road to reach the B5292. Then turn L along this. Within 100 paces turn R up a stepped path to return to the Forestry Commission's attractive Visitor Centre and the car-park, hopefully with some time to spare to have a look round.

Alternative routes

ESCAPES

From the summits of either Barf or Lord's Seat it is possible to return direct to the Forestry Commission's Visitor Centre at Whinlatter by following the marked trails. A useful Guide Map is published by the Commission detailing the routes, and showing the location of each of the helpful Marker Posts. An updated copy can be obtained at the Visitor Centre.

EXTENSIONS

Extensions to this route are best planned by making use of the extended forest trails. There is a permanent orienteering course within the forest area, and details of this and other more temporary features can be obtained from the staff at the Visitor Centre. In the new Guide Map no less than 11 suggested walking routes are listed, and it states that you are welcome to walk where you choose providing you take care to stay clear of harvesting operations.

DALE HEAD, HINDSCARTH and ROBINSON
High Level Route 7

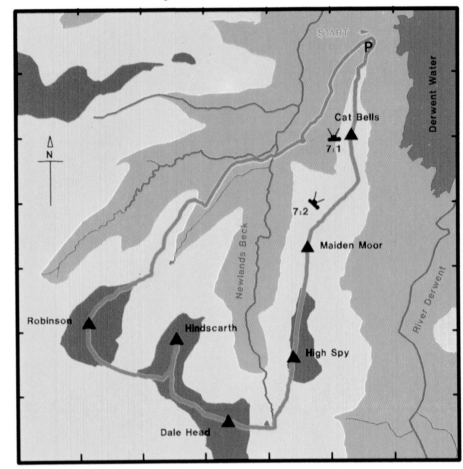

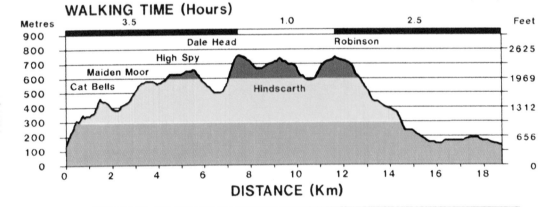

WALKING TIME (Hours)

DISTANCE (Km)

STATISTICS	
START and FINISH - Car Park nr. Gutherscale - OLM 4 / MR 247212	**TOTAL HEIGHT GAINED** - 1190 Metres 3904 Feet

WALKING DISTANCE	Km	Miles
- Excluding Height	18.7	11.6
- Including Height	19.0	11.8

TOTAL WALKING TIME : 7.0 Hours

PRINCIPAL HEIGHTS	Metres	Feet
Dale Head	753	2473
- Hindscarth	727	2385
- Robinson	737	2417

OTHER FEATURES OF INTEREST
- Spectacular panoramic views in all directions; Dale Head Tarn and Little Town

5

The North-west and Westerly Fells

Part 2

HIGH-LEVEL ROUTE

Route 7 · Dale Head, Hindscarth and Robinson

Allow 7 hours

STARTING LOCATION

Car-park near Gutherscale.

OLM 4/MR 247212.

Small car-park – holds 10 to 15 cars.

(Some additional parking nearby).

Not on a bus route!

OVERVIEW/INTEREST

Superior high-level ridge walk.

Climbing gradual and well spaced out.

Stupendous views, particularly across Derwent Water.

Interesting perspectives of other mountain groups.

In good weather the route is suitable for older, stronger teenagers.

FOOTPATHS

The going is invariably sound, firm and rocky.

Paths are clear, except around Dalehead Tarn.

Surfaces, even in the valley, are well drained.

No serious erosion anywhere along the route.

The way to Dale Head   *Allow 3½ hours*

Take the path leading up stone steps from the corner of the car-park on to the ridge above, walking almost due E. Immediately higher ground is reached there are revealing views of Derwent Water; beyond this the peaks of Skiddaw to the NNE and Blencathra ENE stand out. On your R across the intervening flatness of Newlands Valley the peaks of Rowling End and Causey Pike come into view to the W. A good path zigzags up the fell swinging to the S, which from now on will be your predominant direction of travel along the spur rising to High Spy. Further up, Bassenthwaite Lake appears to your rear, to the L of the modest tree-covered plug of Swinside Fell at the foot of the Newlands Valley. The much higher, more majestic summit of Grisedale Pike rises in the NW. A short easy scramble will bring you to the top of Skelgill Bank, and a plaque nearby commemorates a gentleman who believed that 'The best things any mortal hath are those which every mortal shares'.

The path leads along the ridge, with some more scrambling involved up to the top of Cat Bells. From this vantage point a large number of mountains can be seen to the SW in clear weather. These are dominated by Hindscarth and Robinson, and beyond these the NE profile of the High Stile group. Below, the grass-covered, upper reaches of the Newlands Valley are revealed. Along the ridge, the summit of Maiden Moor beckons to the S, while just discernible far away to its L is the peak of Pike of Stickle in the Langdale Pikes SSE, with the Glaramara Ridge to the R of this.

Scramble down from the summit of Cat Bells, continuing along the excellent ridge path leading down across Hause Gate, and then climbing SSW to the top of Maiden Moor. The Helvellyn group comes into view far away to the SE on your L as cairns positioned to the R of the path lead you to

49

7:1 A northward vista from Cat Bells.

the summit of Maiden Moor. From here continue sw first along Narrow Moor, then between Eel Crags and Minum Crag, to reach the rocky peak of High Spy. The top of Dale Head appears ahead, spurring you on. The immediately surrounding crags are well worth more intensive exploration while those to the w provide stunning views of the steep precipitous NE rock and scree slopes of Hindscarth with its satellite crags. Those to the E afford more revealing views down into the contrasting flatness of Borrowdale. Ahead lies Bow Fell beyond the Glaramara Ridge to the s, while more to the w the outline of the Scafell Massif can be detected.

From High Spy a rocky path descends sw down the steep, craggy slopes of the fell to Dale Head Tarn. This is a tiny oasis of water trapped in a small basin within the folds of the lower ground between the soaring heights of High Spy and Dale Head. It is a picturesque setting, and the only stretch of water you will pass during the entire route! As you descend to the tarn, Great Gable appears directly ahead to the ssw, and the rocky buttresses of Dale Head are revealed to the R, with the underlying steep scree slopes plunging down into the tranquil valley below.

Veer round the tarn in a semi-circle to the L, and for some distance here the way becomes less distinct as it traverses up the grassy slopes of Dale Head. Continue uphill skirting the tarn to your R, climbing to the w, to gain the ridge path leading to the summit of Dale Head directly ahead, but still some height above you. You come to a good track on your L and this then winds to the R along a shallower gradient to reach the top of the fell. There are other ascent routes, directly up the steep, grassy fellside, but these are considerably more demanding.

Along the suggested route the final approach to the summit is towards the N and here you are accompanied by both dilapidated iron fence-work and guiding cairns. The top of Dale Head commands a height of 753 m (2,473 ft), and from here some additional mountain peaks can be recognized. Kirk Fell rises to the SSW, one of its slopes dropping down to Black Sail Pass SW, from where the extended ridge rises again to Pillar WSW. In the middle ground in this direction are Fleetwith Pike and Hay Stacks. While observing these views you are standing on the highest point of the entire route.

The way to Robinson   *Allow 1 hour*

The way continues along the rocky band to the WNW, and the descending path crosses several rocky pinnacles before descending in a more orderly way to the wide col below. Part of Buttermere is visible from these slopes. Once across the hause you are faced with another climb, not so arduous this time, to reach the summit of Hindscarth, which juts out as a massive rock spur to the NW of your position running approximately NNE. In ascending from the col, select the narrow side-path veering up the fellside to the R. This traverses the slope ahead in a northwards diagonal, and surprisingly quickly you reach the expansive, rounded summit area. In clear weather it is simply delightful to spend time wandering along the edges of the huge area, and also down the short distance to the second NNE marker cairn. The views from here, at a height of 727 m (2,385 ft), are magnificent. There is not much in the way of additional sightings, but the views of the route you have just traversed are stunning, promoting such thoughts as 'Did I really walk along there?'.

Start your departure from Hindscarth by walking SSW along the broad, well-defined summit path, alongside cairns. Then veer to the R along the ridge path, avoiding retracing your route of approach

down to the L. Your path continues to bend progressively further R as it descends to the hause below, where it resumes a westerly direction. The path coming in on your L is the direct way from Dale Head, which by-passes the interesting summit area of Hindscarth. Turn to your R along this, using it to descend to the col ahead. The way continues up the opposite steep slope along a wire fence to your L.

On reaching a prominent cairn where the fence veers off to the L, turn R to the N, and follow the good, wide path up the gentle slope to gain the summit of Robinson. From these slopes you can see both Crummock Water and Loweswater to the NW, and the large mountain in between these is Mellbreak. The summit area of Robinson standing at 737 m (2,417 ft) is an interesting mixture of stones, grass and rocky ledges, which are overlooked by a large erect cairn. The area makes a particularly good foreground for photographs.

The way back to Gutherscale   *Allow 2½ hours*

Start your final descent to the NE down a gradual slope, towards a cairn on the near skyline. Then follow the cairned route, which soon begins to drop more acutely to your R towards Blea Crags. A steep descent follows down a series of rocky ledges that involve some scrambling, before reaching the long, lower rocky spur. Once this is reached the going becomes less exacting along the rolling, grassy ridge that continues to descend very agreeably along High Snab Bank, still to the NE. The streams in the valleys on either side of the spur, parallel to your direction of descent, are Keskadale Beck on your L and Scope Beck to your R.

Keep along the crest of the ridge until you come to a sign 'Permissive Path' indicating a R turn, which you take. Another steep descent follows, along a grassy path through bracken, down to the R of a small copse of Scots pines below. At the bottom turn L along a dry-stone wall, following a wide path down the valley NE through several stiles and gates. Pass Low High Snab Cottage and pass through an iron gate to reach a metalled lane. High Snab Farm, owned by the National Trust, is

to your L, followed by a delightful former church built by the parishioners in 1877 and closed in 1967; it now serves as Newlands School.

Shortly after this you pass through a gate, and then turn immediately R to cross a tributary stream running into Newlands Beck. The lane leads uphill to Little Town, which is what its name suggests, a tiny cluster of cottages together with a farm. Then turn R at the track signposted 'Public Footpath Skelgill'. Veer to the L through the iron gate as the path narrows, and further on cross the beck, which you then follow as the path continues to bear L. A succession of stiles and gates focus your diagonal direction of travel, still to the NE. When you reach Skelgill Farm turn to the R uphill, and through a gate. A lane leads you back to the car-park.

Alternative routes

ESCAPES
There are several convenient points where this route may be curtailed from either the ridges or cols before you reach Robinson, by turning to your R and descending along one of a number of good paths down into the valley. These routes can be accessed at Hause Gate, near Dale Head Tarn, from the summit of Dale Head and from the summit of Hindscarth.

EXTENSIONS
The mountains climbed on this route belong to a distinct group and as all of the principal peaks are scaled along the main route, it is not practical to extend the walk. If you wish to do more walking, spend longer in the area of High Spy and explore in more depth the interesting crags and rock features in this area. One other possibility is to descend from Hause Gate into Borrowdale, visit Grange, and then climb back onto the ridge by using part of the Cumbria Way Footpath round Nitting Haws to rejoin the main route to the N of High Spy.

7:2 Looking across Derwent Water to Skiddaw and Blencathra.

HAUSE GATE and GRANGE CRAGS
Lower Level Route 8

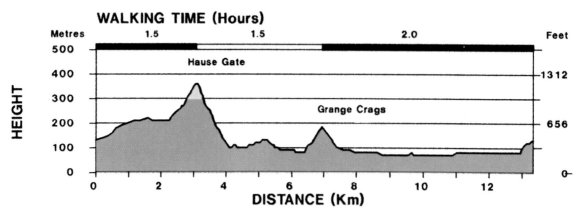

WEST-EAST (Km)

SOUTH-NORTH (Km)

WALKING TIME (Hours)

1.5	1.5	2.0

HEIGHT

Metres: 500, 400, 300, 200, 100, 0

Feet: 1312, 656, 0

Hause Gate

Grange Crags

DISTANCE (Km): 0, 2, 4, 6, 8, 10, 12

STATISTICS

START and FINISH
- Car Park nr. Gutherscale - OLM 4 / MR 247212

WALKING DISTANCE	Km	Miles
- Excluding Height	13.3	8.3
- Including Height	13.4	8.3

TOTAL WALKING TIME : 5.0 Hours

TOTAL HEIGHT GAINED
- 430 Metres   1411 Feet

PRINCIPAL HEIGHTS	Metres	Feet
- Hause Gate	365	1198
- Grange Crags	194	636

OTHER FEATURES OF INTEREST
- Village of Grange, Borrowdale and shores and inlets of SW Derwent Water.

Route 8 · Hause Gate and Grange Crags

Allow 5 hours

STARTING LOCATION

Car-park near Gutherscale.

OLM 4/MR 247212.

Small car-park – holds 10 to 15 cars.

(Some additional parking nearby).

Not on a bus route!

OVERVIEW/INTEREST

This is a walk for the entire family.

The way is undemanding and very interesting.

Grange-in-Borrowdale is visited.

Good views over Derwent Water and up

Borrowdale.

Return along delightful wooded shoreline of

Derwent Water.

FOOTPATHS

First class with only one relatively rough section

over Hause Gate.

Dry underfoot with the help of duckboards across

low-lying swampy areas near lake.

The way to Hause Gate   *Allow 1¼ hours*

Depart from the car-park up the lane sw to Skelgill Farm. Just before reaching the farm gate, take the track off to the L signed 'Public Footpath'. Continue along the broad track uphill, which bears round to the L in a ssw direction. Avoid all branch paths leading off more steeply up the fellside to your L. Extensive views soon open up; on your L is Cat Bells sse, then scanning westwards the Maiden Moor Ridge ssw, Hindscarth sw and Robinson to the wsw are visible. Across Newlands Valley on your R the spurs of Ard Crags leading to Knott Rigg, and Rolling End/Causey Pike can be located to the w and wnw respectively. The rounded shape of Barrow lies to the nw, further round on your R is Bassenthwaite Lake, and the outlines of Swinside backed by the awesome bulk of Skiddaw to the nne completes this attractive, early panorama.

Your path leads below the slopes of Cat Bells, and then it enters the gully shaped by Yewthwaite Gill. Here you climb up into Yewthwaite Comb along the wide, grassy path that swings round to the L before traversing up the steeply rising fellside. It should be recorded that you will have crossed a cobbled area and the beck by a wooden bridge prior to bearing off L, and then climbing se with the water course now to your L. Your path re-crosses the beck and then climbs steeply up the rough fellsides, which consist of an uncomfortable mixture of stones and small boulders. The steepest part of the gradient is soon over as the rock underfoot surrenders to grass. The way is now to the e through quite an unexpectedly remote and confined area. The path then swings first se to a prominent cairn, after which you select the path on the L continuing ne. This leads directly to Hause Gate, a flattish area of elevated land that forms a col in the ridge leading from Cat Bells in the n to Maiden Moor in the sw.

From this rounded spur and immediately below it, revealing views open up into the wide U-shaped valley of Borrowdale. To the nw the majestic lake of Derwent Water comes into view, and the deep blueness of its still waters contrasts vividly with the steep slopes of mighty Skiddaw and Blencathra in the background, the colours of which can vary from the greens of spring and summer, through the browns of autumn to the whites and blues of a winter's day when these high fells are covered in ice and snow. Hause Gate stands at 365 m (1,198 ft) and this represents the highest point along the route. Also, by now, most of your climbing has been accomplished.

The way to Grange Crags   *Allow 1¼ hours*

Cross the spur of the col and locate a steep path descending into Borrowdale alongside a wooden fence. A firm rocky path winds down the fellside from here, first in a series of sharp zigzags, after which it maintains a shallower angle of descent as

8:1 Reflections in Abbot's Bay – Derwent Water.

it traverses down on a long straight diagonal to the SSE. Along here, beyond Borrowdale, there is a revealing view of the extensive fells further to the E, which separate this valley from Thirlmere; the summit of High Seat is on an almost direct line to the E. When your path draws level with the southern tip of Derwent Water the village of Grange appears, and beyond it the impressive jaws of Borrowdale squeeze the valley together in their vice-like grip. The view below of Manesty Park, with the dense wooded slopes sweeping down to the indented SW shoreline of Derwent Water, presents an irresistibly photogenic scene.

Cobbled sections, reassuring signs, gates and stiles come and go before your secure path reaches the Portinscale-to-Grange road below, which you never quite make! Prior to your path connecting with the metalled surface, there is an indistinct path off to your R which you take, and this leads you uphill for about 40 paces, along a diagonal, to a wire fence, which you cross by means of a stile. The way here is signed 'Public Footpath' and a narrow track leads SW uphill through a copse of trees. On emerging from these you pass another sign advising you to keep to the path. (There is a permissive path round the top of this copse, which is reached by turning R higher up on your descent towards the road.)

The path then tracks round the lower slopes of the fells, and generally follows the direction of a stone wall below to the L (SSW). Some wet patches and a watercourse have to be crossed along here. Most of these are best avoided by keeping to the higher ground to their R. However on no account take any of the several ways leading more steeply up the fell to your R, but instead continue S in the general direction of the valley.

Across the watercourse, and after another stile, be careful to pass between a stone wall to your L and a fenced-in cultivated area to the R. Soon, you will see yellow waymarker signs as your way continues E down the fell towards the village of Grange. Follow the line of a stone wall and proceed through the gateway ahead, directly in line with the village. The gate to be used is located at right angles to a white gate marked 'Private High Close'. Follow the diagonal path to your L across the field to the road below, opposite the Borrowdale Gates Country House hotel. Turn R along the road into Grange-in-Borrowdale.

Grange is a delightful spot, usually bustling with visitors who somehow never manage to spoil the charm of the place. The River Derwent is a joy to watch here as its wide course gurgles contentedly under the two attractive, arched, stone bridges that span its pebble-lined bed. There are some large, smooth grooved rocks by the side of the river. The grooves were caused by rock debris frozen in the ice of a moving glacier. This rock debris acted as a rasp on the surface of the rock underneath, polishing the rock and scoring the grooves. The glaciers finally melted about 10,000 years ago.

Cross the bridges to reach the main valley road, the B5289, and turn R up this. Pass the Lakeland

Rural Industries Craft Shop on your L and immediately after this turn L climbing up the six slate steps and crossing a stile to gain entry to the footpath, signed 'Grange Fell'. Head along this grassy path up the fellside, initially to the SE. Your way soon bends round to the L, (E), passing beneath a single electricity cable. The rocky slopes rising steeply ahead are part of the extensive Grange Fell complex, which you do not have to scale today! Your path veers further to the L, now travelling NE. A short distance ahead there is a branch path off to the L, which you take, and after crossing a stone wall by an imposing l-stile, a clear path leads NW to the top of Grange Crags. Although this rocky promontory reaches a height of only 194 m (636 ft), it provides an excellent viewing position, especially over the village of Grange, spreadeagled down below to the W, and along the long ridge of Maiden Moor and High Spy towering above.

The way back to Gutherscale   *Allow 2 hours*

Retrace your steps back over the l-stile to the main path, and turn L along here to resume your route. Your way then passes through a gate in a wall and following this a distinct rocky and grass path descends into the valley ahead. At the next fork branch L, and then immediately cross a wall by means of another l-stile. Your path swings round to a more northerly bearing and the watercourse of Comb Gill appears below. The path reaches civilization once more at a National Trust group campsite in the vicinity of Troutdale Cottages, by which time you are travelling NW.

Follow the walled lane down to the valley road at Derwent House, cross the road to reach the footpath on the far verge, turn R along here, and walk beside the road for about ½ km (500 yd) before taking the public footpath off on your L. Pass through the gate/stile here and continue NNW across the flat meadowland on a diagonal, which will lead you to the banks of the River Derwent, flowing to your L. Follow the tree-lined banks to an imposing footbridge across the river. The marshy, low-lying ground to the S of Derwent Water has to be crossed next, but this is aided by sophisticated

duckboards which even have 'passing places' built into them! The path leads round the indented SW shore-line of the lake, passing through a gate and over footbridges. Veer to the R now, following the maze of footpaths that closely hug the edge of the water. There are several alternative ways through the attractively wooded shores along here, round Great Bay, Myrtle Bay, Abbot's Bay and Brandelhow Bay, in your progress NW to the steamer landing-stage at High Brandelhow.

From here, continue along the excellent footpath further to the N, passing Otterbield Bay, and through a k-gate near to a landing stage. Veer L here away from the lake and after two wrought-iron gates turn R along the metalled lane that descends to Cumberland Education Committee Hawse End Outdoor Activities Centre. About 100 paces further on, take the path off on your L, through the trees to the W with the shape of Causey Pike visible on the horizon ahead. This path climbs to the road a short distance away. Turn L, go past the cattle grid and the entrance to Gutherscale Lodge and then take the next turning on your R, signed 'Skelgill ½'. Your car-park is about 150 paces down this lane.

Alternative routes

ESCAPES

From the village of Grange it is possible to make directly to the SW shore-line of Derwent Water by heading N along the minor road round the W side of the lake, and then taking a footpath off to the R at Ellers Beck, MR 252184, to join up again with the main route.

EXTENSIONS

From Hause Gate turn R and walk along the ridge southwards for as long as you care to. Either Maiden Moor or High Spy are sensible objectives for this. Then descend to the E, veering NE, along part of the Cumbria Way, down the path between Maiden Moor and High Spy. This path will lead you into the village of Grange to re-connect with the main route.

HAY STACKS and HIGH STILE GROUP

High Level Route 9

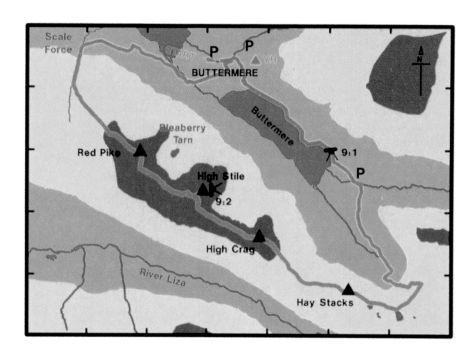

SOUTH-NORTH (Km)

WEST-EAST (Km)

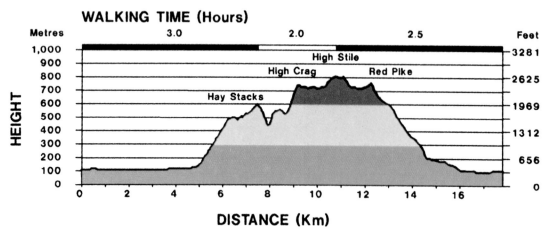

WALKING TIME (Hours)

DISTANCE (Km)

STATISTICS

START and FINISH			TOTAL HEIGHT GAINED		
- Buttermere - OLM 4 / MR 175170			- 1020 Metres 3346 Feet		
WALKING DISTANCE	Km	Miles	PRINCIPAL HEIGHTS	Metres	Feet
- Excluding Height	17.8	11.0	- Hay Stacks	597	1959
- Including Height	18.1	11.2	- High Crag	744	2443
TOTAL WALKING TIME : 7.5 Hours			- High Stile	806	2644
			- Red Pike	755	2479

OTHER FEATURES OF INTEREST
- Good views down into Buttermere and Ennerdale Valleys; Scale Force.

6

The North-west and Westerly Fells

Part 3

Route 9 · Hay Stacks and High Stile Group

Allow 7½ hours

STARTING LOCATION
Buttermere car-park.
OLM 4/MR 175170.
Holds up to 40 cars and some coach parking nearby.
(Additional parking above village).
Not on a bus route!

OVERVIEW/INTEREST
Tranquil start along wooded shores of Buttermere.
Stunning views at both low and high levels.
Demanding climbs.
Fascinating geological features.
Delightful hamlet of Buttermere village.

FOOTPATHS
For most of the way the paths are good and obvious.
Serious erosion on steep scree slopes of High Crag, and summit of Red Pike is badly worn.
Return path above Crummock Water is boggy in places.

The way to Hay Stacks   *Allow 3 hours*

Leave the car-park by the entrance lane and return to the valley road, turning R down it. From the village square, rewarding views immediately appear of High Snockrigg ahead E, and panning around to the R, of Fleetwith Pike SE and of Hay Stacks SSE, your first major objective. Further round, the High

Stile Range soars dramatically to the S with the separate peaks of High Crag, High Stile and the lower slopes of Red Pike clearly distinguishable. Sourmilk Gill plummets dramatically over the lower slopes between High Stile and Red Pike.

Take the next turning on the R beyond Syke Farm, signed 'Public bridleway – Lakeshore path'. Pass through Wilkinsyke farmyard, through a gate and over a stile, and continue along a wide, stony path heading ESE. From here there is a sighting of the tip of Buttermere Lake over to the R (S). At the division of the ways ahead, turn R towards the lake along the path signed 'Lakeshore footpath'. Over to the R, the attractive outline of the white village buildings may be observed standing out against the dominant darker shape of Mellbreak rising above it across Crummock Water WNW.

Pass through a gate and, following a short descent, walk along the NE shore of Buttermere Lake with the imposing view of Fleetwith Pike and Hay Stacks, separated by a massive combe, appearing across the water to the SE. The path wends through a delightful copse of deciduous trees, mainly oak with a sprinkling of holly, silver birch and hawthorn. An interesting feature along here is a narrow tunnel blasted through an outcrop of rock to provide a former working route. Keep always to the lower lakeside path, avoiding less distinct paths to the L leading up the fellside. Towards the head of the lake, the famous and often photographed Buttermere pines come into view

59

hugging a sweeping bay in the lake, and these present a perfect foreground to the more distant vista of Scarth Gap visible across the lake on the R (S). The path eventually leads back to the road; turn R along this and proceed to Gatesgarth. Pass the farm and a car-park, and then turn R along a wide stony track signed 'Bridleway', which leads off S, veering SE.

Avoid a steep path to the L straight up Fleetwith Edge, and continue along the gently rising broad path that threads its way towards the head of the glaciated valley. When the main track veers to the L take a grassy, cairned side path off to the R (SSE) heading to the R of the waterfall ahead. Cross the beck by the wooden footbridge, and the way then crosses a tributary stream with the main water course of Warnscale Beck cascading down a series of minor waterfalls on your L. The path now gains height quickly as it winds up the steep craggy fell-side, and the gradient becomes quite challenging. During this part of the ascent there are good views back down the valley of Buttermere and Crummock Water. The stony path threads its way through boulders, and re-crosses the stream.

Next swing to the R away from the beck, avoiding a L fork ahead opposite a disused building high up on the fellside above; your direction is now S. The track bears round to the L and a small marker cairn is visible on the near horizon. At the next junction select the sharp R-hand turn and climb the steep slope due S up a shallow ravine. The flat-topped massif of Grasmoor is visible to your rear, to the R of the lakes N, and near this point a path over from Honister comes in on your L. Next you pass four cairns in quick succession on your L, and then take a R fork continuing WSW, through wild and craggy mountain uplands. The outlines of the Gables and Pillar rise ahead on your L, SSW and SW respectively, and here you should keep to the main rocky path in the view of a pronounced boulder way over on your L.

Soon Blackbeck Tarn appears on the L (S); descend and cross the exit stream, and then proceed uphill around the spur of the fell as the path continues to ascend. Here there are superb views on your R down into the Buttermere Valley, with a particularly good exposure of Fleetwith Pike NE,

9:1 The Buttermere Pines and Hay Stacks.

Hindscarth and Robinson NNE and Grasmoor N. Next, you pass the delightful small and remote Innominate (no name) Tarn to your L, and the path continues W, leading upwards to the several summits of Hay Stacks, height 597 m (1,959 ft). The vista from the summits is remarkable and includes:

SW	Pillar.
W	Ennerdale.
NW	High Crag.
N	Buttermere and Grasmoor.
NNE	Robinson.
	Skiddaw (in the far distance).
NE	Hindscarth.

ENE	Dale Head.
E	Helvellyn Range.
ESE	The Gables.
SSE	Lingmell.
S	Black Sail Pass.

The way to High Stile   *Allow 2 hours*

Circle round a tiny tarn on your R, and descend down a steep rocky path past a small cairn to the R, heading W in the direction of Ennerdale and High Crag. The path bends R, rising slightly, and then descends rapidly towards Buttermere NNW. Here there is some fine scrambling down alternative routes. The paths swing about on the way down,

and depending upon which particular way you choose, the final descent to the top of Scarth Gap is either direct or along a traverse NNW. In any event, make for the large cairn at the crest of the gap.

Cross the main path leading N to S through Scarth Gap, and head due W up the steep rocky crags along a twisting route through the severe scree slopes, which are badly eroded; you will need to exercise care here! The remains of a long-abandoned iron fence mark the continuation of the way upwards into a short, sharp scramble, after which the path levels off to a less severe rate of climb. Next, the way descends slightly to a col before the final ascent of High Crag NW. Pass a small tarn to your L and then ascend by the path to the L of the rusty iron-railing posts, where shortly the path veers off further to the L (WNW) traversing up a grassy slope. Continue along the final zigzag climb to reach the summit of High Crag, height 744 m (2,443 ft).

The path continues along the flattish ridge WNW, with a revealing view down over Buttermere Village on your R (N). Down the other flank lies Ennerdale with its extensive coniferous forests, snaking lake and the meandering River Liza. You are now proceeding along a superb ridge route between two particularly attractive but contrasting valleys. The path undulates before finally ascending to the summit of High Stile. Along this section the ground to the R falls away dramatically in a series of precipitous rocky crags and gullies intermingled with steeply angled scree slopes, which bear the hallmarks of severe erosion, including ice-shattering.

Soon the immense rocky buttress of High Stile looms ahead, dominating the skyline, while down below on your R the start of the grassy Newlands Valley appears NE. Also in this NE panorama the splendid ridge up from Causey Pike via Sail to Crag Hill may be observed dominating the middle skyline, while the Skiddaw massif rises majestically on the far horizon. The final cairned ascent is to the NNW, and over to the R through gaps in the intervening fells Blencathra may be seen on a clear day.

Towards the top of the main ridge path, veer off to the R (N) to head along the High Stile promontory protruding northwards, and make your way to the summit at 806 m (2,644 ft), and the highest

9:2 Buttermere, Honister Pass and Fleetwith Pike from High Stile.

point of the route. Continue along this alternating rocky and grassy promontory, descending a little at the end to an obvious viewing platform. Below in the valleys the lakes of Ennerdale, Loweswater, and Crummock Water all come into view in a sweep from W to N, while nestling in the middle of much higher terrain the nearer waters of Bleaberry Tarn enhance the views across to Red Pike NW. In clear weather the following high peaks may be recognized:

N	Grasmoor.
NE	Skiddaw.
ENE	Newlands, Keswick and Blencathra.
E	Robinson and Hindscarth.
ESE	Dale Head.
SE	Helvellyn Range beyond Fleetwith Pike, and the Langdale Pikes.
SSE	High Crag, Hay Stacks and the Gables beyond.
S	The Scafells.
SSW	Pillar
NW	Red Pike.

The way back to Buttermere village

Allow 2½ hours

Return to the main ridge path and follow the line of cairns W. Continue down the slope over rough, rocky ground to reach a col in the ridge between High Stile and Red Pike, after which the path rises steadily to the summit of Red Pike, 755 m (2,479 ft). Again, excellent views may be observed from this peak. The mountains have been identified in previous listings in this chapter. Choose the red gravel and stone path leading steeply down NW for the start of the descent. At the end of the steep section the ground falls spectacularly on the R. Some distance on, take the L fork away from the sharp edge on your R, and continue down along the wide, eroded rocky path through the moorland heathers WNW. (Be careful here not to proceed too far to the W or you will reach the high ground leading to Little and Starling Dodd!)

On reaching lower ground and towards the approach to Scale Beck the path swings round to the R (N), and then continues downhill towards Crummock Water, levelling off to a less severe angle of descent. Another path down from Red Pike converges from your R, but this is a more exasperating way down, twisting and turning uncertainly through the steeper, heather-clad fell-side. The path becomes assisted in the form of a series of rocky steps, which descend steeply in a chain of zigzags to the bottom of Scale Force, the highest single drop, of some 37 m (120 ft), in the Lake District. At this point go round to your L to view the falls, which are quite spectacular.

The route continues downhill, with Scale Beck on your L, towards Crummock Water, and as the path bends round to the R in the direction of Buttermere keep to the higher ground as there is a boggy stretch ahead. Pass a single cairn, and continue along a line of cairns before turning sharply downhill to a lower level, nearer to the shoreline of Crummock Water. A good firm path now becomes established, and this gradually descends to the head of the lake. Turn L through a gateway, then cross over Scale Bridge, and finally follow the well-established pathways back to Buttermere village.

Alternative routes

ESCAPES

The most obvious route is from the top of Scarth Gap (MR 189133). Turn R along this well-defined track, and descend to Buttermere Lake, taking a L fork on the way down. Proceed along the SW shore of Buttermere through Burtness Wood, and at the W tip of the lake cross the beck by the footbridge and follow the well-defined paths back to Buttermere village.

EXTENSIONS

The main route described is quite challenging, but a further extension is to gain height by first climbing Fleetwith Pike along its 'Edge'. Then, after proceeding ESE to Bell Crags, locate the main path leading up from Honister to Hay Stacks. Turn R (WSW) along this path to rejoin the main route suggested just over 1 km (½ mile) further on to the WSW.

MOSEDALE and CRUMMOCK WATER

Lower Level Route 10

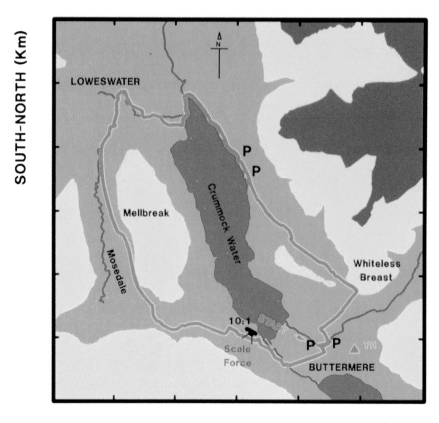

SOUTH-NORTH (Km)

WEST-EAST (Km)

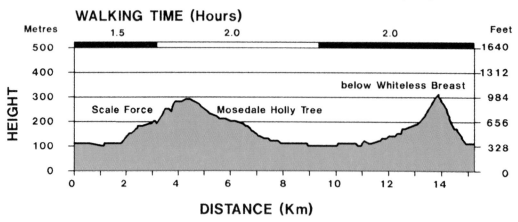

STATISTICS

START and FINISH
- Buttermere - OLM 4 / MR 175170

WALKING DISTANCE	Km	Miles
- Excluding Height	15.2	9.5
- Including Height	15.3	9.5

TOTAL WALKING TIME : 5.5 Hours

TOTAL HEIGHT GAINED
- 440 Metres   1444 Feet

PRINCIPAL HEIGHTS	Metres	Feet
- Mosedale		
(highest point)	295	970
- below Whiteless Breast		
	305	1000

OTHER FEATURES OF INTEREST
- Scale Force and Crummock Water.

Route 10 · Mosedale and Crummock Water

Allow 5½ hours

STARTING LOCATION
Buttermere car-park.
OLM 4/MR 175170.
Accommodates up to 40 cars and some coach
parking nearby.
(Additional car-parking above village).
Not on a bus route!

OVERVIEW/INTEREST
Undemanding route with a minimum of climbing.
Scale Force is visited.
Remote moorland valley of Mosedale.
Tranquil rural setting round Loweswater village.
Variety of rewarding views.
Ideal walk for a family group.

FOOTPATHS
For the most part the paths are clear and the going
is easy.
Some squelchy sections before Scale Force.
Marshy access route to shores of Crummock Water
beyond Loweswater village – alternative route in
wet conditions.

The way to Scale Force

Allow 1½ hours

At the car-park there is an immediate starting
bonus with extensive views to the S of, from L to R,
the lower slopes of High Crag, High Stile and Red
Pike, and also towards the source of the Buttermere Valley the crags of Hay Stacks SE and
Fleetwith Pike ESE. From the car-park turn immediately R around the Fish Inn, continuing down the
wide gravel path towards the lakes. The path bends
sharp L and the route passes through a k-gate. The
impressive waterfall of Sourmilk Gill can be seen
ahead, cascading down the steep mountainside as
glimpses of Buttermere Lake ahead, and Crummock Water behind to the R, come into view. Pass
through the k-gate on the R signed 'To Scale Bridge
and Scale Force'. Mellbreak Fell, which you will
walk around, now comes into prominent view
across the fields on your R (NNW), as too does the

pronounced peak of Hen Comb, visible on the
horizon WNW. To the rear on your R beyond Buttermere village the distinctive crest of Whiteless
Pike rises majestically from the valley.

Cross the stream connecting the two lakes at
Scale Bridge, pass through the gate and turn R
along a narrow gravel path that leads uphill. Grasmoor comes into view on your R (N). The path continues through a sprinkling of trees, including
hawthorn, crab-apple, ash, hornbeam, holly,
silver birch, and further on also oak and rowan.
The path swings abruptly to the L, and for a short
time you are faced with a steeper climb before the
path swings back R, resuming its previous comfortable gradient. In this section there is an area of
boggy ground and the path appears less distinct
before it becomes re-established as a sandy, stoned
route marked by cairns WNW. Turn around to
observe the summit of Robinson peeping up above
High Snockrigg ESE, and Dale Head to its R (SE).

The path bears L, and having passed through a
repaired gap in a stone wall, approaches an
impressive wide wooden footbridge ahead. However, before crossing this veer L to view Scale
Force, the highest single fall in Lakeland, some
37 m (120 ft) high.

The way to the N shores of Crummock Water

Allow 2 hours

Retrace your steps to cross Scale Beck at the footbridge, and climb up the narrow rocky path ahead,
which immediately swings round L. You will soon
be walking along a good narrow path that traverses
the adjacent fellside leading first W and then WNW
as it gains height. Pause when you come to the
cairn on your L to take in the remoteness and scale
of the valley ahead with the encircling peaks of
Gale Fell, Great Borne, Floutern Crag and Cop, and
Hen Comb protecting its upper reaches SSW to
NNW. The path now veers R towards Black Beck,
and a further cairn is passed on the L. Descend,

cross the narrow beck, and climb the opposite grassy slope NNE.

Red Pike now looms into view to the rear SSE as you proceed along the grassy path on the L (NNW). You are now heading towards Mosedale, and you will need to circumnavigate some wet, boggy areas straddling the slopes ahead. Another path joins from the R; continue ahead to the L passing a rusty iron gate on your L. You are now walking along the E side of Mosedale, a sheltered U-shaped valley. You will soon observe a solitary holly tree to your L as the path commences a long gentle descent.

Ignore several narrow tracks leading off on your R uphill, and continue due N beside an iron railing. The two pronounced fells ahead are Darling Fell on the L and Low Fell to the R. Follow the main track round to the L of the V-shaped plantation of pines, and this path then bends round progressively to the R. The dark silhouetted majestic mountain shape ahead is Whiteside ENE, and having passed through a gate, a revealing view of the high mountains dwarfing the N tip of Crummock Water reappears, including the unusual pointed shape, when viewed from this angle, of Grasmoor E. The track widens into a distinct lane as it passes between protective stone walls.

Your way now crosses relatively lush meadowland, and farm animals grazing in a tranquil lowlands rural scene. You pass Kirkgate Farm on your L, and as you walk along the lane there are impressive views on the R of the end of Mellbreak, which plunges steeply and dramatically to the valley floor in the form of three immense rock buttresses, Raven Crag, White Crag and Dropping Crag. Cross Park Beck at the stone-arched Church Bridge, and the Kirkstile Inn is on your L with its inviting S-facing grassy terrace.

Having passed/visited the inn, take the first lane off on the R signed 'No road to the lake', and continue down this with the beck below to your R. When the road bends to the L take the side lane off on the R signed 'Dead end'. Cross the stream at the bridge, pass the entrance to Lowpark Farm on your R and immediately turn L where the path is now adjacent to Park Beck on the L. Go through a wide k-gate and take the top path round to the R, veering away from the beck. Crummock Water can be seen

ahead below the slopes of Grasmoor. Cross the stile at the stone wall and continue to the L beside the wall as long as possible to avoid marshy ground ahead on your R. Then turn R, and cross the stream by the stone slab provided, after which turn L over the next stile. Then follow the line of pine trees down to the lake shore. Turn L over a stile and cross the narrow concrete causeway to start the delightful part of the walk round the lake.

CAUTIONARY NOTE After heavy rains, a section of the suggested route can be nasty, and in these conditions follow an alternative, but less attractive way from Loweswater village by continuing along the road past the church on your L and then turning R down the road which links with the B5289. Take the immediate footpath off on your R, turn L at Gillerthwaite and R at Muncaster House. Continue along the path to reach the lake shore at exactly the same spot as on the preferred route.

The way back to Buttermere village

Allow 2 hours

The path leads round a pumping-house and then across a series of feeder streams with sluices owned by North West Water, the Victorian architecture of which is fascinating. Continue around the lake crossing a stile, a footbridge, the waterworks sluice-gates, and a pleasant natural beach frequented by families. The path then leads off uphill to the R, quickly gaining a modest height above the lake as it passes through Lanthwaite Wood, a mixed grouping of mainly deciduous trees. Veer R along a more imposing path, and this continues SE at a fairly constant elevation. The most interesting route forward is to keep to the path nearest to the lake passing a boat-house on your R. Your way is next through High Wood, which contains a recently planted area where you are alerted that this is private woodland. The path crosses several stiles and footbridges as it winds along the attractive tree-fringed lake shore.

The delightful walk around part of Crummock Water comes to an end at a stone wall, where steps lead up to the road (B5289) at a k-gate in Fletcher

Fields. Turn R down the road, and almost immediately veer L off the road through a car-park, heading for the crag ahead, Rannerdale Knotts.
Continue SSE along a wide cart-track, which
snakes gradually up the fellside. A pleasant grassy
path leads round the fell to the L, across a stile. In
May the rounded slopes in this area are a mass of
bluebells.

Cross Squat Beck at the footbridge, climb over
the wall by the l-stile and then turn L along a
narrow track leading uphill to higher Rannerdale,
with the fell of Low Bank on your R. The path
crosses the beck and at this point turn around to
obtain a revealing view down to Crummock Water
and Loweswater NW. A grassy path leads up to the
hause ahead. At the top turn R, past a small cairn,
along a path that descends from Whiteless Pike on
the L. From this attractive area there are extensive
views of the panorama surrounding Buttermere
village, and the names and positions of the main
mountain groups should be pleasurably etched
into your memory by now. There is also a fine view
into the great glaciated high combe, which houses
Bleaberry Tarn. The exit stream Sourmilk Gill can
be traced cascading down over the steep fellside
directly ahead, beyond Buttermere village. Walk
down the rounded slopes, and select the L path,
which descends to a stone wall on the L. Follow
this line down and pass through a gate below. The
way now leads back to the valley road, turn L along
this and after a short distance pass the Bridge
Hotel, then turn R into Buttermere village and the
car-park at the far end.

Alternative routes

ESCAPES

There are several easy ways to shorten this walk,
which makes it particularly flexible for families.
These include walking just to Scale Force and
back; from Scale Force, leisurely ambling round
Crummock Water instead of following the longer
and more demanding way along Mosedale; and
towards the finish, avoiding the climb up Rannerdale by turning R instead of turning L after crossing
the stream and wall. Then, on this latter alterna-

10:1 Scale Force.

tive, follow the path in the opposite direction
round the rocky spur of Rannerdale Knotts on the
L, back to the road. After a short distance, take a
minor track off to the L in order to avoid prolonged
walking by the roadside. This track rejoins the
road further on before Buttermere village is
reached.

EXTENSIONS

The obvious extension for the very fit is first to
climb Red Pike by way of Bleaberry Tarn. This
route is along well-defined footpaths, and apart
from the serious erosion of the paths, particularly
on the higher slopes, the way should present no
problems to the experienced walker. For those who
tackle this extension, join the suggested main
route at Scale Force.

Another possibility is to climb Mellbreak
instead of proceeding down Mosedale, and then
continue N along this ridge to rejoin the main route
at Loweswater village.

PILLAR and RED PIKE
High Level Route 11

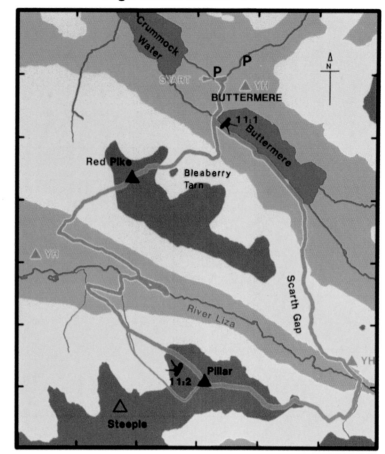

SOUTH-NORTH (Km)

WEST-EAST (Km)

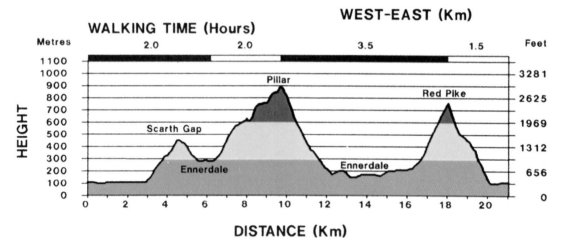

WALKING TIME (Hours)

HEIGHT

DISTANCE (Km)

STATISTICS

START and FINISH		
- Buttermere - OLM 4 / MR 175170		

WALKING DISTANCE	Km	Miles
- Excluding Height	21.1	13.1
- Including Height	21.6	13.4

TOTAL WALKING TIME : 9.0 Hours

TOTAL HEIGHT GAINED
- 1650 Metres   5413 Feet

PRINCIPAL HEIGHTS	Metres	Feet
- Pillar	892	2927
- Red Pike	755	2479

OTHER FEATURES OF INTEREST
- Buttermere, westward views from Pillar, Ennerdale Forest and River Liza.

7

The North-west and Westerly Fells

Part 4

Route 11 · Pillar and Red Pike

Allow 9 hours

STARTING LOCATION
Buttermere car-park.
OLM 4/MR 175170.
Holds up to 40 cars and some coach parking nearby.
(Additional parking above village).
Not on a bus route!

OVERVIEW/INTEREST
Really outstanding route.
Probably one of the finest high-level day treks in the whole of Lakeland.
Wide variety of superb landscapes, including Buttermere and Ennerdale.
Physically extremely demanding.
The ultimate in terms of satisfaction upon completion.

FOOTPATHS
The paths with two exceptions are remarkably good.
No entirely satisfactory route down from Pillar!
Descent from Red Pike down steep, seriously eroded slopes!

E	High Snockrigg blocking Robinson beyond.
SE	Fleetwith Pike.
SSE	Hay Stacks.
S	High Crag and High Stile.
SW	Red Pike (summit not visible).
WNW	Mellbreak.
NNE	Whiteless Pike above Low Bank.

Leave the car-park by the entrance road and turn R round the Fish Hotel, following the public bridleway which leads SW. There are revealing views along here. Ahead to your L is Sourmilk Gill, and Crummock Water over to your R (NW). Continue down the path through gates, heading SSW towards Sourmilk Gill. Over to your R the pointed peak of Hen Comb appears to the W. Turn around now to pinpoint the long edge of Grasmoor summit N, as Buttermere appears through the trees ahead on your L (SE). Cross Buttermere Dubs at the footbridge and select the L path round the SW shoreline of the lake.

The path winds along the lake under a canopy of mainly deciduous trees. Soon, over on your L at the head of the lake, the sweep of the famed Buttermere Pines comes into view. Pass footbridges, k-gates and confirmatory signs before, near the commencement of a stone wall on your L, you take a narrow, stony path leading off uphill on your R. Veer to the R at the joining of routes ahead, and

The way to Black Sail Hut (Youth Hostel)

Allow 2 hours

Before leaving the car-park look E and, turning round clockwise, position the following high mountains that surround Buttermere village:

69

follow the stony path as it twists upwards to Scarth Gap between the mountain peaks of Hay Stacks and High Crag.

Towards the top, turn around for a lingering look backwards to view the Whiteless Pike Ridge leading up to the massive shape of Grasmoor to the N; Robinson, Hindscarth and the ridge leading to Dale Head NNE, and nearer to the distinctive pointed summit of Fleetwith Pike NE. Through the gap ahead the progressively revealing skyline is equally but differently impressive. The bulk of Great Gable rises on the L to the SSE, the graceful slopes of Kirk Fell more to the R leading down to Black Sail Pass, and further to your R still the long profile leading to the summit of Pillar to the SW.

The descent into Ennerdale is along a well-defined, cairned route down a rugged slope. During the relaxing walk down, the extensive coniferous forestry plantations that occupy much of Ennerdale become more prominent. At a point where your path bends to the L, the impressive ser-rated profile of Pillar Rock rears up across the valley to the SW on your R, and must be a tantaliz-ing sight for climbers. The path continues to descend along the tree-line on your R, as Green Gable appears to the L of Great Gable. A wide fores-try track is reached at the bottom of the slope. Turn L down this, now walking ESE. This leads, a short distance ahead, to the Black Sail Youth Hostel.

11:1 Early morning sunlight on Buttermere.

The way to Pillar   *Allow 2 hours*

Fork R, cross the River Liza by the footbridge and then proceed up the path that climbs SSW to the top of Black Sail Pass. Higher up there is a superb view down along Ennerdale over your R shoulder to the WNW, with the valley flanked to the L by Pillar and on the R by the High Stile group. Ahead to the L of the col, the dark brooding rocky shapes of Boat How Crags and Kirkfell Crags loom up to the S and SSW respectively.

When you reach the top of the pass your contin-uation route is to the R (WNW). However, advance for a short distance, walking slightly downhill, in order to take in a sighting of the famous Mosedale Horseshoe and to pan your eyes round many of the

peaks that make up this magnificent high-level route. Over to the L is the craggy sentinel-peak of Yewbarrow SSW, with its N ridge sweeping down to the now dangerously eroded Dore Head Screes. To the R of these is the dominant bulk of Mosedale Red Pike to the WSW. This in turn leads to the main ridges of the Pillar group of mountains, of which Great Scoat Fell marks the WSW extreme.

Retrace your steps the short distance to the path heading off WNW and walk up it. When more height is gained, the Irish Sea may be observed on a clear day through the gap in the mountain chain to the SW beyond Dore Head. Part of West Water appears SSW, and then further away the shimmer-ing shape of Burnmoor Tarn S comes into view. Just before the slope you are treading up steepens appreciably, the far-distant rocky pinnacles of Sca Fell appear round the shoulder of the nearer Kirk Fell to the S. In virtually the opposite direction, and also a great distance away, the outline of Skid-daw can be observed on the skyline to the NNE.

The next part of the ascent is along a steep rocky path, and some easy scrambling is involved. This is followed by a long, sweeping traverse beneath the highest level of the ridge, and along here the higher peaks leading to the summit of Pillar appear ahead WNW. Continue climbing towards these along the cairned, rocky path. To your rear L the full extent of the Scafell group is now revealed, with the separate peaks of Scafell Pike and Great End prominent SE. To the R of these massive fells is the lower, pyramid profile of Harter Fell, which nevertheless towers over its immediately surrounding landscape. Further to the R is the more irregular, jagged outline of Ulpha Fell to the S.

To the immediate R are a series of deep gullies and chasms, which are worth your inspection from the safety of the top ridge. A further series of slopes, differently graded in terms of steepness, have to be climbed before the ground levels off into the wide expanse of the summit area of Pillar, with its topography of a shelter, a trig. point and a large summit cairn. These are at a height of 892 m (2,927 ft). This peak, the high point of the route, commands extensive views in all directions when the weather is favourable, and the following features can be observed from its trig. point, starting with the Scafell grouping:

SSE	Scafell group and Harter Fell.
S	Illgill Head and Whin Rigg Ridge.
SW	Wasdale Red Pike and Haycock.
W	Scoat Fell with Steeple.
WNW	Ennerdale Water.
NNW	Crummock Water.
N	Buttermere Red Pike and Grasmoor.
NE	Skiddaw, over Causey Pike and Robinson. Blencathra.
ENE	Helvellyn group.
ESE	Glaramara.
SE	Great Gable and Bow Fell.

The way to Red Pike   *Allow 3½ hours*

Depart from the summit area heading NW, passing a smaller shelter to your R, and quickly locate a cairned path leading down towards the head of Ennerdale Water. Be careful here of the precipitously steep edge to your R. When the lower slopes of the mountain come into view, take a bearing on the position where the stream High Beck enters the forested area, i.e., to the NW, and steadfastly descend on this line of travel. Before you lose too much height pause to enjoy the vista unfolding before you of lower Ennerdale, with its wide irregular lake flanked to the N by Great Borne and to the S with Crag Fell and Boathow Crag.

A long descent across less steep, grassy slopes, following a line of intermittent old iron fenceposts, will bring you to the boundary of the forested area. Here Steeple and Black Crag jut out above you on the L. On no account enter the forest before High Beck is crossed, and therefore ignore the first inviting stile leading down into the trees. On the far side of the stream your route joins up with the alternative descent route, which is described next.

This alternative was suggested by one of the Forestry Rangers, but it is debatable whether it offers a balance of advantage over the descent route previously described. Start this alternative by descending from the summit of Pillar to the SW, heading down to the narrow ridge connecting Pillar with Little Scoat Fell. The comfortable starting slope soon changes to a steep climb down through loose scree and firmer rock as several ways down twist and turn through the craggy wilderness, before a firmer rock-face is reached at the hause of Wind Gap.

Turn sharp R at the bottom of the col, heading down a faint, narrow path that descends steeply towards the NW. The compacted path then squirms down the very severe, loose-scree slope. Fortunately, this is soon over and as firmer, larger rocks are engaged, cairns point the correct route across these infrequently used piles of debris. Keep walking down the fellside in an uncompromising NW direction, heading towards the meandering stream below of High Beck. At a convenient point lower down, cross the stream. You will have to abandon a line of cairns to do this, but for once this is permissible, as the stream is more difficult to cross further down. Continue to descend until you reach the boundary of the forest plantation, where this alternative route joins up with the way down described initially.

Both routes now continue eastwards for a short distance along a faint path by the side of the forest fence. Cross this fence at the next stile and follow a better established path down beside an internal wire fence on your R. Veer L by a weathered stone wall and continue to descend to the NNW. Cairn markers re-appear along here. Cross the forestry road on the diagonal and continue down the path on the far side, the start of which is located by a cairn. The next section is currently quite difficult; however, sticks with red tape have been positioned to mark the intended way through this unpleasant area. Eventually, a stile is reached with an orange marker circle on a wooden post. The path beyond leads to the Forestry Commission's 'Nine Becks Walk', which is signed as such. Turn to the R and continue along this narrow but established way E towards upper Ennerdale. This forest trail is marked with posts carrying a blue circle.

The trail leads slightly uphill before, at the next beck adjacent to a line of more mature conifers, it turns sharply to the L and descends towards the River Liza below to the N. The path reaches a forestry road and after using the bridge along this to cross the stream on your R, turn immediately L down the continuation of the trail to reach the river directly below. Turn R along the river bank and follow the trail upstream to the ESE. The trail leads to a wide forest road that crosses the River Liza by a substantial bridge at this point.

Climb on to the road and cross the river by turning L. Then turn L again into the major road and walk down the valley, now travelling WNW. After about ½ km (500 yd) turn off to the R along a path signed 'Nine Becks Walk' and a short distance further on, veer R again, up an attractive minor forest road that immediately bends to the L. The lane levels off and then commences to descend gradually to the L. Just before it drops, look out for an important marker on your R indicating the continuation of the Nine Becks trail that you follow here. The sign is low down and can easily become obstructed by foliage!

There is a very indistinct exit route from the road and the way along the next section of the path under the trees only becomes intermittently well established as it runs diagonally to the NW, rising at first and then levelling off. A stream is crossed by a footbridge and the continuation path soon reaches the edge of the trees at a wire fence. On the other side, cross a short stretch of open fellside to connect with the path coming up from High Gillerthwaite. Turn R along this clearly defined way and make for the gate and stile ahead, which provides access to the open fellside.

A long, severe climb now follows that will test aching leg muscles and lung capacities as you trudge up the relentlessly steep slopes. The path ascends to the NE towards the shallow col linking Little Dodd to the NNW with Red Pike to the ENE. Then, quite unexpectedly, you arrive. The summit of Red Pike provides an array of views in the soft, yellowing evening light, which are beyond comparison. The blend of long mountain spurs linking the flat valleys and lakes with the surrounding high massive mountains is superb, and inevitably much is lost in any attempt at translating this scene into words. You must see it for yourself, glowing in the warmth of your exertions and the contentment derived from your achievements.

The summit of Red Pike stands at 755 m (2,479 ft), and on clear days the following mountains and lakes are visible from here:

SE	Scafell group.
SSE	Pillar.
S	Steeple and Scoat Fell
SSW	Haycock.
W	Ennerdale Water.
WNW	The Dodds and Great Borne.
NW	Hen Comb with Blake Fell and Carling Knott behind.
NNW	Loweswater and Mellbreak.
N	Crummock Water.
NNE	Grasmoor.
NE	Whiteless Pike with Crag Hill and Sail beyond.
	Causey Pike with Skiddaw on horizon.
ENE	Blencathra, also on the far horizon.
ENE to E	Robinson, Hindscarth and Dale Head.
ESE	Fleetwith Pike.
SE	High Stile.

11:2 Descending westward from Pillar into Ennerdale.

The way back to Buttermere   *Allow 1½ hours*

Start the descent ESE along the wide path marked by cairns. Small, round Bleaberry Tarn then comes into sight below. The way is down a steep, danger-ously eroded path, which twists and turns drop-ping to the tarn. You should be particularly careful descending here. Pass the tarn, keeping it on your R. Great combes open up below the summits of High Stile and Red Pike. The remoteness and wildness of these bowls, intensified by their lining of shattered rock-faces, contrast vividly with the serenity of Buttermere and the orderly neatness of the village, with smoke slowly rising from the chimneys of the buildings there, indicating the warmth and cosiness that awaits you down below.

Next cross the stream, which falls as Sourmilk Gill, and continue walking along the stony path ESE. A long traverse follows, which starts by lead-ing you some distance away from Buttermere vil-lage towards the head of the lake. Then follows a series of steep zigzags along a renovated pathway that is not entirely sympathetic to tired and aching leg muscles and sore toes! Following a gate, there is a final descent down a long straight traverse through mixed woodlands. This takes you to the lower path round Buttermere that you used on your outward route. Retrace your steps from here back into Buttermere village.

Alternative routes

ESCAPES

The most sensible way of curtailing this long, demanding route is, when you descend into upper Ennerdale, to walk westwards down the valley, cutting out the ascent of Pillar. Rejoin the main route lower down the valley at MR 165135, just above the bridge across the River Liza.

Having climbed Pillar and descended back into Ennerdale, should the prospect of climbing Red Pike appear too daunting, continue up Ennerdale from MR 165135 and return to Buttermere via Scarth Gap, retracing your outward steps from the top of the hause.

EXTENSIONS

The route described is sufficiently demanding for even strong walkers, and therefore extensions to this particular route are not recommended. For those few who must, there is an even longer, more arduous descent route from Pillar by way of Steeple and down Long Crag, back into Ennerdale!

73

ENNERDALE
Lower Level Route 12

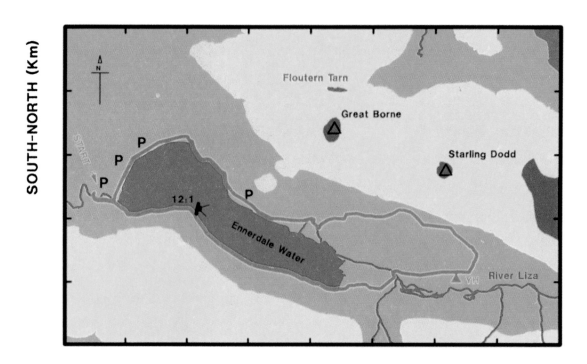

SOUTH-NORTH (Km)

WEST-EAST (Km)

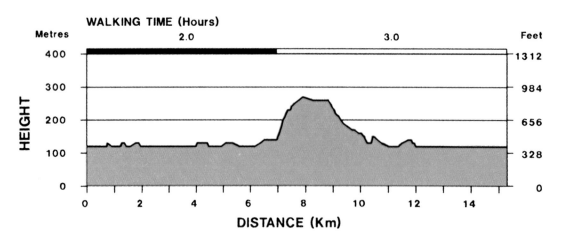

STATISTICS

START and FINISH			TOTAL HEIGHT GAINED
- Forestry Car Park - OLM 4 / MR 085154			- 240 Metres 787 Feet

WALKING DISTANCE	Km	Miles
- Excluding Height	15.3	9.5
- Including Height	15.3	9.5

TOTAL WALKING TIME : 5.0 Hours

OTHER FEATURES OF INTEREST
- Ennerdale Water, views of flanking Pillar and High Stile Ridges.

Route 12 · Ennerdale

Allow 5 hours

STARTING LOCATION
Forestry Commission car-park to W of Ennerdale Water.
OLM 4/MR 085154.
Holds 15 to 20 cars.
Not on a bus route!

OVERVIEW/INTEREST
Delightful route with plenty of variety.
Start is along wild SE shoreline of Ennerdale Water.
Return through forested areas.
Suitable for strong, older children.

FOOTPATHS
Paths good and enjoyable to walk along.
Forest trails waymarked.
Route mainly dry.
Some minor wet patches; and becks to be forded.

The way to High Gillerthwaite *Allow 2 hours*

From the car-park turn L down the lane towards Ennerdale Lake. After crossing the stream keep to the path ahead, as the lane bends R to the cottages, and pass through a gate. The lake comes into view in front to the E. Further away over on your L the great dark mass of Great Borne looms up ENE, while to your R there is a more restricted view of Crag Fell SE. Follow the wide gravel path down to the lakeside, passing a footbridge and then a weir on your L. Bear to the R along the obvious path round the S shore of Ennerdale Water. Following this, select all alternative paths nearest to the lakeside.

The imposing mountain shapes beyond the head of the lake include Red Pike and High Stile to the E, with the Dodds to their L. A k-gate gives entry to the National Trust land at Anglers Crag, and the path rises to scale the crag with some easy scrambling involved. Soon the majestic outlines of Steeple and Pillar come into view on the R of the lake to the ESE. Then, part way round the shore,

you enter a long, narrow wooded area containing a mixture of birch, hawthorn, holly, oak and rowan. Stiles, footbridges and the like are crossed as the path winds ESE.

At the end of the lake, having emerged from the trees, cross a small feeder stream by a footbridge and continue up a wide grass track between the bracken, making for the L lower corner of a conifer forest ahead E. Look around to the W down Ennerdale Lake to observe the fine sight of Anglers Crag plunging down spectacularly into the deep, dark waters below. Follow the path beside the conifer forest of spruce and firs on your R through, in quick succession, a gate/stile, a l-stile over a wall, across a forest road and then down a narrow path squeezed between a stone wall and a wire fence. At the next stile, just before reaching a sheep pen, take a diagonal to your L across the fields, heading NE to a footbridge over the River Liza.

Across the bridge and below the wooded slope to your L, turn away R and walk by the side of the fence to the l-stile over the wall ahead. There is a notice here, 'Beware Bull in Field'. You are, however, on a public footpath. Continue along the grassy path E to pass through a cluster of buildings at Low Gillerthwaite Field Centre. Walk up the lane to reach the main forestry road and turn R. There are now fine views of Pillar Rock and the sharp ridge descending from Steeple SE. Pass the Youth Hostel, and when you come to the cattle-grid take the path off on your L, crossing a stile near a sign that reads 'Red Pike and High Stile'. This is at High Gillerthwaite.

The way back to W of Ennerdale Water *Allow 3 hours*

Follow the grassy path that snakes up the steep fellside to the NNE between lanes of conifer trees, to reach the area just below the top fringe of the forest. Locate a wooden post with a blue ring to your L; veer L at this point and cross into the forest at the p-stile in the fence, walking NNW. Just before entering the enclosed area, turn around to view the rising slopes of Red Pike NE, High Stile ENE, and Pillar and Steeple to the SE.

Turn R along the forest road, which bends to the L uphill, in the direction NNW. Deer are sometimes sighted in this area. Avoid the grassy track off to your R, and continue along the wide, gravel road westward as it levels off. When you reach a vehicle turning circle, ignore a path off to your L. The going underfoot changes to a grassy cart-track as the route bends to the R. Then the way heads W through a gap in the fence to the L of a stile. The path narrows appreciably as it leads towards a gate and a stile, which provide access to open fells between Starling Dodd NE and Great Borne NW.

Ignore these and turn L downhill through an opening in the conifers, heading S. The gap separates larches from spruce on your R. There is a good elevated view from here of Anglers' Crag across Ennerdale Water to the W. The path leads down on a long diagonal to cross Smithy Beck. There is a clear view from here of Great Borne with its formidable rock-strewn slopes, high above on your R (NNW). The path joins the 'Smithy Beck' forest trail at a red-banded marker post supporting a sign to that effect. Veer to the R down this trail, walking W.

Orange-ringed marker posts appear on your R as the trail leads down to a forest road, onto which you turn L. The road immediately bends to the R, and further on when it bends back sharply L, turn along a path to your R and walk downhill W. Just beyond Marker Post 3 1/QF follow the narrow path on the R and cross Smithy Beck again, at the narrow footbridge. Then turn R passing Marker Post 29/ZB, and continue along the trail as it winds slightly uphill. At the next ringed marker post turn sharp R up a narrow, rocky gully, obscured by the branches of overhanging trees. At the top of this gully the trail veers to the L, and it then descends on a long diagonal W to reach the forest road below, passing Marker Post 27/KM. Some of the forest trees in this vicinity have been named, e.g *Larix leptolepis* (Japanese larch).

Follow the forest road down to Bowness Knott Car Park (toilet facilities here), and then take the path off to the L, which leads to the top of a grassy knoll. From here there are unobstructed views of the precipitously steep rock-faces of craggy Bowness Knott, and of its sheer scree slopes. Beyond it, the bulky outline of Great Borne rises to the NE. Veer L at the top and descend to the second, lower rocky outcrop, passing through a gap in the stone wall on your L. Then walk down a narrow, grassy track, which leads NNW to a grouping of oak trees close to Ennerdale Water. Cross the fence at the p-stile and continue along the raised lakeside embankment. A good wide path then leads by the side of the lake, over p-stiles and through k-gates, with only one slight deviation away from the

shoreline. Walk along this path around the NW fringe of the water back to the car-park.

Alternative routes

ESCAPES

The only obvious escape route is after you have crossed the River Liza by the footbridge at the head of Ennerdale Water. Veer L, and immediately turn into the forest road at the top of the rise ahead. Turn L and walk down this road to the Bowness Knott Car Park, to rejoin the main route.

EXTENSIONS

At High Gillerthwaite, continue straight up the grassy path to reach the hause between Red Pike and Little Dodd. Then follow the ridge W round the shoulder of Little Dodd to the green-topped summit of Starling Dodd, 663 m (2,085 ft). Descend, first NNW, and then WNW, to reach a flat moorland area. Turn L at this hause and descend southward to reach the boundary of the forested area at the gate and stile mentioned in the description of the main route. Enter the forest at this point to rejoin the main route down.

12:1 The dawning of a glorious summer's day over Ennerdale.

BURNMOOR TARN and SCA FELL
High Level Route 13

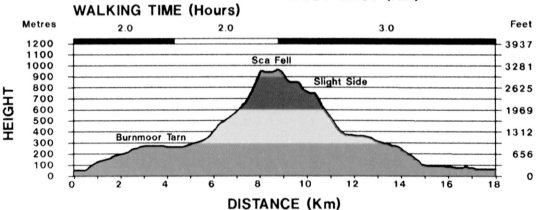

STATISTICS

START and FINISH
- Dalegarth Station - OLM 6 / MR 174007

WALKING DISTANCE	Km	Miles
- Excluding Height	18.0	11.2
- Including Height	18.2	11.3

TOTAL WALKING TIME : 7.0 Hours

TOTAL HEIGHT GAINED
- 940 Metres 3084 Feet

PRINCIPAL HEIGHTS	Metres	Feet
- Burnmoor Tarn	255	835
- Sca Fell	964	3162
- Slight Side	760	2499

OTHER FEATURES OF INTEREST
- Chasms and rock faces on Sca Fell; views of Upper Eskdale

8
The Central Fells
Part 1

Route 13 · Burnmoor Tarn and Sca Fell

Allow 7 hours

STARTING LOCATION
Dalegarth Station car-park.
OLM 6/174007.
Extensive parking facilities.
Not on a bus route!

OVERVIEW/INTEREST
Straightforward approach to a difficult summit to reach.
Burnmoor Tarn is visited.
Distant views interesting but not spectacular.
Superb rock-faces and awesome deep chasms at summit of Sca Fell.
Quite strenuous but no serious scrambling involved.

FOOTPATHS
Mixed; good in parts, erosion on paths leading to the summit of Sca Fell, indistinct in places on both the way up and on the descent.
Some wet patches.

The way to Burnmoor Tarn   *Allow 2 hours*

Turn L from the car-park and pass Dalegarth terminus railway station on your L. The pinnacle of Harter Fell appears ahead on the R (ESE). You are now walking up the U-shaped glaciated valley of the River Esk, where lush meadows and deciduous tree-lined watercourses abound. Take the side road on the L at Brook House Hotel, and pass through the hamlet of Boot. Then proceed along the stony path leading uphill, and having passed through a gate take the grassy R fork NNE signed 'Bridleway'.

A good path winds uphill through bracken, and as you gain height you have a pleasant view to your rear of Boot, and part of the lovely Eskdale valley SW. Ulpha Fell is also visible over on your R (SE). Be careful now to proceed through a gate on your R (SE). The pointed fell ahead is Great Barrow E. Soon you are passing a steep slope to the R with Whillan Beck, the exit stream from Burnmoor Tarn, down below. Pass through three gates as the valley starts to widen out, giving more extensive views of the pleasant, rounded, moorland landscape ahead.

You then cross Eskdale Moor along a comfortable gradient, although there are some isolated boggy patches in this area. The high ground to your L (NW) marks the SW edge of the ridge, Whin Rigg and Illgill Head, which rises gently above the infamous steep Wasdale Screes. The immense mountain ahead to your R (NE) is Sca Fell, your main objective. Quite suddenly, round a bend in the near fellside, the peaks of, from L to R, Yewbarrow, Mosedale Red Pike, the Pillar Ridge and Kirk Fell (N to NNE) appear.

Then, over the brow of the fell ahead, the extensive placid waters of Burnmoor Tarn come into view. This is a very tranquil spot where the quietness and serenity of the tarn in a wide open setting blends perfectly with the grandeur and majesty of the surrounding massive mountain shapes. Continue down to the tarn along the grassy path, and pass the water to your L. Cross Bulatt Bridge over Whillan Beck.

79

13:1 Buttress above Deep Gill on the summit of Sca Fell.

The way to Sca Fell   *Allow 2 hours*

Beyond the bridge, fork L round the head of the tarn, following the cairned path NW. At the hillock ahead veer R along a wide grassy path NE, which then bends L. More interesting mountain shapes appear ahead, including Haycock over on the L (NW), and a little further on, the bulk of Great Gable is progressively revealed NE. At the brow of the pass, near a cairn on the L, turn to the R and climb across the open fellside towards the summit of Sca Fell, heading directly to the R of the top of a distinctive gully, through which Groove Gill flows ENE. Soon some indistinctive tracks heading in your direction of ascent may be followed. The famed Mosedale Horseshoe is now in view over on your L. After a time, steeper slopes are reached, and the climbing becomes progressively more strenuous. Change your direction slightly to a NE

diagonal as views of Wasdale, and then glimpses of Wast Water and Wasdale Head, are revealed down below on your L (NW).

When you attain your immediate target of climbing above the gully, the irregular summit skyline rocks of Sca Fell reappear to the E. Then traverse higher round the slope to the NNE where, in the 'Piles of Stones' area, you will locate a path that will guide you ENE to the summit of Sca Fell. This path winds up the higher fellside at an agreeable rate of climb, and soon the details of the extensive rock-shattering below the summit ridge can be observed in some detail. Cairns appear, as to the N the far-off summit of High Crag comes into view, together with the broad ridge leading from it to High Stile.

A rocky path now becomes firmly established and the general direction of the climb changes subtly to ESE. Some areas of moderately difficult, loose scree are encountered next, and these intensify as the summit is approached. The final section of the climb is once again quite strenuous. The rocky track eventually levels off, and there are some nearby shelters. The exact summit rocks lie a little higher to your R, but first, if the weather is clear, explore the extensive, fairly level ground ahead on your L (NNE). This broad area with precipitous edges on most sides is a veritable jumble of rocks of all shapes and sizes effectively bonded together by a vegetation of mosses, lichen and bilberry.

The features of many famous rock buttresses, and intervening chasms and gullies, can be seen, including part of the exits from Lord's Rake and Deep Gill, as you tread carefully along the edges of Scafell Crag and Symonds Knott. Retrace your steps SW, and walk to the summit cairn and shelters, which lie at a height of 964 m (3,162 ft). An extensive panorama of mountains and other features can be observed from the summit area of Sca Fell. Start by looking NE towards the highest mountain in England, and then sweep eastward to observe in succession:

NE	Scafell Pike and Ill Crag.
ENE	Esk Pike.
E	Bow Fell.

ESE	Crinkle Crags.
SE	Coniston Fells.
SSE	Dow Crag.
S	Harter Fell.
SW	Eskdale.
WSW	Burnmoor Tarn.
	Whin Rigg and Illgill Head.
W	Wast Water.
WNW	Seatallan.
NW	Yewbarrow and, beyond it, Haycock.
	Mosedale Red Pike and behind it Scoat Fell.
NNW	Pillar and further away High Stile Range.
N	Kirk Fell and Great Gable.
	Grasmoor and NW Fells.
NNE	Skiddaw.

The way back to Dalegarth   *Allow 3 hours*

Leave the summit along the jumbled rocky promontory protruding SSE. Follow the westward edge of this broad band down across Long Green to Slight Side in the general direction SSE, avoiding the cairned paths turning down more steeply to the R. Below is the Upper Esk Valley with the infant stream threading its way along it. For most of the way down the descent is gradual, with one modest uphill section before the final descent to Slight Side is reached S. Then there is a minor scramble to gain the interesting, smooth rock formations, that mould the summit of Horn Crag.

Continue your descent along the cairned path, which swings down between SE and SW. Once through the testing rocky gully, there is an easy path, which alternates between grass and scree, descending to the elevated mossy plateau below. The path veers SSW to cross the high grassy moorland, and as you proceed the nearer view of the Coniston Fells will enable you to identify, from L to R, Swirl How, Grey Friar, Brim Fell, Coniston Old Man and Dow Crag. Do not be tempted here to drop down to the L towards the beck below.

The path next winds between somewhat enclosed rock formations, hugging the R-hand side of the intervening col. Be vigilant here to keep to the cairned route, which is not very distinct but

which veers R round a craggy outcrop before resuming first a S and then SSW direction. Soon on the opposite fellside to your L the Roman Fort of Mediobogdum can be spotted. The path swings round WSW to follow the contours of Eskdale below on your L. A number of gates through a sheep pen then have to be negotiated before the path reaches the valley road at a stile near to Wha House Farm. Turn R here, passing a Youth Hostel and the Woolpack Inn on your R. After Penny Hill Farm turn R down a track signed 'Public Footpath Stony Tarn via Eel Tarn'.

Pass through a gate signed 'Christcliff', and then walk past a further gateway leading to Eel Tarn before selecting a footpath through a gate on your L signed 'Footpath Boot' incorporating a yellow waymarker. Cross the field and climb over a wall-stile before crossing the next field, making for and then passing through a gate leading to farm buildings, and signed 'Woolpack Boot'. After passing through a further gate, a narrow lane leads back to the road. Turn R along this and follow it back to the car-park at Dalegarth.

Alternative routes

This high-level route is essentially a straightforward, long up and down, and as such it is not really suitable for either shorter walks or optional extensions.

ESCAPES
If problems arise, the route is best abandoned in the vicinity of Burnmoor Tarn. From this area a safe route leads back to Eskdale on the E flank of Whillan Beck, via Eel Tarn, where there is a choice of ways down into Eskdale.

EXTENSIONS
The obvious extension for the very fit and experienced is to continue to Scafell Pike, but this involves demanding scrambling along Lord's Rake or one of its variants, together with either a return to Sca Fell or a long, demanding descent back to Eskdale down Mickledore and then round Great Moss.

ESKDALE and HARTER FELL
Lower Level Route 14

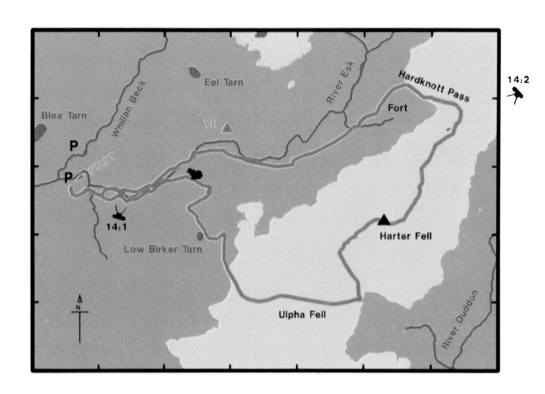

WEST-EAST (Km)

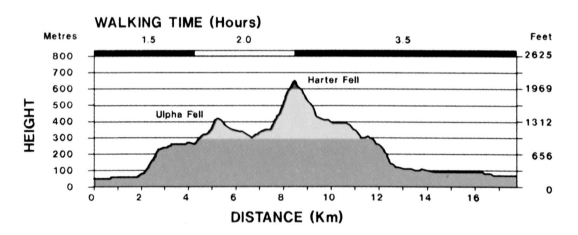

STATISTICS

START and FINISH
- Trough House Bridge CP - OLM 6 / MR 172003

WALKING DISTANCE	Km	Miles
- Excluding Height	17.7	11.0
- Including Height	17.9	11.1

TOTAL WALKING TIME : 7.0 Hours

TOTAL HEIGHT GAINED
- 750 Metres   2461 Feet

PRINCIPAL HEIGHTS	Metres	Feet
- Ulpha Fell	420	1380
- Harter Fell	653	2140

OTHER FEATURES OF INTEREST
- Eskdale, Low Birker Tarn and coniferous forests. Remains of Mediobogdum Fort.

Route 14 · Eskdale and Harter Fell

Allow 7 hours

The way to Low Birker Tarn *Allow 1½ hours*

Turn L from the car-park along the wide gravel lane signed 'Stanley *Ghyll* Footpath Only'. Bear L along the track signed 'Stanley *Gill* Birker Moor' and 'Waterfalls', which winds gradually uphill veering L. Go past the bridleway on your R leading to Forge Bridge, and continue along the bridleway on L, signed 'Boot and Upper Eskdale' E.

The path then crosses a field, leads through another gateway and after this down to a wooden footbridge across a tributary of the River Esk, in an area of mature woodland. Across the bridge, pass through a gate in the stone wall ahead, and select the main track heading ESE between other paths peeling off to the L and R. Your first sighting of the craggy summit of Hårter Fell appears ahead E, and nearer on your R are the slopes of Hartley Crag ESE.

A well-defined, grassy cart-track passes through an extensive area of gorse bushes, which are seen at their best in May. The way meanders uphill; avoid here the public footpath descending to your L. The path fords a stream and winds uphill, where soon an unrestricted view of the upper slopes of Sca Fell may be seen over on your L (NNE) in the far distance, with the Slight Side Ridge, which leads to its summit, occupying the middle ground. When you come to the wall ahead, bear round and above this feature, ignoring the public bridleway through the gap. Pass a track off on your R, proceed through a gap in the next wall and then tread through an area of more dense gorse bushes E.

Soon, you pass a delightful small tarn surrounded by spruce trees on your R. The patch continues through gateways and across streams to Low Birker Guest House, which caters for natural healthcare and therapy. Here take the grassy path beside a wall, which leads uphill to the open fells SE. At this spot there is a sighting of the pronounced, pointed peak of Bow Fell through a gap in the nearer fells over on your L (NNE).

The rising path crosses another stream and steadily gains height as it bends round the spur of the fellside. Ignore the path off on your R leading through a gate and continue E as the path veers to the L. After passing through a k-gate the path turns abruptly R round the crag ahead WSW, and from here there is a superb view on the R down along lower Eskdale to the coast. The grassy path changes to a stony one, and as you gain more height the views of the distant mountains on your R become more extensive, with the Mosedale Horseshoe including the Pillar group N. Now turn round further to your R to absorb upper Eskdale and the superb surrounding high volcanic mountains of Crinkle Crags, Bow Fell and the Scafells NE to NNE. The long ridge of Whin Rigg and Illgill Head is also visible to the NW. By this time the stony path is zigzagging up the steep, rocky fellside. A stream is crossed and just before a derelict stone building is reached take the side path uphill on your L.

The path quickly narrows to a single file as it winds round a boggy area to the L. Veer to the R of

83

the crags ahead, following compass bearings swinging between s and sw in order to avoid difficult terrain, until you locate Low Birker Tarn on your R (w). The footpath in this area is not good and the faint tracks that you have to negotiate here will almost inevitably involve some crossing of open, unmarked fellside. Walk round the L-hand side of the tarn.

The way to Harter Fell   *Allow 2 hours*

Descend to the L of a small outcrop of rocks ahead with a larger boulder beyond s. The going here is along a grassy, cairned track and this relatively distinct way continues s for some time to rise eventually to attain the grassy, wide col between the southernmost rocky outcrops of Ulpha Fell. After passing through the higher ground of the hause to the SE, the path veers round to the L (NE). Be careful because the path markings on the Ordnance Survey 1 : 25000 scale can be misleading!

The summit of Harter Fell, your principle objective, now rises across the moorland straight ahead NE. Occupying the far horizon to the R of Harter Fell are Grey Friar ENE, Dow Crag E and Walna Scar SE. At the end of the rocky outcrops be particularly careful to head down due E in order to avoid the worst of the awful, boggy, badly drained moss to your L. On this stretch, keep always to what higher ground there is on the R, and continue downhill without deviating from your E compass bearing. Make for the pointed apex on the w side of Dunnerdale Forest, directly below which a stone wall coming in from the R converges with the apex.

Climb the l-stile over the wall, and a path then leads down SE to a stream and following this to a gate on your L, which provides access into the forest. Your route is now uphill under a dark canopy of dense and mature conifer trees, mostly spruce. The well-defined path veers NNW, but after heavy rain it can be very boggy in the clinging peat, and exposed tree roots in this area are extremely slippery. Marker posts indicate the way, and look out for a further unusual sign of a carved squirrel in a tree stump as you head along the main path NNW.

You emerge from the forest area at a wooden gate. Now take the path on your R, which climbs steeply uphill E passing some wooden posts with red-topped rings. A good, clear, narrow path winds through coarse grass and rocks with the edge of the forest also rising to your R. Higher up, the Duddon Valley comes into view over on the R (SSE), and to your rear is the faraway outline of Black Combe, which overlooks Barrow SSW.

Eventually the steep slopes ease off and the landscape opens up. Near to the top, Low Birker Tarn can be seen again, this time considerably below you, due W. The profile of Muncaster Fell may also be seen pointing down to the coast over to the R of the tarn. At a cairn, a better-defined path converges from the L; turn R uphill along this route. There are now extensive views of the Duddon Estuary and Morecambe Bay stretching away far below to the s. When the path divides take the higher branch on the L, which leads directly to the summit rocks.

The highest elevation of Harter Fell is 653 m (2,140 ft), and this is the height of the craggy outcrop over to the E of the summit cairn. The top of the fell is made up of jumbled masses of quite large rocks, and the two pinnacles require some care to scale. The views from the summits are very impressive, apart from Seathwaite Tarn ESE, the principal mountains and other main geographical features have already been identified.

The way back to Eskdale   *Allow 3½ hours*

Start to descend to the E, and quickly locate a narrow path leading steeply down, first through a tangle of rocks, and then across grassy slopes. Head along this path towards the N tip of Dunnerdale Forest below to the NE. The path descends through a small gully, crossing several small watercourses, and there are a few squelchy areas here to exercize your jumping ability. The route descends to a stile over a wire fence.

The way then follows the line of a fence bordering the forest of spruce trees to your R and leading N. Wrynose Pass can be seen to your R (NE) with Grey Friar further to the E. The path then veers

14:1 Sca Fell and Slight Side from Eskdale.

slightly away from the forest boundary up the fell-side. You next pass a small tarn on your L near a stile, where a cairned path leads off ENE. Follow this path through a gap in a stone wall, and afterwards up a hillock to your L as it first veers round to the NW and then descends to the road along a wide, grassy sward. Turn L downhill along the road. Hard Knott towers above to your R.

Descending down the road, there are fine, elevated views ahead looking directly down Eskdale, with the protective walls of the Roman Fort of Mediobogdum now visible among the rolling fell-side to the R. Take the path off on your R, signed 'Public Footpath' and follow this wet, soggy way across several watercourses down to the E walls of the fort. Your way is round these walls in a sweeping semi-circle, keeping to the line and elevation of the former fortification. From the fort, walk downhill along a grassy track adjacent to a stone wall on your R. Squeeze through the narrow gap in this wall and descend down the grassy path towards the road. Climb the l-stile on your L over a wall to reach it.

Near the cattle grid a short distance ahead, take the path on the L signed 'Public Footpath Eskdale and Muncaster'. Cross the venerable stone bridge and proceed up the rocky footpath round to the R. Pass through a couple of gates and then take the R fork, which descends to, and along, a wall W. The path passes through a series of gates, stiles and footbridges as it continues down the valley W, before it climbs diagonally to join a major pathway ahead; turn R down this. Soon you reach a three-dimensional direction sign and your way continues ahead W along the path indicated 'Bridle-way Penny Hill'. More stiles and gates have to be

negotiated before you reach Penny Hill Farm.

Proceed to Doctor Bridge. Cross the River Esk here and take the footpath to your L adjacent to the stream signed 'Public Footpath St Catherine's Church'. Continue SW beside the meandering river. The path parts company with the exact course of the stream for a time and your direction reverts to W, with more gates of various descriptions to go through. Look out for a sturdy and newly constructed bridge over the Esk near Gill Force and turn L to cross the river again at this point.

Across the bridge turn immediately R, and proceed along the path that rises above the stream. Pass over a stile and then you will see St Catherine's Church on the far side of the Esk. After another stile, pass through the gate on your L, and then proceed uphill along a path leading away from the main river but following the course of a tributary stream, to rejoin your outward route; turn R down this wide path and retrace your steps to the car-park.

Alternative routes

ESCAPES

The most obvious way to curtail this walk is at the point where you emerge from Dunnerdale Forest at MR 212993. Instead of turning R here and climbing to the summit of Harter Fell, continue downhill NW along the footpaths, which will lead you back to Eskdale to the E of Penny Hill Farm. Here you can rejoin the suggested main route.

EXTENSIONS

Previously it was mentioned that Harter Fell is an isolated mountain, and because of this, convenient extensions, which do not involve additional strenuous climbs to surrounding high fells, are not numerous. One modest addition worth considering, however, is to turn R when you reach Doctor Bridge and proceed to the Woolpack Inn. From here there is an interesting circuitous route, back to Boot and thence to the car-park, via Eel Tarn.

14:2 Cockley Beck Bridge and Harter Fell.

SCAFELL PIKE and BOW FELL

High Level Route 15

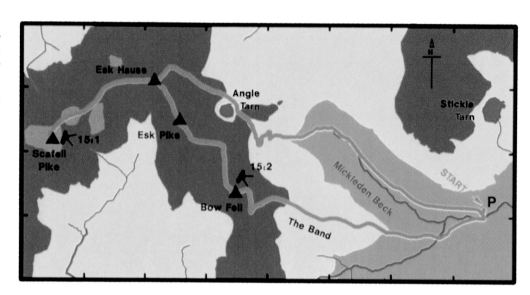

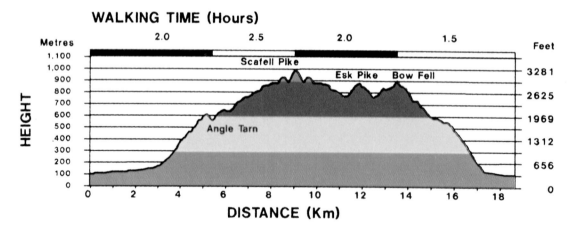

STATISTICS

START and FINISH
- Dungeon Ghyll Car Park - OLM 6 / MR 286061

WALKING DISTANCE	Km	Miles
- Excluding Height	18.6	11.5
- Including Height	18.9	11.7

TOTAL WALKING TIME : 8.0 Hours

TOTAL HEIGHT GAINED
- 1290 Metres 4232 Feet

PRINCIPAL HEIGHTS	Metres	Feet
- Scafell Pike	978	3210
- Esk Pike	885	2903
- Bow Fell	902	2960

OTHER FEATURES OF INTEREST
- Rossett Gill, Angle Tarn and panorama from highest point in England.

9

The Central Fells

Part 2

Route 15 · Scafell Pike and Bow Fell

Allow 8 hours

STARTING LOCATION
Car-park at Old Dungeon Ghyll Hotel.
OLM 6/MR 286061.
Holds about 40 cars.
CMS bus route 516.

OVERVIEW/INTEREST
One of the great walks of the Lake District.
Reaches highest point in England.
Although long and challenging, the climbing is
well spaced out.
Some easy scrambling over rock formations.
Excellent panoramic views.
Within the capabilities of fit and hardy teenagers.

FOOTPATHS
Very adequate footpaths not too badly eroded.
The worst section is towards the top of Rossett Gill.
No significant wet areas.
The way is clear and the paths relatively easy to
follow.

The way to Angle Tarn   *Allow 2 hours*

From the car-park pass behind the Old Dungeon
Ghyll Hotel travelling wsw. Here there is an imme-
diate view of high fells over on the L including Side
Pike SSE, and Pike of Blisco SW. After passing
through a k-gate, a magnificent view is revealed of
the additional mountain peaks of Great Knott SW,
Crinkle Crags WSW, the Band leading to Bow Fell
WNW and the lower slopes of the Langdale Pikes N.
The way continues along Mickleden.

Soon round a bend ahead, Rossett Gill and Pike
come into view to the NW. Then the helmet
summit of Pike of Stickle looms up on your R
(NNW). Mickleden is a wild and remote glaciated
valley and the area is noted for *Digitalis* (foxglove).
The broad gravel and stony path leads NW to Rossett Gill and Stake Gill at the head of Mickleden.
Ahead, the craggy skyline is dominated by Bow
Fell and Rossett Pike NW, with the fault line of
Rossett Gill straddling these two rock forms. Cross
the beck by the wooden bridge near a stone sheep
pen down on your L. Then take the L-hand fork up
Rossett Gill and signed 'Esk Hause'. The path has
suffered badly from erosion, but extensive restor-
ation work has been superbly carried out on the
lower sections.

Keep to the distinct, rocky path as it climbs
round a sizeable bluff to your R, after which you
cross a section of layered rock before the path traverses to your R and zigzags upwards, following the
course of the stream below on the R. Turn around
to take in the fine view ESE, looking down into
Mickleden flanked by the Langdale Pikes on its L
and by the spur of the Band descending from Bow
Fell on its R. Beyond lie the peaks of Side Pike and
Lingmoor Fell SE. Near this point there is a choice
of ways to the top of the pass, either straight ahead
up the steep-sided gully adjacent to the watercourse, or by a route off to the L (W), which traverses upwards along a more comfortable gradient.
Both ways converge again near the top. The gully

*15:1 Looking towards Bow Fell from the summit of
Scafell Pike.*

route does have some unstable scree to contend
with and there are several mini routes through the
rock-fall to choose from.

Near the top, as the steepness of the climb levels
off, there is a massive cairn straddling the wide,
eroded path. A little further on, the enormous dark
mass of Great End looms up ahead to the L of the
path, leading onwards to Esk Hause WNW. Allen
Crags is the mountain shape to the right of the pass
NNW, and from this peak a rocky band leads up to
the less-frequented peak of Glaramara NNE. Then
the tranquil and remote Angle Tarn comes into
view below on your L nestling beneath the precipitous SE slopes of Bow Fell and Esk Pike. These two
mountains are separated by Ore Gap in between.
During your short descent to the E side of the tarn
look to your R for a view of Blencathra on the distant skyline to the NNE. Angle Tarn is a wild,
remote, peaceful and sheltered spot. At the exit
stream there is a restricted view down the great,
long, winding valley of Langstrath over on your R
(NE).

The way to Scafell Pike   *Allow 2½ hours*

Leave the tarn along the eroded path that climbs
quite steeply to the NW from the combe. In depart-
ing, look out for the pointed peak of Sergeant Man
over on your R (E). When further height is gained
look back for a more revealing view of the
Langdale Pikes and identify them from L to R as
Pavey Ark, Pike of Stickle and Harrison Stickle
ESE. The broad path next winds up to the shelter at
Esk Hause, which is an impressive stone cross
construction.

In good weather there are fine views from Esk
Hause of Great and Green Gables NW, with a more
restricted sighting of the summit of Pillar, which
appears to their L. More mountains to be observed
for the first time on this walk appear over on your
R; in the far distance are the silhouettes of, from L
to R (NW), Grasmoor, Crag Hill and the ridges leading up to them from the Newlands Valley, with
Grisedale Pike forming the background. Nearer to,
flanking their R, are the rounded bulks of the Dale

Head Fells N. Immediately on your R are the much closer slopes leading to Allen Crags NE.

Continue uphill wsw, passing the shelter to your R, along a broad eroded path. Soon distant Skiddaw comes into view over on your R (NNE), and almost immediately afterwards Derwent Water appears far below, again to your R, followed by a glimpse of Blencathra peeping out round the shoulder of Allen Crags further R. When the path divides, either choice will lead you westward up to the shallow col between Great End and the rest of the Scafell Ridge. After a short distance a path converges from the L; this is the route down from Esk Pike and you will use it on your return journey. On a clear day there are views from here of Morecambe Bay. The path rises, and in a broad sweep to the w, followed by some steeper turns, reaches the Scafell main ridge.

Veer L along the ridge from the col, following the obvious well-trodden, cairned way over the worn rocks wsw still gaining height. Along this section an extended vista of the famous Mosedale Horseshoe, dominated by the bulk of Pillar NW, is revealed. Beyond this impressive array of mountains to the R lies the High Stile Range NNW. Further over on your far R and on the distant horizon are the extensive Helvellyn and Fairfield mountain chains, separated by Grisedale Hause ENE.

Cross the higher rocky ground between Broad Crag and Ill Crag before descending over really demanding, large boulders and steep scree slopes to the narrow col between Piers Gill and Little Narrowcove. Then follows the final, rocky climb up the steepish slope to the highest point in England, the summit of Scafell Pike, standing at 978 m (3,210 ft). Several smaller satellite shelters are passed in the rocks on the L before you reach the huge, dominant summit shelter, cairn and trig. point complex. The commanding views all round from the top include the following famous mountain landmarks:

WSW	Sca Fell
W	Wast Water.
WNW	Yewbarrow.
NNW	Mosedale Horseshoe including Pillar.
	Kirk Fell and beyond the High Stile Range.
N	Grasmoor and Great Gable.
	Grisedale Pike on the far horizon.
NNE	Robinson, Hindscarth and Dale Head.
	Sty Head Tarn, Maiden Moor and Skiddaw.
NE	Borrowdale, Derwent Water and Blencathra.
	Great End.
ENE	Helvellyn group.
E	Langdale Pikes.
ESE	Bow Fell.
SE	Crinkle Crags.
SSE	Coniston Fells.
S	Harter Fell and coastline beyond.

From the edges of the summit, additional perspectives, including a more revealing exposure of Esk Pike, Bow Fell, Crinkle Crags, the Coniston Fells and Harter Fell, can be viewed. The sight of the infant River Esk far below starting its far from direct journey to the coast among this gigantic sweep of Lakeland Fells completes a picture of enrapturing mountain scenery.

The way to Bow Fell   *Allow 2 hours*

Commence the return by retracing your final approach steps along the cairned path, descending first to the NE and then veering E to reach the narrow col. Continue to retrace your approach route along the main band, passing between Broad Crag and Ill Crag. Then re-cross the intervening rocky band to reach the hause once again before the ground rises to Great End. Descend to your R here along the wide path that swings to the E, and continue along this path until you come to the major division of the ways previously mentioned. At this junction select the R-hand route, which climbs steeply as it bends further to the R to scale Esk Pike.

The path, over worn, rocky ground, gains height rapidly in a series of twists and turns. Then, following a short traverse, it reaches the summit of Esk Pike. Looking backwards to your R (w), the majestic outline of the Scafell Ridge becomes increasingly exposed as you reach an increasingly more advantageous elevation. From the summit descend along the distinct cairned path SE to Ore Gap, where a path on the L initiates a descent route down to Angle Tarn below. Ignore this and continue along the cairned path to the summit of Bow Fell by next traversing round the arc of a circle as the path bends from SE to S. A wide, gravel path provides a final zigzag approach to the L (SE) to reach the extensive pile of large boulders that form the considerable, distinctive summit peak of Bow Fell. Scramble up these to complete your final climb of the day. You are now at a height of 902 m (2,960 ft).

On a fine evening, in the gathering twilight, as the sun sinks towards the Scafell skyline, the views from the summit of Bow Fell can be superlative. This stupendous all-round vista includes:

E	Langdale Pikes and Great Langdale Valley.
SE	Side Pike, Lingmoor Fell and Windermere.
SSE	Pike of Blisco, Red Tarn and Wetherlam.
S	Crinkle Crags, Coniston Old Man and Dow Crag.
SSW	Duddon Valley and Harter Fell.
WSW	Eskdale, Muncaster Fell, Eskdale and coast.
NW	Scafells.
NNW	Pillar, Great End, Gables and Esk Pike.
N	Grasmoor, Crag Hill and Grisedale Pike.
NNE	Glaramara and Skiddaw.
NE	Langstrath and Blencathra.
ENE	Helvellyn Range and Fairfield. (Some panorama – I hope you have enough film!)

A few words of caution concerning compass bearings: Bow Fell contains a mixture of rock and minerals that are magnetic. Therefore, compass readings in this vicinity are suspect!

The way back to The Old Dungeon Ghyll Hotel
Allow 1¼ hours

Descend through the maze of rocks, first to the SE and then veering to your R to follow broadly a dominant SSE direction as the way down twists and turns over boulders. Soon, an intermittent path over more worn rock is reached as the route next turns to the L (ESE) and then ENE. Another, less interesting cairned path descending from the summit comes in on your L. Turn R down this more established way. This leads you to a steep scree gully facing SE. Descend carefully down this eroded way to reach the landmark of the Three Tarns below.

Turn L at the Three Tarns and continue your long descent along the Band, a rocky spur from Bow Fell, which first runs ESE and then sweeps round to SE. This part of the way down is gradual to start with, and there are a few wet, peaty patches to contend with. However, the final descent to the valley floor is down a steepish scree path that contorts sharply to reach Stool End Farm. Turn R between the farm outbuildings and proceed along the metalled farm lane to the valley road. Continue down the road a short distance and then turn L and cross over the bridge to reach the car-park.

Alternative routes

ESCAPES

There are several convenient opportunities for curtailing this long and demanding route.

The first of these is at Angle Tarn, where instead of continuing NW to Esk Hause; slightly uphill past the tarn, take the L-hand fork in the path SW and follow this narrower path up to Ore Gap to rejoin the return way back over Bow Fell at the top by turning L down the path coming down from Esk Pike.

Another improvisation is to take a similar escape to the L at Esk Hause. Instead of proceeding to the Scafell Ridge, turn off up the path to Esk Pike SE, rejoining at this point the recommended main return route.

Both the above curtailments do not, unfortunately, involve climbing Scafell Pike, but a third possibility which does, is to complete the main route as far as the return to Esk Hause. Then, instead of climbing Esk Pike and Bow Fell, continue retracing your approach route down past Angle Tarn, through Rossett Gill and along Mickleden.

15:2 Crinkle Crags, Great Knott and Wetherlam bathed in late evening sunshine.

EXTENSIONS

There are two different possibilities for extending the route.

The first is to include Great End, and perhaps also a variety of other optional, short extra excursions to several of the additional vantage points along the Scafell Ridge. These could include visiting Ill Crag and Broad Crag.

For the very fittest and experienced fell-walkers who are adept at scrambling, there is another way of extending the route. This is from the summit of Scafell Pike, to continue sw and to scale Sca Fell, after which you return to Scafell Pike to commence the main return route via Bow Fell, etc. The usual approach to this additional 3,000 ft peak is to descend to Mickledore and then to traverse through Lord's Rake, either direct or up Deep Gill, returning via the alternative.

PIKE of BLISCO and BLEA TARN
Lower Level Route 16

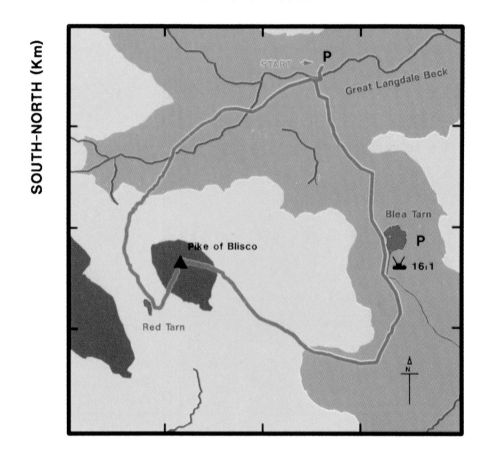

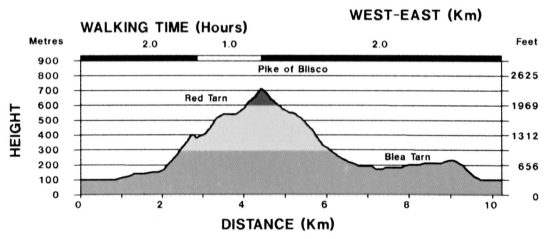

STATISTICS

START and FINISH
- Dungeon Ghyll Car Park - OLM 6 / MR 286061

WALKING DISTANCE	Km	Miles
- Excluding Height	10.2	6.3
- Including Height	10.4	6.5

TOTAL WALKING TIME : 5.0 Hours

TOTAL HEIGHT GAINED
- 690 Metres   2264 Feet

PRINCIPAL HEIGHTS	Metres	Feet
- Pike of Blisco	705	2304

OTHER FEATURES OF INTEREST
- Fine views of Langdale Valley, Oxendale and Mickleden; Red and Blea Tarns.

Route 16 · Pike of Blisco and Blea Tarn

Allow 5 hours

The way to Red Tarn   *Allow 2 hours*

From the car-park turn R along the valley road towards the head of Great Langdale Valley. You will immediately be surrounded by the most magnificent mountain amphitheatre, which from L to R includes Pike of Blisco SW, Great Knott WSW, Crinkle Crags W, the Band leading to Bow Fell WNW, and Rossett Gill and Pike NW. More to your immediate L and R are Side Pike SSE and the rising slopes of the Langdale Pikes NNW respectively.

In a short distance the road bends sharply to the L and here branch off through the k-gate signed 'Public Road to Stool End – Cul De Sac – Footpaths to Oxendale and Bow Fell'. Beyond the farm take the L-hand fork uphill signed 'Path to Band' SW. Continue past a branch path on your R which climbs up along the Band, and keep to the lower path on the L. Next cross a l-stile over a stone wall and walk W along the still fairly flat valley bottom of Oxendale. Your way now passes through several k-gates. The route here is indicated by helpful yellow-arrowed marker signs. Cross the splendid footbridge over Oxendale Beck, built in memory of two young mountain enthusiasts.

The route continues along the obvious rocky path, which soon rises steeply to gain the col of Browney Gill on your L (SSW). This hause separates Pike of Blisco from Great Knott. When you have gained sufficient height look around to your R to see the summits of the Langdale Pikes, with the separate peaks of Pike of Stickle and Harrison Stickle prominent NNE. The rocky path has been buttressed in several sections here by reconstruction work in the form of stepped terracing. This sensitive repair-work blends in particularly well with the surrounding contours.

The route continues through a high-level combe. A deep gully develops down below on your R, while striking rock buttresses appear to your L as the path continues to snake upwards. Near the top, turn around to observe a splendid view of the Band and Bow Fell in the foreground, and directly behind the profiles of Allen Crags and Glaramara N. When the path divides, take the L fork and cross the main path from Pike of Blisco to Crinkle Crags at right angles. Your narrow path levels off and leads SSE to Red Tarn. The landscape now becomes wilder and more remote as the distant skyline of the Coniston Fells appears ahead SE to S.

The way to Pike of Blisco   *Allow up to 1 hour*

Depart from Red Tarn by continuing S along your arrival path as it veers to the L. When the path starts a shallow descent, locate a large rock above on your L with cairn stones on top, and another smaller cairn further up the fellside, more to the L of the lower rock. Turn abruptly L here, traversing up the fellside away from the lower path along a narrow grassy track NNW. The path you are now on is faint, but it does continue up among the grassy fellside towards some rocky crags that lie ahead to

95

your R. The path becomes reassuringly more definite higher up as more cairn markers appear. This path soon meets the eroded main route up to Pike of Blisco. Turn R along this wide series of intermingled paths and climb them as they twist and turn up the steep slope to bring you to the twin summits of the mountain; your direction up these is generally NE.

Pike of Blisco is a fine, isolated mountain composed mostly of hard, volcanic rock, but there are some exposed, intermingled minor areas of softer sandstone and shales. It stands at 705 m (2,304 ft), at which height it commands comprehensive views in all directions, particularly down to the east. By taking observations from its twin peaks, and also from the surrounding rocks, you can obtain an extensive range of sightings. In addition to the mountains previously observed and recorded, the new vistas from these summits include the following:

- Extensive views of the lower easterly fells and of Lake Windermere down below to the ESE.
- The peak of Dow Crag, appearing through a gap in the nearer Coniston Fells over to the S.
- The coastline SW, to the L of Harter Fell.
- More revealing aspects of Great Langdale Valley, with its protective, southern mountain chain of Side Pike and Lingmoor Fell NE.
- The Helvellyn Range dominating the far horizon to the NE.
- The high mountains of the High Street Ridges lying to the ENE.

The way back to The Old Dungeon Ghyll Hotel
Allow 2 hours

Start your descent to the E along the much-used, eroded path flanked by cairns. A short distance down this path, near an outcrop of rocks, locate a faint side path leading off across the bilberry-strewn fellside, heading SSE in the direction of Wetherlam. Follow this route and shortly a small tarn will be observed ahead, beyond an outcrop of irregular rocks on your L. Head towards this tarn, which is your next certain landmark. Intermittent cairns appear near two outcrops of rock, which you

pass between as you progressively descend in a SE direction. Your descent here is in a fairly direct line with the large white hotel situated on the E shore of Windermere.

On this cross-country stretch of the walk there are some boggy areas to cross as you descend in the straightest line possible towards the mountain pass road ahead at Wrynose Bridge. The exact path can easily be lost from time to time along this little-walked route. Eventually, small watercourses emerge on your L. Near Wrynose Beck, which you follow down with it on your L, a distinct path becomes established down rounded grassy slopes.

In descending further the grandeur of the upper reaches of Little Langdale Valley is progressively revealed. In additiion, the profile of the Coniston Fells allows you to identify Wetherlam SSE, Coniston Old Man SSW and Swirl How SW. Follow the grassy paths down to the road at Wrynose Bridge, and then turn L down this, immediately crossing the bridge. There is a reasonably wide, grassy verge on the exposed R-hand side of the road for most of your short journey along this part of the route.

The road bends L round the rocky spur of Hollin Crag and Stack, as the valley through Side Gates comes into view over on your L. After a short descent along the Wrynose Road, a vehicle lay-by is reached situated on the L side as you approach it. Turn L off the metalled surface here opposite the sign 'Public Footpath' and proceed NNE across the fellside with the rising ground of Hollin Slack on your L, and skirting Blea Moss on your R. Initially a definite path is hard to locate, but persevere, keeping to the higher ground and detouring round the worst of the boggy patches and surface water that confront you.

Keeping to a more-or-less constant height, and bearing NE, you will soon reach a narrow but good path coming in from your R. Near here over on your R, part of little Langdale Tarn can be seen popping up over the nearer skyline E. The path now rises along the course of a drystone wall, and as you gain height the Langdale Pikes once again become progressively revealed directly ahead. Harrison Stickle is the dominant peak seen from this angle, with Pavey Ark behind it to the R. Then the rocky shape of Side Pike looms up anew further over to your R (N).

Your path crosses a side stream and rises to Blea Tarn. Go through the k-gate and take the lower of the two paths ahead leading off to your L, around the W shore of the tarn in a northerly direction. Do not cross the stream on your R! The path circumnavigates the tarn at a fairly constant elevation, passing through extensive clumps of large rhododendron bushes. You will sight glimpses of the tarn down on the R through this dense foliage.

The path climbs slightly, veering L away from the tarn, and after passing through a k-gate the way leads to the narrow road connecting the two Langdale valleys, near to a cattle-grid. Cross the road and the l-stile on the far side, and then proceed along the lower of the two footpaths that lead downhill, adjacent to a wall on the L. There is a memorial stone seat near this point dedicated to two people who loved the Lakeland Fells, and carved in stone are the poignant words 'There is a comfort in the strength of love'.

Now descend along the agreeable path down towards the multi-coloured campsite below. Pass through a stile at the fence directly ahead and continue down through a copse of conifer trees, mainly larch. You next cross a field, pass through a gateway with a white marker post, and descend through a k-gate to reach the campsite. Turn L along the internal camp lane, and then pass through the narrow wall stile next to a gate to reach the valley road once more. Turn R along the road and follow it back to the car-park at the Old Dungeon Ghyll Hotel.

16:1 Early morning reflections in Blea Tarn.

Alternative routes

ESCAPES

Apart from abandoning the walk and retracing your steps there are no convenient escape routes before you reach the summit of Pike of Blisco. From here, if you wish to cut short the excursion, ignore the suggested R fork, a short way down from the top on your return route, and instead keep to the main, eroded path down. This easy-to-follow route will take you to the road connecting the two Langdale valleys. Turn R up this narrow road for a short distance and then leave it to the L by means of a stile. You have now returned to the prescribed main route, and therefore turn L downhill along the path and follow the directions previously provided.

EXTENSIONS

The obvious extension is to scale Side Pike, and for very strong walkers it is possible then to continue along Lingmoor Fell Ridge and effectively complete Route 20 as well, returning to the Old Dungeon Ghyll car-park along Great Langdale Valley from the E! The start of these extensions is from the point where you have crossed the road near the stone seat memorial after having visited Blea Tarn. Here take the higher path, which rises steeply to the NE to gain the interesting rocky summit of Side Pike.

GREAT GABLE and GLARAMARA
High Level Route 17

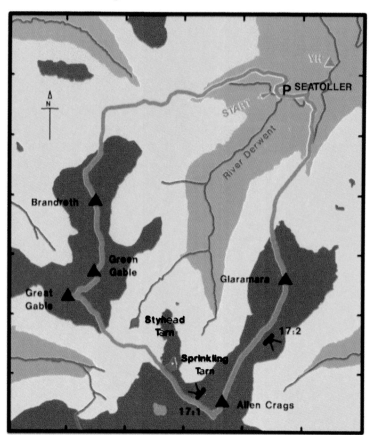

SOUTH-NORTH (Km)

WALKING TIME (Hours)   WEST-EAST (Km)

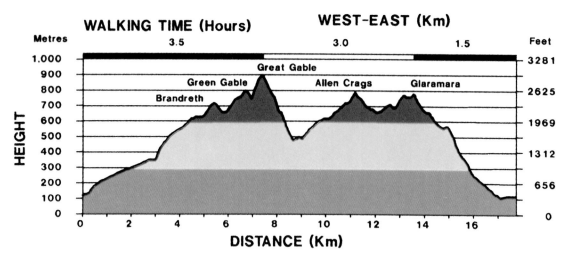

DISTANCE (Km)

STATISTICS	
START and FINISH - Car Park, Seatoller - OLM 4 / MR 245138	**TOTAL HEIGHT GAINED** - 1380 Metres 4528 Feet

START and FINISH
- Car Park, Seatoller - OLM 4 / MR 245138

WALKING DISTANCE	Km	Miles
- Excluding Height	17.7	11.0
- Including Height	18.0	11.2

TOTAL WALKING TIME : 8.0 Hours

TOTAL HEIGHT GAINED
- 1380 Metres   4528 Feet

PRINCIPAL HEIGHTS	Metres	Feet
- Green Gable	801	2603
- Great Gable	899	2949
- Allen Crags	785	2572
- Glaramara	781	2560

OTHER FEATURES OF INTEREST
- Magnificent views of Central Fells, including Scafell Pike;   Styhead and Sprinkling Tarns.

10
The Central Fells
Part 3

Route 17 · Great Gable and Glaramara

Allow 8 hours

STARTING LOCATION
National Trust car-park at Seatoller.
OLM 4/MR 245138.
Holds about 30 cars.
CMS bus route 79 – 'The Borrowdale Bus'.

OVERVIEW/INTEREST
Superb route over demanding rugged terrain.
Two strenuous, quite different climbs.
One popular, the other neglected.
Visit to Sty Head and Sprinkling Tarns.
Some minor scrambling necessary.
Few level bits!
Excellent open views along entire way.

FOOTPATHS
Good and easy to follow.
The only severe erosion is on the long descent from Great Gable to Sty Head.
Some peaty hags on return route.

The way to Great Gable   *Allow 3¼ hours*

Leave by the path at the rear of the car-park winding uphill to the NE. Cross the stile, turn R beyond, and immediately take the L fork, continuing uphill. Ahead, just before a tiny beck crosses the path, take the narrow path off to your L and follow this steeper way up the fell beside the watercourse. Soon the path reaches the main track coming up from Seatoller. Turn R along this, and it almost immediately bends sharp L westward, along a comfortable gradient. Turn around for a good view of the Glaramara Range to the S. There are a number of k-gates and stiles to go through as the broad stony path traverses gradually up a wide rolling valley along the course of the narrow, tree-fringed Hause Beck, which the road also follows.

The path converges with the road some way on. Bear R here, and then take the first narrow path off on your R. Continue along this track as it widens and re-crosses the road near some quarry spoil-heaps at an iron gate. At the entrance to the Honister Quarry go through the small gate on the R, and at the end of the adjacent car-park climb the stone steps and go over the p-stile, where you will pass a sign marked 'Public Footpath Gray Knotts Public Bridleway Great Gable Dubs'. Then climb more steps, cross another p-stile and turn L along a narrow path beside the road. Turn L off the road at a wooden gate signed 'Public Bridleway'. You next cross part of the quarry yard and proceed up the broad gravel path leading up the fellside WNW.

After about 100 m (yd) take the L-hand fork, which is a relatively new route leading more steeply uphill. A good rocky path with steps in places winds up the fellside to merge with the older, eroded route some distance ahead. Just prior to reaching the former loading-ramp from the abandoned quarry rail-track, take the cairned path off to your L (SW). Avoid, to their L, the worst of the few nasty, peaty hags ahead, and as the re-established path veers further L, the craggy outline of Grey Knotts appears on your horizon to the S.

99

Soon the summits of Pillar SSW and those of the High Stile range WNW can be observed over on your R as the stony, cairned path continues its gradual upwards incline. The path then veers further towards S. The next peak to establish itself is craggy Hay Stacks WSW, and then to the R of Hay Stacks the formidable long profile of the Scafell Range comes into view WSW. When more height is gained the first glimpses down the attractive Buttermere Valley, of Buttermere Lake and part of Crummock Water NW, present a pleasant contrast to the grandeur and starkness of the surrounding high mountain scenery.

Be careful not to follow the branch in the path leading down on your R, which goes to Hay Stacks. Next, the contrasting valley of Ennerdale comes into view down on your R (NW). Following this, the dark, massive, rounded shape of Great Gable appears ahead of you to the S. There are at least two recognized routes to the main path leading up Green Gable, the gateway to Great Gable, along

your direction of approach. The higher one, which is well marked by cairns and which sweeps further L keeping to firmer ground, is the recommended route. It swings from SSE to SSW through this section of the way.

When you have gained sufficient height, look around for a view of Dale Head, Hindscarth and Robinson, the splendid high mountain range beyond Buttermere NNE. Green Gable should now also be in view to the L of Great Gable. The path veers round the contours of the fellside as a number of small tarns are passed on your R, and from here the higher ground of Green Gable lies ahead to your R (S) at Gillercomb Head. The ascent of this commences with a steep, rocky section through which a well-worn path snakes up the craggy slope. The gradient eases off near the top and the final approach to the summit is across rounded, grassy slopes SW. Behind you there is a revealing view of far off Skiddaw and Blencathra NW.

17:1 Looking towards The Gables from the approach to Esk Hause.

Although the views from the summit of Green Gable are partly obscured by the dominating bulk of Great Gable to the sw, there are rewarding views of varied mountain scenery in other directions, including such well known landmarks as:

w	Kirk Fell.
s	Great End and Scafell group.
SSE	Bow Fell, Crinkle Crags and Sprinkling Tarn.
SE	Allen Crags and Langdale Pikes.
E	Glaramara.

Leave the summit of Green Gable by dropping down the steep, cairned path leading off L (s) to Windy Gap down an eroded scree slope. During this passage, over to your L, the rounded Styhead Tarn appears below, and then at a higher elevation the shimmering waters of Sprinkling Tarn can be made out SE. Start the climb of Great Gable by traversing upwards along the worn stony path that climbs to the L of a rocky outcrop ahead ssw. The path turns R to negotiate a rocky funnel. Soon you will come across a good, cairned path that is composed of small, whitish stones. Eventually the steepness of the slope decreases and the final approach to the summit is across a wide expanse of fairly level rocks and stones sw.

The summit of Great Gable is a boulder-strewn peak standing at 899m (2,949 ft). A magnificent panorama extends for miles in all directions. Starting by looking s to the paramount Scafell Ridge and scanning clockwise, you can see the following peaks:

S	Scafells.
SW	Wast Water.
W	Yewbarrow.
NW	Kirk Fell and Pillar Ridge beyond. Ennerdale and High Stile Range in the distance.
NNW	Grasmoor.
N	Grisedale Pike.
NNE	Skiddaw.
NE	Blencathra.
E	Helvellyn group and Fairfield.
ESE	Langdale Pikes.
SSE	Great End and Bow Fell beyond.

The way to Glaramara   *Allow 3 hours*

Leave the summit along the cairned path that descends steeply to the SE. During this section, there are particularly good views of the Glaramara Ridge, your final major objective, over to your L (E). The demanding, loose-scree path drops down to the sw end of Styhead Tarn. Due to constant heavy use this part of the route is inevitably seriously eroded. At the end of the tortuous descent your path crosses, at Sty Head, the former important trade and communications route between Borrowdale to the NE and Wasdale to the sw. A large first-aid box, which actually constitutes the Mountain Rescue Community Rescue Post, is passed on your R.

Continue along the path leading uphill E. In gaining height again you are rewarded with closer views of the awesome bulk of Great End towering up on your R (SSE). Further over to the R (sw) is the competing splendour of Piers Gill, a great fault chasm tearing into and up the otherwise relatively uniform shape, when viewed from this angle, of Lingmell. Lingmell is another gigantic and splendid mountain spur running NW from the central Scafell Massif. There is also a revealing view from here, to your rear, of the side elevation of Great and Green Gables NNW with the intervening col of Windy Gap separating their respective bulks. The alternative path down to Styhead Tarn by way of Aaron Slack is clearly visible between these two massive mountain shapes.

A good winding path that gains height at a comfortable gradient leads to the delightfully serene and irregularly shaped Sprinkling Tarn, which is passed on your L. Allen Crags lies beyond these sheltered waters SE, and makes a perfect backcloth to the scene.

Continue upwards along the firm and well-cairned path that brings you to Esk Hause. After passing a massive cairn that attempts to obliterate your wide path, select the lower L fork when the path divides. The correct path leads off SE in the direction of Allen Crags, and following this the wide expanse of Esk Hause is quickly attained.

At Esk Hause a Pandora's box of both completely new and extended mountain scenery opens up. These views are particularly revealing in the quadrant between E and S, where the Langdale Pikes and the slopes of Bow Fell and Esk Pike are to be seen, flanking the lower broad band of ground leading down to Angle Tarn (not in view). By contrast you may also look along the length of the Scafell group of mountains further round to your R (WSW), with their series of receding silhouettes.

Take the path off on your L, which climbs quite sharply ENE and you soon reach the summit of Allen Crags 785 m (2,572 ft), the NW sentinel to the Glaramara Ridge. The summit of Bow Fell appears once more over on your R (SSE) as you near the top of Allen Crags. The other consolidating views from the summit will all be familiar to you by now.

Descend along the path towards Glaramara NE. During the first part of the ensuing ridge walk good views open up on your L (N), among which the extensive Dale Head Range and the pinnacle of Grisedale Pike, in the far distance, may be observed. Also a long way off over on your R is the Helvellyn group E.

The broad, craggy, undulating ridge which you are now walking along extends for some 2.5 km (1½ miles) to the summit of Glaramara. In between there are several craggy outcrops of igneous rock and intermingled small tarns of incredible beauty. The rocky path eventually leads upwards to the ENE for the final climb to gain the summit of Glaramara. The last section of this approach is along a well-cairned stone path, which ascends quite steeply through rocky buttresses and boulders, and depending which particular route you select and whether you visit all the pinnacle rocks, some minor scrambling may be necessary.

The summit area of Glaramara is deceptively large with masses of jumbled boulders and shattered rock. There are several competing peaks, of which the highest lies furthest away N. This has a height of 781 m (2,560 ft). Most of the views from these various vantage points will be known to you by now, but there is a particularly revealing sight down along Borrowdale below, with Derwent Water nestling within its wide northerly embraces in the faraway distance NNE.

The way back to Seatoller   *Allow 1½ hours*

Commence your final descent by taking the rocky path down to the NE. Your route veers to the L of a series of small tarns below. Initially the stony path descends steeply over rocky outcrops. Soon to your L there is a formidable pitch of rock to be negotiated. This is at Combe Head and you will have to be prepared to stretch for secure hand and footholds while climbing down this challenging section.

The short excitement is soon over, and at the bottom of the rock face continue along the narrow path N in the direction of Borrowdale and Derwent Water. Your path hugs the broad ridge descending N over Raven and Capell Crags before dropping down the more rounded features of Thornythwaite Fell. Avoid all side paths off to your L, which descend more rapidly, keeping always to the crest of the broad spur. Your path generally snakes between N and NE down steep rocky and rough peaty ground among which there are some extensive hags.

The path eventually swings to the R off the continuation of the rocky spur, and you then descend along a steeper fall line. While proceeding through this section, watch out for a small rock pitch that you suddenly and quite unexpectedly encounter, and which has a nasty short drop to your R. The path next converges on a watercourse, Combe Gill to the R, gurgling merrily down into Borrowdale. A k-gate leads through a stone wall and the final approach to the lane below is along a grassy path down gently sloping ground. Follow the wall down by selecting the R-hand fork in the path, and this will lead you to a l-stile that provides access to the lane from Thorneythwaite Farm. Turn R along this lane and when you reach the main road ahead turn L and walk along the road back to the village of Seatoller.

Alternative routes

ESCAPES

The route is long and quite exhausting, and particularly on the final descent from Glaramara does pose some minor navigational challenges. For these reasons it is fortunate that there are at least two convenient ways to curtail the planned expedition. The first of these is at Windy Gap where, instead of climbing up Great Gable, turn L and descend SE down Aaron Slack to Styhead Tarn. From here either rejoin the recommended route by turning R and walking part way round the tarn to the first-aid box, or turn L and simply walk down by the side of Styhead Gill to Seathwaite. Then follow the valley road back to Seatoller.

The other curtailment is a variation upon the previous one. This is achieved by first climbing and descending Great Gable along the intended route. However, when Sty Head is reached turn L, passing the tarn on your R, and proceed down the path beside Styhead Gill as described in the previous variation.

EXTENSIONS

You will need to be fit to contemplate any serious extensions to this demanding route. However, there are possibilities for doing this, and one exhilarating addition is when you reach Sty Head to continue along the exacting Corridor Route to the summit of Scafell Pike. After which you walk along the Scafell Ridge to Esk Hause to resume, at this point, the continuation of the main route previously described.

17:2 The tops of the Langdale Pikes from the Glaramara Ridge.

WATENDLATH and LODORE
Lower Level Route 18

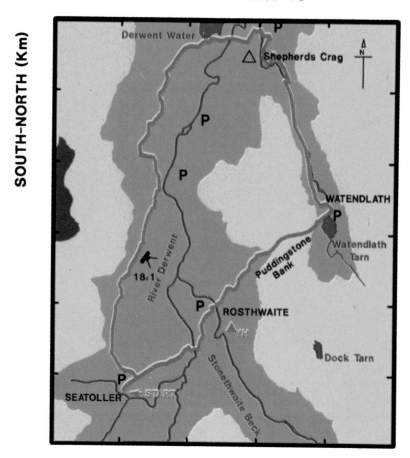

SOUTH-NORTH (Km)

Derwent Water

△ Shepherds Crag

P

P

P

WATENDLATH

P

Watendlath Tarn

Puddingstone Bank

18:1

River Derwent

P

ROSTHWAITE

YH

Dock Tarn

P

SEATOLLER

START

Stonethwaite Beck

N

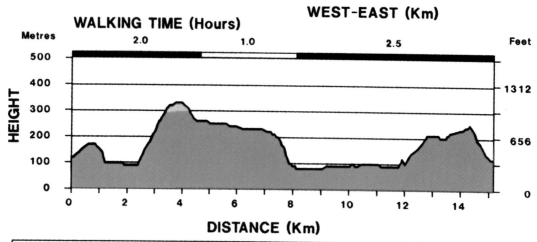

WEST-EAST (Km)

WALKING TIME (Hours)

| | 2.0 | 1.0 | 2.5 | |

Metres — Feet

500 / 400 / 300 (1312) / 200 (656) / 100 / 0 (0)

HEIGHT

DISTANCE (Km)
0 2 4 6 8 10 12 14

STATISTICS

START and FINISH
- Seatoller Car Park - OLM 4 / MR 245138

WALKING DISTANCE	Km	Miles
- Excluding Height	15.1	9.4
- Including Height	15.2	9.5

TOTAL WALKING TIME : 5.5 Hours

TOTAL HEIGHT GAINED
- 510 Metres   1673 Feet

PRINCIPAL HEIGHTS	Metres	Feet
- Puddingstone Bank	330	1080

OTHER FEATURES OF INTEREST
- Seatoller & Rosthwaite villages, Watendlath Fells, Borrowdale & River Derwent.

Route 18 · Watendlath and Lodore

Allow 5½ hours

STARTING LOCATION

National Trust car-park at Seatoller.

OLM 4/MR 245138.

Holds about 30 cars.

CMS bus route 79. 'The Borrowdale Bus'.

OVERVIEW/INTEREST

Undemanding route through alternating scenery of enclosed woodlands and the lower open fells.

Wide variety of views.

Visit to Watendlath and walk along River Derwent.

Plenty to interest all ages, including the Lodore Waterfalls.

FOOTPATHS

Footpaths for most of the route clear and firm.

Virtually no boggy places.

The way to Watendlath

Allow 2 hours

Leave the car-park at Seatoller by the broad path at the rear, which leads uphill to the NE. Climb a p-stile, face immediately R and continue uphill along a broad cart-track, which is the higher of two ways ahead. Pass through a gate and proceed along a broad stony path adjacent to a wall, ignoring a track off on your L that leads steeply uphill. Enter the woodlands ahead by means of a p-stile. Continue along the main, fairly level, track, generally NE. At the point where your path bends to the R and commences to drop, passing through a convenient gap in a stone wall, there are views through the Jaws of Borrowdale to the N. The descent to the valley floor is relatively steep for a short distance as the narrowing path swings sharply to the L and zigzags down the lower slopes.

At the bottom, cross the wire fence by means of a p-stile, to gain access onto a broad level path, which is part of the Allerdale Ramble. Turn R and descend gently downhill. Go past farm buildings on your L before a k-gate affords entry to a broad meadow in which an imposing Youth Hostel building is situated. Before you reach this establishment turn sharp L along a metalled track leading down from the Youth Hostel. Pass through an iron gate and cross the River Derwent. The lane passes the dwellings of 'Castle Lodge' and 'Peat Howe' on your L, after which immediately take the footpath off on your L signed as such. Go through the gate where you pass 'Peathow Barn' house on your R.

Cross a p-stile, and proceed alongside a wire fence, which gives way to a stone wall on your R. Along here views of the High Spy and Maiden Moor Ridge appear over to the L (NW). Next turn R through a gateway and cross the subsequent field at a diagonal, making for the cluster of buildings ahead. Continue through a stile and maintain the same diagonal to reach the path adjacent to a stone wall ahead. On attaining this wall look back to observe Glaramara SSW. Through the next gate turn R into the lane, and then almost immediately L to pass 'Larch Cottage' and 'Nook Farm'. Pass 'Yew Tree Farm' to your L and then turn R and walk down the narrow lane to the main valley road (B5289) passing through Rosthwaite.

Turn L down the road for a few paces and then turn off to your R up a lane leading to 'The Hazelbank Hotel'. You then cross a bridge and take the path to the L of the hotel entrance gateway, and which is helpfully signed 'Watendlath Footpath'. Through the next gate a more open, stony path meanders uphill, veering to the R. When further height is gained, extensive views to the rear progressively appear of the higher fells around Dale Head W, and of the higher Central Fells beyond Seathwaite SW. As you climb higher still, Great End and Great Gable can be identified from here on clear days in the SW. At the next gate turn L to the NE.

Overleaf

18:1 A peep down into Stonethwaite and Greenup.

105

Your path next passes through a series of minor obstacles including a k-gate, gate and also a stream more than once, as the summit of Dale Head appears to your rear L,(W). Go past a path forking off on your L at a k-gate, which leads to Keswick and the Bowderstone. Look around again further on for a really memorable sighting of the successive mountain chains forming the high mountainous arches of the Central Fells, dominated from this particular viewing angle by the profiles of:

SSW	Glaramara.
SW	Great End.
WSW	Great Gable.
WNW	Dale Head.

Next, cross a narrower path at right angles to the route, then your broader way NE starts to descend, progressively more steeply, over exposed bedrock. There is a well-protected copse of conifer trees down to your R, comprised mostly of larch and spruce with an area of less mature Scots pines. The path descends steeply to the hamlet of Watendlath, which is a popular spot. The renovated buildings of this farmstead are set in a wild and remote landscape, although the placid waters of the nearby tarn and fishermen patiently plying their expertise does tend to mellow the overall starkness of the location.

The way to Lodore Waterfalls *Allow 1 hour*

Skirt the northern fringes of the tarn, and having passed through a k-gate your exit path is through a gate on your L, with Watendlath Beck flowing out of the tarn to your R. The path down starts by hugging the line of the beck, but soon it veers off slightly uphill to the L, skirting a drystone wall before it resumes its general direction of travel down the valley NNW, winding along a separate course some distance away from and above the stream. Several small footbridges over tributary watercourses, gates and steps have to be negotiated as the path descends to the riverbank once more.

After several more gates and footbridges are passed, the path leads to an unusual triangular directional stone set in the ground near to a sparsely wooded area ahead (MR 268182). Turn R here along the route signed Keswick, and cross Watendlath Beck at the sturdy footbridge. After about 50 paces turn L over the l-stile and take the R path heading N. Ignore a faint track to the L, but then veer to your L down a better established way which leads NW between two wire fences. Follow the path down as it bends to the R and then veer L, passing a stile on your R. Stoop under the fallen tree, which is a permanent feature, and take the next path off downhill on your L. A short distance below there is an excellent view of the Lodore Falls, over on your L.

The way back to Seatoller *Allow 2½ hours*

Descend to the footbridge to your L and re-cross the beck. Pass behind the hotel and walk down to the busy B5289 road. Turn L, and within 250 paces take the footpath off to the R, through a wall stile beyond a gate. The continuation way is signed 'Public Footpath Manesty' at this juncture. Make for the impressive footbridge ahead which you use to cross the River Derwent. Continue along the raised footpath round the southern shores of Derwent Water.

Pass through a gate and directly opposite Great Bay at the S end of the lake select the grassy path on your L leading away from the lakeshore SW. Your path meanders through an outcrop of gorse bushes, before bearing further to your L (SW). After a k-gate and using duckboards the minor road from Grange is reached, along which you turn L. Continue up the road until you reach the Borrowdale Gates County House Hotel, immediately after which you take the public footpath leading off on your R at a gate, and follow this diagonally uphill along a narrow stony path SW. At the top of the incline, pass through a gateway and then turn L, adjacent to a drystone wall on your further L, along the rough cart-track.

Proceed through the farmstead ahead by passing in succession a gateway, a bridge and k-gate. This is Hollows Farm and through this continue down the narrow farm road that veers to the L. At the interchange ahead take the track off to your R and walk along the slate pathway SSW. Keep to the main wide path, ignoring side paths uphill on your R in several places. Your way now follows the wide meanders of the River Derwent. After this select the path branching away from the main stream to the R, crossing a side tributary by a bridge at which there is a notice, 'No camping in woodland beyond this point'.

Your path now winds quite steeply uphill and soon you will locate the entrance to a disused quarry that is well worth your passing attention. Return to your path and continue along this through the trees SE until it merges with a more pronounced path coming in on your L, and along which you proceed by turning R. When you reach a large cairn, ignore the steeper path leading off on the L to an isolated crag above, but continue to head S to the top of the col ahead. The path leads up the narrowing gully to reach the hause where ahead the summit of Glaramara is exposed to the S. To the R of this, the rocky, precipitous down fall of Great End also appears, with the main Scafell Ridge beyond, including the sighting of Scafell Pike SSW.

Rosthwaite comes into view again down across Borrowdale on your L (ESE). When the path divides, choose the narrower side path that descends to the L to reach the impediments of the bridges, stiles and gates beyond. Your path continues SSW and has now become pleasantly grassy in parts. There is a further series of obstacles to contend with, but be careful to avoid a path over a l-stile on your L. At a double gate select the L one, and descend alongside cairns down a grassy path to the track ahead. Turn L, continuing downhill along this broad track, and the dwellings of Seatoller will soon come into view down below on your R. Pass through two k-gates and when the main track swings round abruptly to the R veer off sharply downhill to your L to join the wide path below. Turn R along this path and retrace your outward steps back to the car-park at Seatoller.

Alternative routes

ESCAPES

Once Watendlath Tarn has been reached there are no significant short cuts, although the rising ground beyond Grange can be avoided by keeping to the valley footpaths alongside the River Derwent, using these to return to Seatoller.

EXTENSIONS

This is a complete walk in itself and opportunities for significant extensions without resorting to considerable extra climbing effort are consequently somewhat limited. Two possibilities which do exist are: to climb to the top of Brund Fell, which overlooks Watendlath from the W; and/or take in Dock Tarn.

Brund Fell is reached by turning L (NW) at the top of the hause above Watendlath at the end of your climb out of Borrowdale. To get to Dock Tarn use the same diversion point but instead of turning L, on this occasion, turn R (SE) and follow the path SSE to the tarn. Walk round the tarn and proceed to Watendlath along the alternative path, which starts from the E side of Dock Tarn. This will bring you back to the main route at Watendlath.

CRINKLE CRAGS and BOW FELL
High Level Route 19

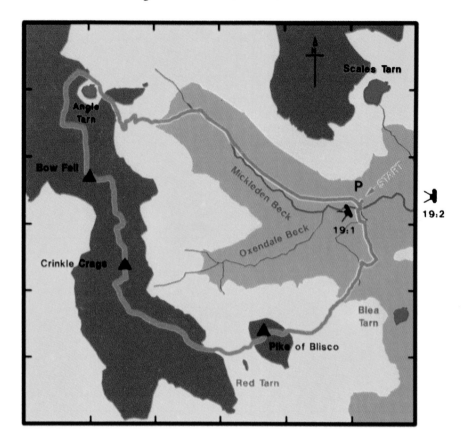

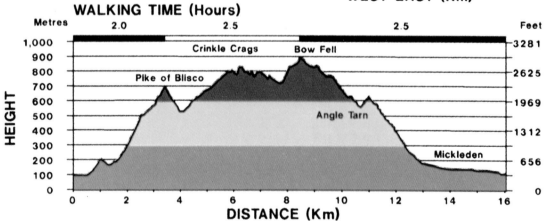

STATISTICS

START and FINISH
- Dungeon Ghyll Car Park - OLM 6 / MR 286061

WALKING DISTANCE	Km	Miles
- Excluding Height	16.0	9.9
- Including Height	16.4	10.2

TOTAL WALKING TIME : 7.0 Hours

TOTAL HEIGHT GAINED
- 1290 Metres   4232 Feet

PRINCIPAL HEIGHTS	Metres	Feet
- Pike of Blisco	705	2304
- Crinkle Crags	859	2816
- Bow Fell	902	2960

OTHER FEATURES OF INTEREST
- Great Langdale Valley, Red Tarn, Angle Tarn and Mickleden

11
THE CENTRAL FELLS
Part 4

HIGH-LEVEL ROUTE

Route 19 · Crinkle Crags and Bow Fell

Allow 7 hours

STARTING LOCATION
Car-park at Old Dungeon Ghyll Hotel.
OLM 6/MR 286061.
Holds about 40 cars.
CMS bus route 516.

OVERVIEW/INTEREST
Rewarding route with plenty of variety.
Not too demanding for a high-level walk.
Spectacular scenery.
Some fairly easy scrambling on Crinkle Crags.
Visit to Angle Tarn.

FOOTPATHS
Clear and easy to follow.
Mostly over exposed bed-rock.
Few wet patches.
Considering high usage, not too badly eroded.
Worst section is the higher reaches of Rossett Gill.

The way to Pike of Blisco   *Allow 2 hours*

Return to the main road, and turn R towards the head of the valley. An interesting view of the mountains opens up immediately ahead with, from L to R, Pike of Blisco SSW, Great Knott SW, Crinkle Crags WSW, the Band leading to Bow Fell W, Mickleden and Rossett Gill WNW, and the Langdale Pikes NNW. The road turns sharp L, and then sharp R at a campsite. Side Pike marking the end of the Lingmoor Fell spur looms up on your L ahead SE.

Turn L at the second bend and squeeze through the narrow opening in the stone wall to the R of a gate signed 'Public Footpath'. In the campsite, turn down the path on the R, and pass over a watercourse beside a stone wall on your R. Pass through a k-gate, and continue along a path uphill to a gap in the stone wall ahead. Veer to your R, cross the meadow, and pass through a second gap in a wall to enter a small copse of conifer trees, mostly Scots pine and larch. Cross the wire fence by a p-stile, and continue along a good gravel and then grassy path that leads uphill across open fellside SSE. Look to your rear for a revealing view of the Langdale Pikes NNW.

At the brow of a hill the path converges on the road from Great Langdale to Little Langdale via Blea Tarn, and here use the stile to reach the road. Proceed downhill for a short distance, and just beyond the road sign indicating a sharp bend to the R, take the well-defined track off to the L (SSW turning SW). There are splendid views along this stretch looking up the twin valleys of Oxendale and Mickleden, with the intervening rocky spur of the Band separating these two contrasting basins.

Follow the broad track that ascends along a comfortable incline WSW to reach the summit of Pike of Blisco. The path follows the course of Redacre Gill. Towards the top the path becomes stony, and on reaching the brow of the steepest part of the ascent follow the distinctive cairned route to your R, still WSW. The path twists and turns among rocky slabs as it snakes its way to the twin summits about 150 paces apart. These peaks of volcanic rock lie at

111

705 m (2,304 ft), and as the summit of Pike of Blisco is relatively isolated it commands impressive views in all directions. Start by looking SE and pan round to the W:

SE	Windermere.
SE/S	Wetherlam and the other Coniston Fells.
SW	Red Tarn.
W	Great Knott and Crinkle Crags.
NW	Bow Fell.
NNW	Glaramara.
N	Langdale Pikes.
NE	Helvellyn group.
NE/E	Great Langdale Valley.
ENE	Side Pike and Lingmoor Fell; and beyond the mountains of the High Street Fells.

The way to Bow Fell   *Allow 2½ hours*

Descend along the well-marked cairned path leading down SW in the direction of Red Tarn, which deserves a brief visit. The path crosses Browney Gill exiting from Red Tarn to your L, and it then passes round Great Knott in a broad westerly sweep. The ground steepens as the route progressively swings from WNW to NNW as it nears the first peak of Crinkle Crags. Along this stretch there are views of the coastline to the S through gaps in the intervening mountains, of which the peak of Dow Crag in the Coniston Fells is particularly prominent.

The path approaches Crinkle Crags from a westerly direction, and then meanders N over the various undulating rock formations of quite impressive sizes and irregular shapes. The rock-shattering is intense in this area, and is probably due to glacial action followed by subsequent exposed weathering, resulting in severe frost fracturing. The ground drops to a pronounced col before the narrow gully that houses 'Bad Step' is reached. The accepted scramble is up the rock face to the N and on the R of the gully. Apart from a little stretching for hand and foot holds the route

19:1 Early morning start up Crinkle Crags.

should present minimum difficulty as there is virtually no exposure. A less adventurous way round the step is to select the path on your L, rejoining the main route at the top of the gully. There are several summit crags on the Crinkles as the name suggests, and the highest of these is given as 859 m (2,816 ft). The changing panoramas from these crags are formidable and always rewarding, but the highlights are similar to those seen from Pike of Blisco and Bow Fell.

Now take care to keep to the highest ridge path between N and NNW, and on no account deviate along any of the tempting ways down on your L as these will lead you astray towards Lingcove Beck, where you will face the indignity of having to climb back to the higher ground at the Three Tarns. Eventually the Crags give way to lower ground, and the correct descent is NNW down a rocky zigzag path that leads to a hause of the Three Tarns.

After passing the tarns, a well-cairned path, which further up fans out into several alternatives, leads steeply up N through a shallow gully and then through the labyrinth of rocks that form the extensive summit pinnacle of Bow Fell. Bow Fell rises spectacularly to 902 m (2,960 ft), and is the highest point of the walk. On a clear day, especially in the late evening sunlight, the views from the top of this mountain are awe-inspiring. The magnificent and extensive mountain scenery includes:

E	Langdale Pikes and Great Langdale Valley.
SE	Side Pike and Lingmoor Fell, with Windermere beyond.
SSE	Pike of Blisco and Red Tarn; Wetherlam in distance.
S	Crinkle Crags and the Coniston Fells.
SSW	Duddon Valley and Harter Fell.
WSW	Eskdale, Muster Fell and coast.
NW	Scafell group.
NNW	Pillar, Great End, Gables and Esk Pike.
N	Grasmoor, Crag Hill and Grisedale Pike.
NNE	Glaramara, with Skiddaw beyond in the far distance.
NE	Langstrath and Blencathra.
ENE	Helvellyn group and Fairfield.

A few words of caution concerning compass bearings. Bow Fell contains a mixture of rocks and minerals that are magnetic, and therefore compass readings in this area are suspect!

The way back to The Old Dungeon Ghyll Hotel
Allow 2½ hours

Descend from Bow Fell down the rock-strewn slope in the direction of Esk Pike NNW. The path twists steeply through a tangled mass of boulders formed from volcanic rocks. The path eventually flattens off somewhat, and next there is a long traverse NNE along a cairned route, following a good, gradually descending path that winds through a further scattering of boulders. The ground levels off at Ore Gap, and here select the branch path off to the R (N). This path descends moderately at first, and then more steeply to reach, after joining up with the path down from Esk Hause, the delightful Angle Tarn nestling beneath the formidable NE precipitous buttresses of Bow Fell.

Angle Tarn is a favourite resting spot, and is a typical example of a gouged-out high corrie glacial basin, the exit of which has been effectively dammed by moraine debris. Geological field studies are sometimes undertaken at this interesting location. One last short ascent up the opposite fellside SE is required to reach the top of Rossett Gill.

The subsequent steep descent is over rough rocky ground, at first down an enclosed gully representing a fault line, and then over more open ground as the stony path twists and turns down the fellside to the head of Mickleden below. The final stages of this path have been refurbished, and a particularly good job has been made of this section of the route. There is an alternative route off to your R (SSE), which avoids the steepest section of the Gill, and which at one time was a mandatory way up.

At the valley floor the path along Mickleden is joined by the route coming down from Stake Pass. Continue along the flat valley path beside Mickleden Beck, which in its upper reaches has a number of miniature waterfalls. The Langdale Pikes loom up on your L and on the other flank of the valley the Band sweeps impressively down to Stool End Farm. Towards the end of the walk the path leads through a series of k-gates before you pass behind the Old Dungeon Ghyll Hotel on the higher path to return to the car-park.

Alternative routes

ESCAPES

There is one recognized escape route and this is from near Red Tarn, following the descent from Pike of Blisco. At this juncture instead of climbing W to circumnavigate Great Knott, turn abruptly R (NNW) and descend along the clearly established footpath down into Oxendale by Browney Gill. Then follow the path back along this remote valley

to Stool End Farm. From here continue down the farm lane to the Great Langdale Valley road and the car-park.

EXTENSIONS

The possibilities for optional extensions for the very fit are abundant. A modest extension is to continue from Bow Fell along the mountain chain via Esk Pike to Esk Hause, and then to descend to Angle Tarn to rejoin the main route. More strenuous extensions still are to continue from Esk Hause onto the Scafell Massif either to Great End or SW to climb Scafell Pike. The latter is a really daunting itinerary and should only be attempted by strong walkers, and then only in favourable weather conditions.

19:2 Heavy powder snow on Crinkle Crags and Bow Fell.

LINGMOOR FELL and SIDE PIKE
Lower Level Route 20

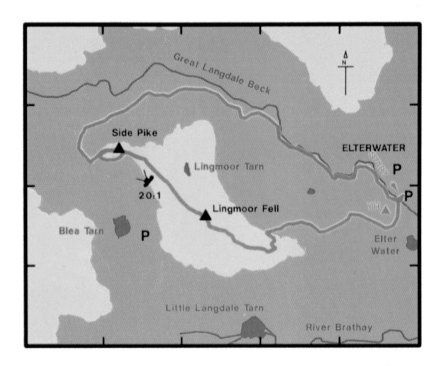

SOUTH–NORTH (Km)

Great Langdale Beck

Side Pike

Lingmoor Tarn

20:1

Lingmoor Fell

Blea Tarn   P

Little Langdale Tarn

ELTERWATER   P

P

Elter Water

River Brathay

WEST–EAST (Km)

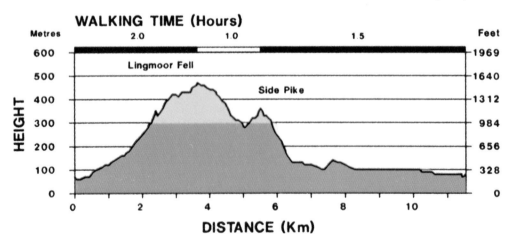

WALKING TIME (Hours)

Metres				Feet
600	2.0	1.0	1.5	1969

Lingmoor Fell

Side Pike

HEIGHT

500		1640
400		1312
300		984
200		656
100		328
0		0

0   2   4   6   8   10

DISTANCE (Km)

STATISTICS

START and FINISH
- Elterwater Car Park – OLM 6 / MR 328047

WALKING DISTANCE	Km	Miles
- Excluding Height	11.5	7.2
- Including Height	11.6	7.2

TOTAL WALKING TIME : 4 5 Hours

TOTAL HEIGHT GAINED
- 570 Metres 1870 Feet

PRINCIPAL HEIGHTS	Metres	Feet
- Lingmoor Fell	469	1530
- Side Pike	362	1187

OTHER FEATURES OF INTEREST
- Extensive views of Great and Little Langdale Valleys; disused slate quarries.

Route 20 · Lingmoor Fell and Side Pike

Allow 4½ hours

STARTING LOCATION
National Trust car-parks at Elterwater.
OLM 6/MR 328047.
In total the 2 car-parks hold about 50 cars.
CMS bus route 516.

OVERVIEW/INTEREST
One of the great little walks of Lakeland.
A microcosm of the fells.
Splendid close and distant scenery.
Very varied terrain.
The perfect introduction to fell walking.
Eminently suitable for the whole family.

FOOTPATHS
All conceivable types of walking surfaces.
The going for the most part is firm and enjoyable.
A few boggy stretches.
The occasional scramble.

The way to Lingmoor Fell   *Allow 2 hours*

From Elterwater village take the road S towards Little Langdale, which immediately crosses Great Langdale Beck. Bear L along this road and pass a white cottage on the R, named 'Bridge End'. The Elterwater Youth Hostel is passed to your R, and then the Elterwater Country House Hotel to the L. After passing the entrance drive, select the minor lane off to the R proceeding uphill.

Continue uphill along the good surfaced lane, and at the next fork turn R. A cottage named 'Ullet Nest' is passed on your R, after which keep to the lane until a vehicle-wide path is reached, leading off more steeply uphill on your L at an acute angle to the lane. Take this path signed 'Public Bridleway' passing between two stone pillars and walk uphill, crossing another path at right angles. The continuing wide path of grass and stones bisects a wood of mixed deciduous and coniferous trees. Emerging from this canopy, you have the first clear views of the surrounding mountains, and ahead of you the open fells beckon.

Near a stile and a grouping of silver birch trees look below to the orderly neatness of Great Langdale Valley, then train your eyes upwards W to E to identify in turn the Langdale Pikes NW, Sergeant Man more to the N, Silver How further to the E beyond the village of Chapel Stile, far away to the NE the ridges leading to Fairfield and the Helvellyn Range, and finally look between NE and E to the High Street Fells. Continue uphill along the broad, grassy path, which zigzags to the main ridge. The path leads to a stone wall with a gate/stile positioned at your approach point; climb over this to reach the ridge leading to the summit of Lingmoor Fell.

Turn R along one of several narrower paths which wind uphill. From now on keep in contact with the continuation of the stone wall that you recently crossed by the stile. Before proceeding to the summit look out for and visit a large cairn over on your L. This is easily located after crossing the stile and turning R. Proceed uphill for a few paces, turn almost 90° to the L and cross the rough fellside, where you will see the cairn directly ahead on bearing SSE. From the surrounding vantage points there is a sighting of tranquil Windermere far away to the SE, and of the grandeur of Wetherlam directly to the S. Retrace your steps NE, passing some disused quarry workings on your L, and make for a cairn ahead with the helpful stone wall located beyond. Follow the path upwards to the L (NW); you are now back on the main route, where shortly you will observe a pronounced cairn, which you pass on the L.

Proceed along the path W avoiding dangerous ground on your R, which is clearly identified by a notice reading, 'DANGER, no path, Unstable Clifftop'. The way ahead is obvious as the path undulates, progressively gaining height. Next locate a line of cairns, and at the second of these select the R fork, which leads uphill on bearing NW. Continue along this narrow, stony, cairned path, which zigzags steeply up the fellside to reach a wire fence

117

20:1 Side Pike caught between Bow Fell and The Langdale Pikes.

coming in on your R. Follow the line of this fence slightly uphill and cross it at the stile provided to reach the summit of Lingmoor Fell.

The summit of Lingmoor Fell is 469 m (1,530 ft), and the highest point of the route. The extended views from here include a sighting of all the Langdale Pikes NW, a more complete exposure of Bow Fell WNW, with the route from Pike of Blisco and Crinkle Crags leading up to its pointed summit. Then turn about and focus on the far distant Pennine chain to the SE. Almost beneath your feet nestles tiny Lingmoor Tarn.

The way to Side Pike   *Allow 1 hour*

The path from Lingmoor Fell descends quite steeply W before regaining height, as the E-facing, sheer rock slabs of Side Pike come prominently into view. Here the upper reaches of the Great Langdale Valley can also be seen, with Mickleden, the intervening Band, and Oxendale in view. Blea Tarn is also visible below. Your route continues to descend

along a rocky path where some easy scrambling is necessary. After crossing several boggy areas the sharp descent terminates in a pleasant grassy col. To reach this follow a wall on the L downwards to cross a stile, then continue along the path, which increasingly becomes better defined.

The daunting, rocky, E buttresses of Side Pike loom up ahead as you approach the bottom of the descent. Cross the wire fence at the stile. Then locate the indistinct path and follow this upwards, initially to your R. Next comes the interesting part as the path becomes more definite and leads off SW at a constant height round the impressive vertical rock pitches on your R. The path threads its way between the wall of the mountain and a needle-shaped outcrop of rock. The path very clearly guides you along the correct way. Do not be tempted to descend from the path at this point and go round the outside of the outlying rock, as this is relatively dangerous.

Afterwards, continue along the narrow but obvious path and take the R higher fork NW. This rocky section of the path leads first diagonally, and then twisting and turning, towards the outline of the Langdale Pikes directly ahead across the valley. The way then follows a line to your R (NNE), still climbing quite steeply to connect with a major cairned path. Following a R turn, this will guide you uphill to the summit of Side Pike. Although Side Pike is a modest 362 m (1,187 ft), it is a mountain of immense stature with extensive rock formations. The views from these rocks on fine days are superb:

SE	Route from Lingmoor Fell.
S	Blea Tarn and Wetherlam.
SW	Pike of Blisco.
W	Crinkle Crags.
WNW	Bow Fell and Mickleden.
NW	Langdale Pikes.
N	Sergeant Man.
E	Great Langdale Valley.

The way back to Elterwater   *Allow 1½ hours*

Start the descent by retracing your final approach steps, which will now guide you WNW. Return to the point where the main cairned path was reached, and then follow the marked route to the R, making for a distinctive cairn on the near horizon W. Here you will locate another stone wall to follow downhill. Initially keep this to your R, but after a short distance the path breaches it through a convenient gap, and shortly, the correct cairned route down will come into view.

The direction of descent now varies between SW and W. There is one more tricky bit; first some scrambling down rocky ledges is necessary, and then a rocky traverse downwards to the R leads to a grassy path veering off L, where another fine view of Blea Tarn can be seen. Proceed along this zigzag to reach a further large cairn, turn downhill to the R (NW), and follow the path down into Great Langdale Valley. You will soon reach an indistinct sheep track off to the R, follow this and make a final line of descent towards the most easterly edge of a copse of spruce trees in the valley below. These trees border a good path, which when followed to the E will bring you to the Cumbria Way footpath at Side House. This well-trodden route will guide you back to Elterwater.

The final part of your journey along the valley is interesting and relaxing. After passing Side House and immediately after climbing the next stile, take the upper footpath. From here yellow arrowhead guide markers indicate the correct way. The route passes through a gate, and then continues eastwards along the course of a stone wall on the L, as it meanders round the lowest slopes of Lingmoor Fell. An attractive neat cottage named Oak Howe is passed on your L. From here the path leads gently down to Great Langdale Beck, and then a broad farm track follows the raised river bank. This track leads to a small shaded pool where the water is usually of swimming depth.

Beyond the pool, keep to the path still following the stream. A culvert appears on your R, but before you become completely marooned, a stile followed by a sturdy wooden footbridge provide an escape route. Cross these and continue along the path, which can be quite wet and boggy. Keep to the riverbank, and after ducking under a water-pipe you will come to a second pool just past an imposing footbridge over the main river. A good,

wide path continues down the valley, round a slate slag spoil, and then slightly uphill to a metalled quarry road. Turn L and follow this road down to Elterwater village.

Alternative routes

Lingmoor Fell and Side Pike provide a discrete, isolated expanse of fell-walking, and as such opportunities for escape routes and extended walking are limited.

ESCAPES

The only sensible escape route is not to scale Side Pike. This ascent is best avoided by selecting the path down to your L (S and then SW) at the col between Lingmoor Fell and Side Pike. Follow this track down towards the road in the direction of Blea Tarn. A path beside the road will lead you down into Great Langdale Valley after you have turned R along it. Make for the copse of spruce trees below to rejoin the main route.

EXTENSIONS

Two interesting extensions are to visit Lingmoor Tarn and Blea Tarn. There are several, not altogether satisfactory, ways of reaching Lingmoor Tarn from the main ridge path, some of which do involve crossing short distances of demanding fellside. Reaching Blea Tarn, however, presents no problems. When descending from the summit of Side Pike continue down the path towards the road, and just before reaching this turn off L (ESE) along the footpath that skirts the road to Bleatarn House. Here branch R along the road to the vicinity of the car-park located to the E of the tarn. Turn R along the path that leads down to and then, by turning R again, round the W attractively wooded shoreline of Blea Tarn, where huge rhododendron bushes proliferate. Head N along the well-defined track, which will lead you back to the road. Cross the road on a diagonal and turn L down the path on the other side, which descends to Great Langdale Valley. Make for the copse of spruce trees below to rejoin the main route.

SERGEANT MAN and the LANGDALE PIKES

High Level Route 21

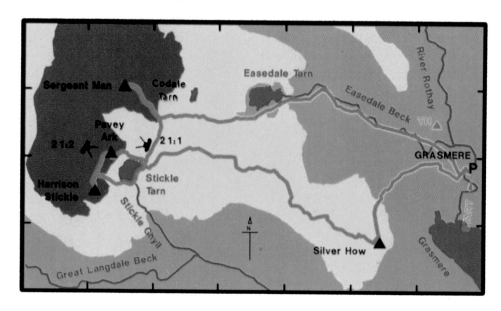

SOUTH-NORTH (Km)

WEST-EAST (Km)

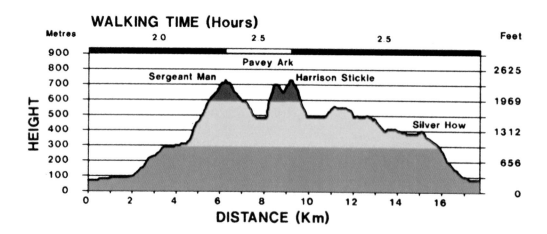

WALKING TIME (Hours)

STATISTICS	
START and FINISH	**TOTAL HEIGHT GAINED**
· Grasmere · OLM 7 / MR 337076	· 1090 Metres 3576 Feet

WALKING DISTANCE	Km	Miles
· Excluding Height	16 0	9.9
· Including Height	16 3	10.1

TOTAL WALKING TIME : 7 0 Hours

PRINCIPAL HEIGHTS	Metres	Feet
· Sergeant Man	736	2414
· Pavey Ark	697	2288
· Harrison Stickle	732	2403
· Silver How	394	1292

OTHER FEATURES OF INTEREST
· Superb scenery within Langdale Pikes; exhilarating scramble up Jack's Rake.

12
THE CENTRAL FELLS
Part 5

Route 21 · Sergeant Man and the Langdale Pikes

Allow 7 hours

STARTING LOCATION
Grasmere – Broadgate Meadow car-park.
OLM 7/MR 337076.
Holds about 80 cars.
CMS bus routes 518 and 555.

OVERVIEW/INTEREST
Superb walk with plenty of variety.
Magnificent open and uninterrupted views.
Challenging exposed scramble up Jack's Rake.
Route physically quite demanding.
Suitable for experienced fell-walkers only.
Visit to Easedale and Stickle Tarns.

FOOTPATHS
With a few exceptions the paths are good.
Erosion surprisingly well contained.
Worst part is steep descent from Harrison Stickle.
Some wet boggy patches in upper Easedale.

The way to Sergeant Man   *Allow 2 hours*

From Grasmere's village green leave along the Easedale Road, which is signposted 'Easedale Tarn'. Views of Helm Crag appear ahead NW. The lane crosses Easedale Gill, and immediately after a sharp R bend, cross the stream to your L and follow the way signed 'Easedale Tarn'. Ahead there is a view of Upper Easedale and the cascading water falling down Sourmilk Gill WNW. Go through the iron gate and follow the wide stony path leading to the falls. Ignore the path through a gate on your L

signed 'Blindtarn Moss', and continue along the obvious main path on the R beside the stream, again signed to 'Easedale Tarn'. Pass through another iron gate and cross the track to Brimmer Head Farm, continuing WNW along the path. The heights seen above Sourmilk Gill are Greathead and Stenners Crags NW.

Pass through a k-gate and climb up the fellside on the L of the meandering course of Sourmilk Gill. From here there are extensive views back down the valley to Grasmere, and nearer to there is a pleasant discrete waterfall with a catchment pool below. The path then bends round to the left and here a jagged skyline appears ahead. This is the top of Shapestone Edge WSW and Blea Rigg SW. When you approach the crest of the incline, look behind to observe the Fairfield Ridge NE and the mighty Helvellyn group ENE, with the great fault of Grisedale between them.

When Easedale Tarn comes into view at the head of Sourmilk Gill the landscape changes abruptly to the W into desolate, wild and remote terrain, devoid of trees and flanked by craggy, rock-shattered high fells. Continue along the path to the L of the tarn WSW, where for a time the course of a significant feeder stream to the R is followed as you combat a harsher gradient beneath your feet.

Your route is marked by reassuring cairns and the path next winds to the L round a rocky outcrop as it rapidly gains height towards a col on the near horizon. Scramble round to the L up the rock-face, making for two small cairns ahead WNW. These are passed to your R and following this the path traverses upwards to the L of these landmarks. There is now a more revealing view of the Fairfield Horseshoe to your rear E. On reaching your immediate horizon the path forks; take the L-hand choice, which will lead you uphill to the W where soon a small tarn comes into view over on your R (NNE).

Scramble across the boulders and locate the cairned path ahead SW, following a fast-flowing infant watercourse, which the path crosses. At the top of this pitch take the path off to the R leading NW, and then veering W. Another path converges acutely from the L, turn R along the merged route and head for the summit of Sergeant Man along the rising path. When you approach a large, angled rock slab to your L, climb up it and peer over its safe edge. From this vantage point there is an incredible view over Stickle Tarn below, to the distant Coniston Fells beyond SSW. To the L of these, Lingmoor Fell and Side Pike rise more modestly SSE, while framing the R edge of the view are the majestic steep slopes of the Langdale Pikes SW. Return to the path and make a final short climb to the rocky summit of Sergeant Man. This relatively isolated peak has an elevation of 736 m (2,414 ft) and the view from its summit provides an understanding of the relationships of many of the major mountain chains and stretches of water situated within its radius.

Train your eyes southwards; in the hanging valley below, beyond the glacial moraines, nestles the corrie waters of Stickle Tarn. Directly beyond the tarn, across Great Langdale Valley, Side Pike can be observed. This is a modest, but nevertheless impressive rock buttress that marks the westerly edge of the Lingmoor Fell Ridge SSE. Beyond on the far horizon are the high fells of Coniston. The individual peaks of Wetherlam, Coniston Old Man, Swirl How and Dow Crag SSW can be discerned. Much nearer, continuing to turn your eyes to the R, are the craggy, precipitous, easterly slopes of Pavey Ark, the most northerly peak of the Langdale Pikes. Behind on the far horizon is the distinctive grouping of Crinkle Crags SW, Bow Fell and Esk Pike WSW, the Scafell Ridge ending abruptly with Great End W and to complete this revealing outline the squarish mass of Great Gable dominates the NW horizon. Apart from Stickle Tarn, several more significant stretches of water come into view, including Rydal Water ESE, Windermere SE to SSE, Elter Water SE and part of Coniston Water SSE.

The way to Harrison Stickle   *Allow 2½ hours*

Descend from the summit by initially retracing your approach steps, this time heading SE to SSE, and return to the large slab of rock previously mentioned. Just after passing this take the R-hand fork, which veers S, away from your approach route. Head towards a distinctive cairn directly in line with the gap formed between Pike of Stickle and Pavey Ark, and descend along the narrow grassy path down towards the tarn. The path soon becomes indistinct in places, and as you lose height there is a multitude of minor paths heading along your descent line. Be careful not to surrender too much height to your R too soon, as this will lead you into relatively difficult terrain. Following these directions you will reach a distinctive path down, which then snakes through a maze of rocky outcrops through a gully before it winds round the lower grassy slopes immediately above the tarn. An established path brings you to the water's edge near a feeder stream at the tarn's NE corner.

Turn R at the tarn, cross the watercourse by the stepping stones and continue along a well-defined path around Stickle Tarn until you reach the bottom of Jack's Rake. This is situated in an area of rock fall and the approach path to the bottom of the rock fissure leads off through a jumble of rock and scree, just before a large boulder jutting out into the tarn is reached. Your way is now abruptly upwards. Soon you can locate the narrow scar of the Rake, seemingly chiselled into the otherwise hardly blemished, exposed rock-face of Pavey Ark above to your L. The climb is fortunately not as difficult as it appears to be from below, and exposure can be minimized within constraining limits to suit the tastes of individual walkers.

When the impassable rock-face ahead is reached the routes to the top divide, your's to the L up

Jack's Rake sw, while the one to the R ascends up Easy Gully NNW. In scrambling up the fissure you will find that this is broken up into several discrete, smaller rock pitches. Pause between each of these sections to regain your composure, there is no hurry and remember that you, not the mountain, are in charge of the ascent! There are plenty of safe and secure hand and foot holds, and there are at least two alternative ways to the top of the cleft. One is less exposed and tucked right into the Rake, and is technically slightly more demanding than the alternative to the L of it, which is considerably more exposed, but which provides more conveniently positioned holds. Parts of both ways can be used to provide an appropriate cocktail to match your abilities and head for heights. Partway up, you will pass a solitary tree and near this spot is a comparatively comfortable ledge where you can use your camera in safety.

On emerging from the Rake proper, be careful to turn immediately R and continue to climb up the near vertical rock-face, which contains excellent hand and foot holds. Look out for a short, level path round to your L and follow this before continuing your scramble upwards over easier, well-worn rocks. This will take you to a shallow gully just below the summit. Turn R when you emerge onto more open ground and locate a path that leads across a stone wall at a stile wsw to the final, easy scramble up the summit rocks of Pavey Ark.

Pavey Ark commands a height of 697 m (2,288 ft), not one of the giants of the Lake District Fells by any means, but it does have a grandeur and presence commensurate with the difficulty with which you have gained its summit. You will probably be familiar with most of the views from the top of Pavey Ark, but from this new vantage point Blea Tarn, situated on higher ground between the two Langdale Valleys, is now visible SSE, and Grasmoor, Sail and Grisedale Pike appear in the NW. The Glaramara Ridge to the WNW completes the new sightings from here.

Retrace your approach steps for a short distance to commence your descent, until you locate a rocky path branching off to the R (wsw). Follow this, passing a grouping of very small tarns on your R. Your route leads along the edge of the rocky

21:1 Gazing at Jack's Rake from the safety of Stickle Tarn.

band linking Pavey Ark to Harrison Stickle. Follow the contour round veering to the s, and never surrender height to your L. Soon the peak of Pike of Stickle, comes into view to your R (wsw). Then, after you have passed a rocky outcrop, the isolated peak of Pike of Blisco appears in front of the Coniston Fells backcloth ssw. Your path continues SE, up a rock-strewn moderate slope to the craggy summit of Harrison Stickle.

Harrison Stickle at 732 m (2,403 ft) is made of rocks formed from volcanic activity, and it is the highest and most prominent separate peak within the Langdale Pikes grouping. Its extensive rocky summit area has several high spots, all of which are worth exploring. In addition to the views you have already experienced, there is a particularly revealing exposure of the SE face of Pavey Ark with its precipitous, almost vertical slopes and with Jack's Rake precariously snaking up it on a severe diagonal. From this peak there is also an extensive view down the wide U-shaped Great Langdale Valley with its green fields, boundary walls and other reminders of habitation.

The way back to Grasmere   *Allow 2½ hours*

Retrace your approach route to the bottom of the slope leading to the summit, on this occasion travelling NNW. Then descend slightly further to the grassy hause to your R. At this expanse, near to a double cairn, veer sharply R and descend by the main path that zigzags down to Stickle Tarn some considerable distance below. Your direction down this steep slope is first to the NE and then predominantly ESE to reach eventually the southern tip of the tarn. The exacting descent crosses boulders, shattered rock, loose scree and bilberry down a severe gradient where at times foot holds are difficult to maintain.

At the tarn follow the path round it, in an anticlockwise direction with the tarn to your L, until you return to the place where you first reached it on your outward route. Here, turn R up the path heading E, along which there are some guiding cairns. Your path bends to the NE before returning to E as it climbs gradually up the rounded grassy fellside. When you have attained the ridge ahead, continue walking in an easterly direction, keeping to the higher ground. You are now on the long broad spur of Blea Rigg, a little further to the SE than you were earlier in the day during your descent to Stickle Tarn from Sergeant Man. This landmass leads, first NE, and then ESE descending to Silver How.

There are numerous routes along the broad spur and it matters very little which particular one you select, providing, as previously mentioned, you keep to the higher ground and continue to travel SE. All the routes undulate and lead up, down

and/or around Castle How, Raw Pike and Lang How in that sequence, before the symmetrical peak of Silver How is attained. One of the paths passes round a delightful tarn which, with its expanse of sheltered shallow water, is a natural habitat for fauna and bird-life of several varieties. Along the whole of this part of the route there is only one bit to be particularly vigilant over, and this is when the main path suddenly descends for a short distance down a rocky gully and it becomes indistinct for some distance before reaching a clearly defined path ahead, which then zigzags down to your R.

The summit of Silver How is reached after a final short climb. The views from this interesting peak overlooking Grasmere village are extensively covered in the companion, lower level route. Suffice therefore to mention here that additional to the panorama behind you to the W, with which you are familiar, the summit of Silver How does provide extensive views in the semi-circle centred on E, in which lies, moving from N to S, Easedale and Helm Crag, Helvellyn and Fairfield, and finally down below, Grasmere Lake and Rydal Water.

Your final descent is along the cairned path N, then veering E down to Grasmere village. After an initial short, steep descent through some scree, the path levels off for a time along a pleasant grassy way. It then bends round to the R, after which it descends past a cairn on the L, to cross a narrow rocky gully with a small watercourse at the bottom, across which you are obliged to scramble. Turn R along the path on the far side leading NE, and you will almost immediately be threading your way through a dense clump of juniper bushes, before you arrive at a k-gate, followed shortly by another. The pathway then descends to a lane near two neat cottages. Turn R along this lane, which leads through pleasant parkland down to Grasmere village.

Alternative routes

ESCAPES

There is one obvious way of shortening this demanding route, and this is when you first reach Stickle Tarn to cut out the exhilarating climb and

descent of the Langdale Pikes by turning back up to Blea Rigg once more and resuming the recommended route again from this juncture.

For those of you who do not wish to go up Jack's Rake but still want to climb Pavey Ark and Harrison Stickle, there is the alternative of proceeding to the summits from Stickle Tarn by means of the path that loops up from the tarn to the N of the rock-faces. Once you have reached the summit of Pavey Ark you are again linked into the main route.

21:2 The exit from Jack's Rake on Pavey Ark – looking down across Stickle Tarn to Lingmoor Fell.

EXTENSIONS

If the route described is not sufficient, one modest extension, from the summit of Pavey Ark, drop down again to Stickle Tarn by the path that loops down to the N, and then re-climb the mountain, this time up Easy Gully.

Another possibility is to visit more of the Pikes, including Pike of Stickle and Gimmer Crag.

SILVER HOW and RYDAL
Lower Level Route 22

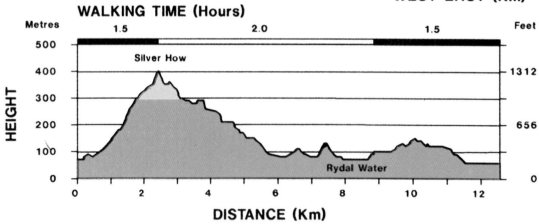

SOUTH-NORTH (Km)

WEST-EAST (Km)

Alcock Tarn

Rydal Beck

P

GRASMERE

P   P

22:1

Silver How

Grasmere

Rydal Water

YH

YH

YH

N

River Rothay

WALKING TIME (Hours)

Metres	1.5	2.0	1.5	Feet

Silver How

Rydal Water

HEIGHT

500 —
400 — 1312
300 —
200 — 656
100 —
0 — 0

DISTANCE (Km)

0   2   4   6   8   10   12

STATISTICS

START and FINISH
- Grasmere - OLM 7 / MR 337076

WALKING DISTANCE	Km	Miles
- Excluding Height	12.5	7.8
- Including Height	12.6	7.8

TOTAL WALKING TIME : 5.0 Hours

TOTAL HEIGHT GAINED
- 540 Metres   1770 Feet

PRINCIPAL HEIGHTS	Metres	Feet
- Silver How	394	1292

OTHER FEATURES OF INTEREST
- Revealing views of Grasmere, Rydal and Langdale Pikes; Wordsworth relics.

Route 22 · Silver How and Rydal

Allow 5 hours

STARTING LOCATION
Grasmere – Broadgate Meadow car-park.
OLM 7 MR/337076.
Holds about 80 cars.
CMS bus routes 518 and 555.

OVERVIEW/INTEREST
Delightfully interesting walk.
Not too energetic.
Should appeal to family groups.
Very suitable for children.
Several connections with Wordsworth.
Superb landscapes, particularly of Langdale Pikes.

FOOTPATHS
Scores high marks in terms of quantity, quality and continuity.
Virtually no erosion or boggy patches.

The way to Silver How
Allow 1½ hours

From the village square in Grasmere select the road running NW, signed 'Public footpath Score Crag Silver How'. From here you have an immediate sighting of Silver How up on your L. Continue along the narrowing lane uphill, passing a cattle-grid. The way then winds up through parkland along a metalled track. Next take the path off to the R, again reassuringly signed. Soon over on your R, through views intermittently obstructed by trees, there are sightings of Helm Crag, Heron Pike and the Fairfield Ridge as the path continues to climb.

When you come to two neat white cottages, cross the stile at the gateway on their L. The path rises more steeply and becomes enclosed. Then the route passes through a convenient gap in the encircling stone wall and from here a good grassy way leads up the open fell side to the SW, through another stile. It veers to the L before scaling the fellside in a series of twists and turns to reach the immediate juniper-bush-fringed skyline.

The path bears L along a less steep gradient SW. Then it crosses a rocky gully down on your L; some easy scrambling is involved here. On the far slope look out for a single guiding cairn, which you pass to your R before the wide grassy way snakes round the fellside SW. A more prominent cairn is passed to your L and directly ahead Silver How comes into view to the S. Your grassy, cairn-lined path tracks towards this along a comfortable gradient to reach the final separate protruding slope of the mountain.

The summit of Silver How is 394 m (1,292 ft) high and commands the following extensive and varied views:

W to NW	Bow Fell, Langdale Pikes and Sergeant Man.
N	Easedale and Helm Crag.
NNE	Helvellyn, Dollywagon Pike and Seat Sandal.
NE	Fairfield Ridge with Grasmere village below.
E to ESE	Grasmere Lake and Rydal Water.
SE	Windermere.
SW	Wetherlam.
WSW	Pike of Blisco and Crinkle Crags.

The way to Rydal Mount
Allow 2 hours

Resume your direction of travel SW, heading towards Wetherlam in the far distance, and retaining the higher ground as the terrain falls. You now follow a grassy path, which in places becomes somewhat indistinct. Soon the egg-timer shape of Elter Water appears below to the S. Follow the path S, gradually losing height and fine-tuning your descent to pass near to the series of cairns strategically positioned along this part of the route. At a second mound of stones, follow the grassy path veering L, still S, downhill towards Elter Water. Next you join another path coming in on your R, and after turning L onto this, continue down as it sweeps round to attain the spur of the fellside leading to Dow and Red Banks. These run SE in the

127

direction of Windermere. Your route then oscillates between E and S along this ridge.

Along the spur there are interesting views down into Great Langdale Valley, particularly of the two tiny enclaves of Chapel Stile SW and Elterwater S. The ridge now undulates in a series of modest hillocks, and soon part of the narrow road snaking over Red Bank between Elterwater in Great Langdale Valley and Grasmere comes into view. Continue SE along the ups and downs. The next helpful landmark is a small tarn nestling in the folds of the fells, which you pass on your L.

Eventually there is a pronounced drop down a rocky traverse. Part-way down, branch to the L to reach a wide main path at the bottom. Turn L along this lower path and after a few paces fork R, making for the end of a stone wall ahead ENE. Your way now follows the course of this wall, with it on your L as you walk up a moderate slope. Pass through a gate before you descend to your L, first towards Grasmere Lake NE and then in the direction of Rydal Water E. Branch L and drop down to the road below. Cross this and smartly leave it again by descending down a track off it on your L, signed 'Public Bridleway' and 'Rydal'.

At the division of the ways ahead proceed L through a turnstile to the R of a gate on which there are restrictive notices addressed to cyclists. A good broad path leads delightfully down through mature deciduous trees. The way brings you to a house on your L, and here turn sharply R along the pathway signed 'Lake Whitemoss Rydal'. This leads down to the southern tip of Grasmere Lake.

Follow the lake shore to your R, almost immediately passing through a gate in a wooden fence. Continue towards the sturdy wooden footbridge ahead over the River Rothay, but do not cross this. Instead take the diagonal footpath leading uphill on your R to reach Loughrigg Terrace WSW, then veer L along this relatively flat and well-walked pathway. Thereafter, ignore all side paths leading more steeply up the fellside. Soon you will see glimpses of Rydal Water ahead to the E. Retain your height by taking the R-hand path, and continue along this well-defined route, still walking E. A rocky outcrop on your L provides a good vantage point of the view back to Helm Crag NNW.

The path continues to meander round the grassy fellside at a constant height as more open views are revealed of Rydal Water down below on your L. Turning around on the R to your rear, the outlines of Silver How and Sergeant Man can be identified to the NW. Your path reaches a flat area of ground at a disused slate quarry, and a quick exploration of the excavated cave, with its saw-toothed archway, off on your R, is an inviting prospect. Then follow the path down to the L beside a wire fence to reach the shores of Rydal Water. Turn R and enter Rydal Woods, a Lake District National Park access area. Your path leads eastward under the attractive shady foliage. Cross the River Rothay by the stout footbridge and then cross the busy main A591 road at a spot where good views of approaching, fast-moving traffic leave something to be desired!

Turn R and pass the closed gateway to 'Dora's Field', of Wordsworth fame, and then turn L down the next lane, signed 'Rydal Mount'. In this tiny hamlet of Rydal there is much of interest. The church on your L is the Church of St Mary – Rydal, and then the entrance to Rydal Hall is passed on your R. This is part of the Diocese of Carlisle and caters for educational and outdoor activities. Then comes Rydal Mount, William Wordsworth's home between 1813 and 1850.

The way back to Grasmere *Allow 1½ hours*

Continue uphill, passing the coach turning area. Beyond this take the L-hand fork signposted 'Public Bridleway Grasmere', and veer L through a gate avoiding a grassy path off, further to your L. Proceed through a second gateway and the path then cuts across the open fellside at a fairly constant height, leading you W back towards Grasmere.

Your path meanders pleasantly round the slopes of the fellside, gradually gaining further modest height. After some distance a house is reached on your R, and here follow the more pronounced upper path, which leads on to a narrow lane passing the dwelling named 'Brockstone'. Descend along the narrow road, where a form by the road-

22:1 The mist rising over Grasmere Lake.

side marks the confluence of a path coming down from Alcock Tarn. The road veers to the L and descends through a grouping of dwellings huddled together round an attractive pool that is popular with ducks. Veer to the R down the road to Grasmere. In a short distance Dove Cottage and the Wordsworth Museum are reached and these provide the opportunity for a further interesting diversion.

Descend to the main road, cross this, and turn along the B5287 loop road into Grasmere village. Your car-park is situated towards the far end of the village. Before you reach this, however, you will come to Grasmere Church, the grounds of which contain Wordsworth's final resting-place.

Alternative routes

ESCAPES
There are a number of ways to curtail this route; you do not need to climb Silver How, and the s tip of Grasmere Lake may be reached by walking round the lakeshore, which is accessed from the road up Red Bank; alternatively, having reached this spot at the s end of the lake after descending from Silver How, you may return direct to Grasmere by turning L instead of R, and following the lakeshore back towards the village; another variation is a direct descent from the summit of Silver How to Grasmere near to the boat and picnic spot at the lake.

EXTENSIONS
The obvious extension for strong walkers is to climb Loughrigg Fell 335 m (1,101 ft). This is achieved by continuing to climb from the southern tip of Grasmere Lake, past Loughrigg Terrace, straight up to the summit of the fell along the well-marked path SE. Descend along the pathways to the E and then N to rejoin the main route adjacent to the disused quarry workings at MR 356058, and continue on to Rydal Water.

129

HELVELLYN
High Level Route 23

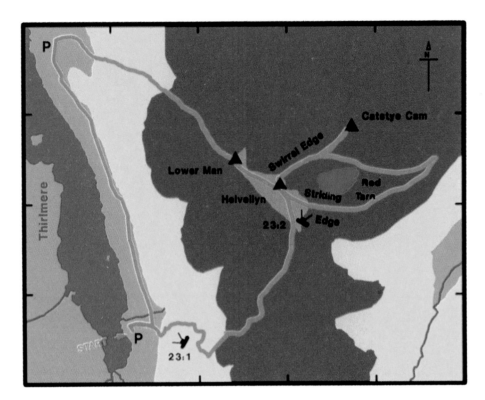

SOUTH-NORTH (Km)

WEST-EAST (Km)

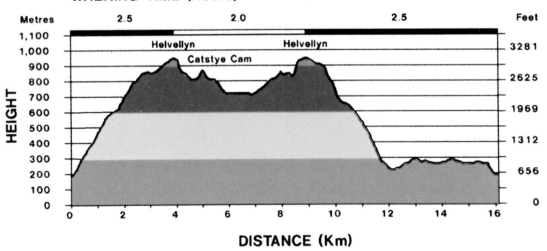

WALKING TIME (Hours)

HEIGHT

DISTANCE (Km)

STATISTICS

START and FINISH
- Wythburn Church CP - OLM 5 / MR 325136

WALKING DISTANCE	Km	Miles
- Excluding Height	16.1	10.0
- Including Height	16.4	10.2

TOTAL WALKING TIME : 7.0 Hours

TOTAL HEIGHT GAINED
- 1230 Metres   4035 Feet

PRINCIPAL HEIGHTS	Metres	Feet
- Helvellyn	950	3118
- Catstye Cam	890	2917
- Lower Man	925	3033

OTHER FEATURES OF INTEREST
- Exhilarating ridge scrambling on Swirral and Striding Edges;   good views over Thirlmere.

13
THE CENTRAL FELLS
Part 6

Route 23 · Helvellyn

Allow 7 hours

STARTING LOCATION
Car-park behind Wythburn Church.
OLM 5/MR325136.
Holds about 30 cars.
CMS bus route 555.

OVERVIEW/INTEREST
Two spectacular ridge routes, Swirral and Striding Edges.
Excitement and exposure in high-level mountain terrain.
Not unduly strenuous – views magnificent.
Visit to Red Tarn.
Suitable for walkers who enjoy the thrill of walking along sharp arêtes.

FOOTPATHS
The scrambles are excellent.
Paths reasonably good.
Severe erosion on the upper part of the descent.
Browncove Crags.
Few boggy areas.

The way to Helvellyn   *Allow 2½ hours*

Leave the car-park at the N end, passing through the k-gate. Turn R up the gravel path beside a stream on your L, and proceed steeply uphill along the path E. Soon part of Thirlmere will appear below you to your rear. To the S of Thirlmere is the symmetrical shape of Steel Fell SSW.

Next, cross a forest road at right angles, and your route continues uphill signed 'Helvellyn'. The path

is now stony, and it leads to a gate and stile that give access to a traverse at a less steep angle of climb along a tastefully refurbished stone pathway. At the first bend ahead, over the tree-fringed skyline on your R, a more revealing view to the W comes into view. The tops of Standing Crag W, leading to Ullscarf WSW may be discerned, and there is an impressive view up the long valley of Wyth Burn to High Raise beyond SW.

Further on the path zigzags up through loose scree, but the going never becomes difficult as you climb well above the conifer tree-line, and the tips of the highest mountains of Central Lakeland start to appear in the far W. Your way emerges from a shallow gully and bears L to provide an approach to the next section of your route, the climb to the high-level band leading to the summit of Helvellyn. From here the distant Coniston Fells can be made out SW. Nearer, the twin peaks of Pike of Blisco appear WSW, while completing this extensive view are the helmet-like summits of the Langdale Pikes, with Harrison Stickle dominating this separate cluster of peaks WSW. The stony path continues to wind across the vast fellside NE, and then it veers more to the N. The gradients vary up an eroded section before the path levels off to a most comfortable rate of climb to attain the main ridge path coming up on your R from Dollywaggon Pike to the S.

Almost immediately over on your R there is, in clear weather, the first sighting of Striding Edge

ENE. The view of the steep arête is particularly impressive from this direction, and the serrated, rocky tip appears unbelievably difficult to traverse. Fortunately, it is nowhere near as awesome to scramble along as it looks from here! At this point you will also be able to see, weather permitting, Nethermost Cove, a fine example of a hanging valley above Grisedale to the E. Towering above and flanking the far side of Grisedale is the broad whaleback shape of St Sunday Crag, one of the principal fingers of rock spreading out from the broad summit of Fairfield. On the far horizon are the Easterly Fells mainly N to S running folds, and dominated by the High Street Range.

Continue climbing to the summit cairns and other features that have been erected on the extensive flattish area marking the highest level of this huge mountain. The summit of Helvellyn stands at 950 m (3,118 ft), and included among the memorabilia situated on this windswept expanse are testimonies to the first aeroplane that landed on a mountain in Great Britain, on 22nd December 1926, and also to a faithful dog that stood guard over the remains of his master, who died in a rockfall on the mountain. There is also a fine stone shelter erected in the form of a substantial cross.

The views from the top of Helvellyn, and from the associated peaks, on a clear day stretch for miles in all directions. The groupings of the most prominent mountains that can be identified from this lofty platform are briefly summarized below. Start by looking to the S, and move round clockwise, making your observations at all times beyond the immediate Helvellyn Range:

SSW	The Coniston Fells.
SW	Crinkle Crags, Bow Fell and Scafell Pikes.
WSW	Great Gable and Pillar group.
W	High Stile group.
NW	The NW Fells, including Grasmoor and Grisedale Pike.
NNW	Skiddaw.
N	Blencathra.
E to SE	The E Fells, including the High Streets.
SSE	The Fairfield Range, and the spurs leading from it to the E.

The way along the ridges back to the summit
Allow 2 hours

Continue along the E edge of the mountain, and shortly you will see Swirral Edge falling away sharply on your R to the NE. This arête then ascends to terminate impressively in the abrupt, isolated peak of Catstye Cam. The glaciated Red Tarn comes into view directly below, in the deep recesses of the wild and forbidding combe formed between Swirral Edge and Striding Edge. Pass the trig. point on your L, and at the single cairn marking the top of Swirrel Edge descend to your R down the steep rocky arête to the NE.

There are several routes of varying difficulty and degree of exposure down this superb ridge of upthrust rocks of all shapes and sizes. Choose the way that suits your abilities best, do not be hurried, enjoy the scramble down and keep your descent always under control. (*Note*: This descent in ice and snow is dangerous and not recommended unless all the walkers are experienced, and are equipped with ice-axes and crampons.) The remote wasteland of surface water, hardy grassland, sedges, and rocks far below on your L is the wild, barren, U-shaped valley of Brown Cove.

At the division of the paths, once off the rocky ridge, select the higher one to your L and follow this stony way to the interesting separate summit of Catstye Cam, 890 m (2,917 ft). From here there is a particularly revealing view of most of Ullswater, snaking away far below to the E, and also a closer observation of the High Street grouping and its complicated satellite ridges ESE.

Turn back and descend for a short distance along your previous approach route to the division of the paths, then turn acutely L and make your way down to Red Tarn below. Your way skirts the tarn in a broad sweep to the E, and in crossing the lower ground before firm rock is again reached, there are some peat hags to contend with. Keep to the higher ground wherever possible, but do not be tempted to turn abruptly to the R and scale the more severe

23:1 Trudging up the lower slopes of Helvellyn above Thirlmere.

*23:2 Walkers on Striding Edge in evening sunshine –
Helvellyn.*

slope here as this leads to difficult terrain and will result in a needless waste of energy. Instead, continue heading E, following a gradual slope upwards along a path that eventually connects with the route to Helvellyn along Striding Edge, coming up from Glenridding and Patterdale. This is near a l-stile over a substantial stone wall appropriately named 'Hole-in-the-wall'.

Turn abruptly R before the stile, heading SW along the flank of Bleaberry Crag to Low and then High Spying Hows, as a prelude to scaling Striding Edge. A long upwards traverse over rough, rock-strewn ground is necessary to reach the firm arête of Striding Edge. The Edge is a series of rock pinnacles with several routes along it, ranging from scrambling over the really quite wide top ridge slabs, to walking up a virtual pathway for most of the way along its sheltered N flank. Again choose a route on which you feel comfortable, and if your initial selection proves more or less demanding than you thought it might be, there are several convenient places for upgrading or downgrading the degree of difficulty and your associated exposure.

The short descent from the last pinnacle of the ridge proper, before the bristly, rock-strewn face of Helvellyn has to be scaled, is the only really demanding section along the whole ridge. Here there are at least two established routes, one down to the L, and the other to the R of the formidable final rocky bluff ahead. Once you have reached the steep, rocky slopes of Helvellyn start by scrambling up the pointed band of jumbled rocks, and then veer L, searching for firm rock ledges that lead upwards to the broad summit ridge just below the top of Helvellyn. Turn R at the top and retrace your earlier steps to the summit. If you reach this for a second time before 9 am you are doing quite well!

The way back to Wythburn Church

Allow 2½ hours

Leave the summit by the broad ridge path, passing the solitary cairn marking the start of the descent via Swirral Edge on your R. Your general direction of travel for some time now is NW. The ridge and the path bend to the R towards N and the descent takes in the separate peak of Lower Man. The more direct way down is before reaching Lower Man to branch L along the wide gravel path leading NW and marked by cairns.

Continue NW along the clear ridge path, which is profusely lined with cairns. Soon you will be descending down the steep, badly eroded slopes to the w of Browncove Crags, on which it is very difficult to maintain a sound purchase. At the junction of the ways below, either path will bring you to the car-park and amenities situated to the N of Highpark Wood, below to the NW. The more favoured route is the newer path to the L here, although its lower slopes can become boggy after prolonged wet weather.

Eventually a reconstructed pathway traverses down the final fell slopes in a series of regular sweeps to the toilets, picnic area and car-parking

facilities below. Various helpful signs are passed together with a series of stiles, footbridges, k-gates and gateways along the obvious way down, before the amenities area is eventually reached at North West Water's Swirls car-park.

Go past these and then turn L through the large k-gate, which provides entry to the forest road leading s. The track winds progressively uphill at a gentle gradient through the conifer forest, which further on has some beech trees interspersed among the evergreens. A l-stile is crossed and the road undulates before petering out into a rocky, narrow waymarked footpath that connects with another forest road some distance to the s. The distinctive markers spaced along the path are blue and white circles. Continue along the second forest road, still heading s, until you reach a stile adjacent to the path up from Wythburn Church that you used on your outward route. Turn R at this junction and descend down the steep path back to the car-park below.

Alternative routes

ESCAPES
The route may be curtailed by excluding the ridges, but this unfortunately misses out the best and most exciting part of the walk. A more acceptable variation might be to complete the walk as specified up to the second ascent of Helvellyn. From here a shorter route back is to retrace your outward steps.

EXTENSIONS
On top of Helvellyn for the second time you could then go round the ridges again, on this occasion in the reverse direction, starting by descending Striding Edge!

Probably a more agreeable option, based on the presumption that familiarity breeds contempt, will be for you, during your prescribed descent from Helvellyn, to continue along the main ridge from Lower Man northwards to Raise and beyond, before tracking back towards Thirlspot. However, prior to reaching Thirlspot, turn s along the path to Swirls car-park to pick up the main route once more.

ULLSCARF and DEAD PIKE
Lower Level Route 24

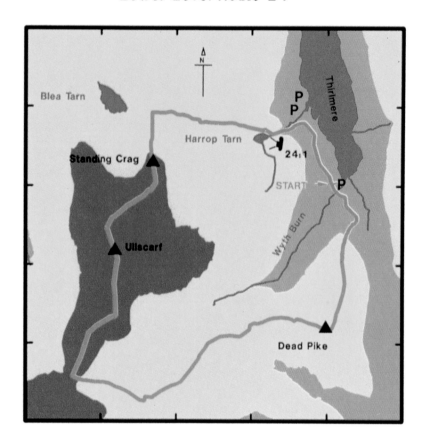

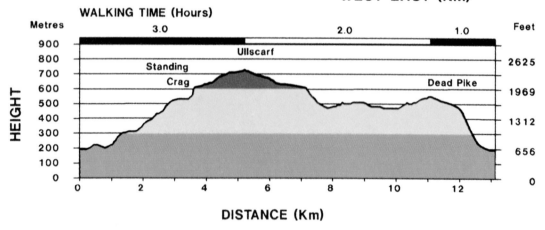

WEST-EAST (Km)

WALKING TIME (Hours)

DISTANCE (Km)

STATISTICS

START and FINISH			TOTAL HEIGHT GAINED		
- Steel End Car Park - OLM 4 / MR 321129			- 700 Metres 2297 Feet		
WALKING DISTANCE	Km	Miles	PRINCIPAL HEIGHTS	Metres	Feet
- Excluding Height	13.1	8.2	- Standing Crag	615	2018
- Including Height	13.3	8.3	- Ullscarf	726	2370
TOTAL WALKING TIME : 6.0 Hours			- Dead Pike	553	1811

OTHER FEATURES OF INTEREST
- Forest trails; good views of Thirlmere, Borrowdale and the Central Fells.

Route 24 · Ullscarf and Dead Pike

Allow 6 hours

STARTING LOCATION
Steel End car-park at Wythburn.
OLM 4/MR 321129.
Small car-park – holds up to 15 cars.
CMS bus route 555 (nearby).

OVERVIEW/INTEREST
Varied landscape – forests, tarns and mountains.
The higher fells provide magnificent open views.
One of the less-frequented routes.
A demanding walk for a lower level classification.
Steep final descent.

FOOTPATHS
To start with, good and clear.
Higher up, of varying quality.
Some improvization required.
Significant areas of wet, boggy ground on the tops.

The way to Ullscarf
Allow 3 hours

From Steel End car-park turn R along the minor road round the W shore of Thirlmere heading N. A short distance ahead at Stenkin Farm take the footpath off on the L. Along this stretch extensive views immediately open up, including the rugged outline of Nab Crags over on your L (W), the wide outlet of Wyth Burn valley below to the L of the Crags, and to your rear the lofty shapes of Dead Pike and Steel Fell S.

When the path splits take the lower R-hand fork, passing the ruined buildings at West Head to your L. Part of Thirlmere is now visible ahead on the R, and also Wythburn Church ENE. Continue through a gateway along a wide grassy path that starts to descend gradually NNW. Beyond another gate the main path leads down to rejoin the road; however, at this point bear round to the L, following the contour that bends round the Binka Stone outcrop. Continue NW onto the Binka Stone, from which there are good views along the length of Thirlmere, particularly to the N. Some wet areas have to be crossed in this vicinity.

From the Stone proceed up the path that leads round the flank of Birk Crag, and then climbs by the side of Dob Gill to Harrop Tarn, NW and then W. In doing this you will be following a distinct, narrow, rocky, cairned path through a dense plantation of sweet-smelling juniper bushes. This path climbs steeply as it twists and turns up the craggy fellside. Your path converges on a wire fence to your R; keep to the rocky path that veers away from this fence as it continues its relentless progress uphill.

Cross the fence at the l-stile on your R some distance further up, and beyond this a good path leads you pleasantly uphill at a more gradual rate of climb beneath a canopy of pines, spruce and Canadian hemlocks. Quite suddenly you arrive at Harrop Tarn, a reeded oasis of mellow colouring with the light filtering across its still waters against a backcloth of overhanging dark conifers and a craggy fell beyond. Ford Dob Gill just below the tarn, and then walk above the tarn along the wide forest bridleway heading W, and waymarked with a blue arrow sign. Your route continues westwards through the forest for about 1 km ($\frac{1}{2}$ mile) or so, gradually climbing, with a small stream on your L. At the next junction veer L along the path waymarked with a blue arrow and signed 'Watendlath Footpath' W.

After a short distance turn L into a broader pathway and continue along this uphill until you come to a narrow path leading off through the trees uphill on your R, and indicated with further blue marker signs, which you follow. You proceed to gain further height along a firm, stony path as this heads W. The path continues to climb steeply through the forest and it will eventually bring you to an imposing wooden caged gate, which provides an exit from the canopy of conifers to the more open fells above. At this point there are impressive views over to your L of the pointed Standing Crag SSW and Low Saddle WSW.

Above the tree-line a broad, grassy path leads

through the dense bracken up the attractive rounded fellside WNW at a gradual rate of climb to reach rougher ground ahead. Here make for the guiding cairn on the near horizon NW. When you have gained sufficient height look around to the E to record the view of the high fells of, from L to R, Helvellyn, Nethermost Pike, High Crag, Dollywaggon Pike, Fairfield and Seat Sandal across the still, deep waters of Thirlmere below. Follow the rocky, cairned path to reach the flat-topped ridge near to an attractive cluster of tiny tarns.

Turn L and proceed along the path as this follows very closely the direction of a wire fence, now on your R. From L to R on a clear day the tops of the following main mountain groupings can be made out as you gain further height:

WSW	Pillar group
W	High Stile Ridge and Fleetwith Pike.
WNW	Dale Head group.
NW	Maiden Moor Ridge.
	Crag Hill, Sail and Causey Pike Spur.
	Grisedale Pike and NW Fells.
N	Skiddaw.

In the near distance the grassy pike of Low Saddle dominates the skyline to the SW while down to the R of this mountain the sheltered waters of Blea Tarn nestle among the folds of the fells. Continue by climbing next to the top of Standing Crag. This is achieved by veering up the path to the L of this formidable rocky outcrop, and then branching off to the R along the grassy path across a stile, followed by a short scramble up the pile of rocks that feature as the interesting summit of this crag WSW. There are more sightings to record on the way up and from the top, including part of Bassenthwaite Lake to the NNW and another view of Thirlmere, which reappears to your rear E. The summit ridges of Blencathra can also be made out to the NNE, and the top of Great Gable is visible for the first time on this route WSW.

Depart from the summit of Standing Crag to the S, following the continuation of the wire fence which is now on your L. A grassy path leads across peaty, exposed moorland, and this climbs steadily towards the summit of Ullscarf in long, gradual

sweeps. In gaining further height you are able to see Derwent Water on your R, in front of the more exposed Bassenthwaite Lake NNW. There are more boggy stretches to cross, and the iron-and-wire fence now becomes reinforced with newly positioned wooden posts before abruptly changing direction with a right-angled turn and continuing northwards. Cross this obstacle here by means of the stile. After this resume your prevailing SW direction of travel, along the continuing line of the rusty old fence-posts, which are now on your R. At a convenient spot along this part of the route descend a short distance to your R (NW) in order to obtain one of the most spectacular views to be seen in clear weather anywhere among the Lakeland Fells. This panorama of almost unbelievable grandeur contains, sweeping your line of vision from L to R, the following impressive mountain shapes:

SSW	Pike of Blisco and Crinkle Crags.
SW	Bow Fell and Esk Pike.
WSW	Great End and the Scafells.
W	Glaramara, Great Gable and Pillar.
WNW	High Crag, High Stile and Red Pike.
NW	Fleetwith Pike, Dale Head and Hindscarth.
	Crag Hill, Eel Crag and Sail.
NNW	Whiteside, Hopegill Head and Grisedale Pike.
	Skiddaw.
NNE	Blencathra.

Below this extensive vista of craggy peaks are the attractive valleys of Langstrath and Greenup WSW, and Borrowdale and Stonethwaite WNW, long slivers of green that snake into the surrounding greyish-purple mountains. Stretches of blue water complete the colour palette in the form of Dock Tarn NNW, and Derwent Water and Bassenthwaite Lake further away. Immediately before you, separating Langstrath from Greenup, is the massive bulk of Eagle Crag with its precipitous, foreboding, dark cliffs that fall almost vertically to the valley below. Return to your previous direction of travel along the ridge path southwards and shortly you will arrive at the summit cairn of Ullscarf. This

24:1 Harrop Tarn above Thirlmere.

mountain stands at 726 m (2,370 ft), and from the top the distant, faint outline of the Pennines can just be discerned on a clear day, far beyond Windermere to the SSE.

The way to Dead Pike   *Allow 2 hours*

Continue along the path leading down S from the summit of Ullscarf, again keeping close to the line of iron fence-posts that are now once more to your L. Soon the summit peaks of the Coniston Fells can be seen peeping up ahead on your R (SSW), as you head towards Greenup Edge. The path descends gradually over a springy sward, and fast progress can be made here, as first Windermere SSE and then Grasmere Lake SE, separated by Loughrigg Fell, come into view down to your L. Soon you will be able to make out the craggy shape of Helm Crag to your L (SE), and then after passing across an extensive wet strip among several small, photogenic, reeded tarns, make for a distinctive cairn positioned on an outcrop of rocks over to your L. This cairn is specifically marked on the 1:25000 map at MR 287109.

At the hause ahead you reach a stony path that crosses your approach at right angles, roughly from E to W, dividing at this crossways two marker cairns. Turn L at this junction and follow the path that descends SE to the lower col ahead, crossing the accompanying beck near a large rock slab on the way down. The path winds round the fellside beside cairns, where unfortunately it can be very boggy. Maintain a line of travel towards an obsolete iron gateway to your L (ENE). Your route continues NNE across Brownrigg Moss, and this is achieved by turning to your L, asccending gradually up the rounded grassy fells, once again alongside a line of rusty iron fence-posts.

At the sighting of a tarn over to your R, proceed along the faint path that traverses the higher ground round Brownrigg Moss, and then continue E making for a pronounced crag along the ridge ahead. Keep the line of the fence-posts within sight as the path of sorts descends marginally over boggy ground to reach another small tarn ahead NE. This is passed to your L, the path bending

round it veering E, and then back to NE after passing the tarn. The path climbs to a more acceptable ridge route, which is pleasantly grassed and comparatively well drained.

At the next division of the paths select the higher one to the R and more to the E. Greenburn Bottom now lies below you down on your R, flanked by Blakerigg Crag and the ridge of Helm Crag. Dead Pike, your next main objective, rises directly ahead, its summit pinpointed by a cairn ESE. When you reach the top, standing at an elevation of 553 m (1,811 ft), you again have outstanding views all round. The various highlights in these have already been positioned.

The way back to Steel End car-park
Allow 1 hour

Descend from the summit of Dead Pike along a grassy track that leads down NE beside yet another fence. Cross the fence at a stile when it veers to the R, and then continue down a narrow grassy path N towards Thirlmere. You are now descending Steel Fell, and as this slope is exceptionally steep and the grass on it quite slippery, go down in a series of zigzags of your own choosing. Further down, strike a diagonal towards a wooden gate in a wall on your R, and pass through this opening.

Continue down the faint grassy path to your R, heading for the lower corner of the conifer wood below. Descend to the stony track at the bottom of the slope and turn L along this through a wooden gate, now heading N. The path drops down to a wider track. Turn R here and continue through an iron gate following the public bridleway. Proceed through West Head Farm to the minor road round the W side of Thirlmere. Turn L and Steel End car-park is a short distance further on.

Alternative routes

ESCAPES

Once the heights of Standing Crag and Ullscarf have been attained, this is not a convenient route for cutting short. If necessary, the final ridge section to Dead Pike can be avoided by walking down the valley alongside Wyth Burn, and there are two ways of doing this. The first is direct from the hause at MR 286106, from here dropping first ENE and then NE following the course of the beck down into the valley. A path down is indicated on the map, but it is virtually non-existent until much lower ground is reached, and before this you have to cross rough terrain and extensive boggy areas with running surface water. The second way of getting down into the valley is to continue further along the main route, but before you go round Brownrigg Moss, at some convenient elevation, strike off across the fellside to your L. From here head NNE, picking your way carefully through the many watercourses to reach the path on the opposite hillside, which then descends down alongside Wyth Burn.

EXTENSIONS

For a lower-level-category walk, the prescribed main route will be long and strenuous enough to satisfy most demands. Strong walkers who want more are recommended to continue across Brownrigg Moss and then take the ridge path E turning SE, and to proceed along this rocky spur over Gibson Knott to Helm Crag. From here they can drop down by Bracken Hause, cross Green Burn, and then climb up the ridge path of Steel Fell over the crags of Cotra Breast, heading NW, to rejoin the main route at the summit of Dead Pike.

Another possibility is, before scaling Standing Crag, continue NW, following the path down to the secluded waters of Blea Tarn. This is a delightful spot to visit both for refreshment and to enjoy the solitude of the enclosing, remote mountain scenery. From here continue NW following the course of Bleatarn Gill to the very different environment of Watendlath Tarn. This is a popular attraction and you will almost certainly have to share this spot with anglers, other walkers who have reached it from the easier routes out of Borrowdale, and tourists. When you have had your fill retrace your steps via Blea Tarn, and from there to the sanctuary of the high fells by climbing Standing Crag. Should walking back over some of the same ground not appeal to you, there is an entirely different route back from Watendlath Tarn. This return is achieved by using the footpath to the E, over High Tove, to reach Thirlmere. From there walk S along the W shore of the reservoir back to the car-park at Steel End.

FAIRFIELD HORSESHOE
High Level Route 25

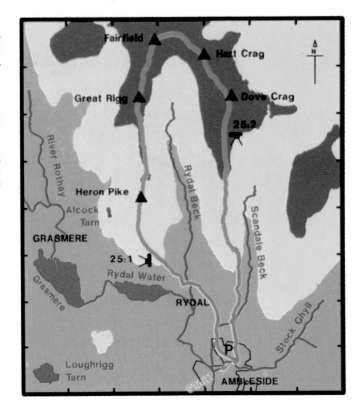

SOUTH-NORTH (Km)

WEST-EAST (Km)

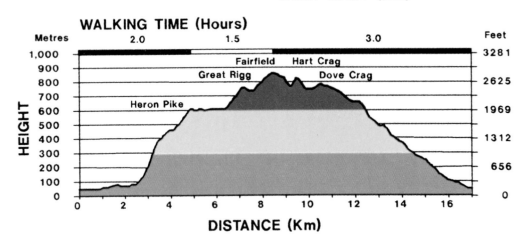

WALKING TIME (Hours)

HEIGHT

DISTANCE (Km)

STATISTICS

START and FINISH		
- Ambleside Main Car Park - OLM 7 / MR 376047		

WALKING DISTANCE	Km	Miles
- Excluding Height	16.9	10.5
- Including Height	17.1	10.6

TOTAL WALKING TIME : 6.5 Hours

TOTAL HEIGHT GAINED		
- 940 Metres 3084 Feet		

PRINCIPAL HEIGHTS	Metres	Feet
- Great Rigg	766	2513
- Fairfield	873	2863
- Hart Crag	822	2698
- Dove Crag	792	2603

OTHER FEATURES OF INTEREST
- Good views Rydal, Grasmere and Helvellyn Group; rocky east butresses of Fairfield Group.

14

THE CENTRAL FELLS

Part 7

Route 25 · Fairfield Horseshoe

Allow 6½ hours

STARTING LOCATION
Ambleside – Rydal Road car-park.
OLM 7/MR 376047.
Large-premium long-stay car-park.
CMS bus routes 505/506, 516, 518 and 555.

OVERVIEW/INTEREST
A splendid, classical ridge walk.
One pleasurable long up and down.
A few intervening peaks thrown in.
Good views over Rydal Water and Grasmere.
Craggy fells and rock-faces to (E) of Fairfield.
Route not too daunting.

FOOTPATHS
Impressively good until descent from Dove Crag.
Then extensive wet and boggy areas.
Virtually no erosion of any consequence.
Paths easy to follow.

The way to Heron Pike   *Allow 2 hours*

Turn L along the main A591 road away from the town. Continue along the main road and just beyond the de-restricted 30 mph road sign pass through the impressive black wrought-iron gates on your R. The way is reassuringly signed 'Public Footpath to Rydal Hall'. A broad, immaculate pathway winds through attractive parkland to reach Rydal Hall. In this mature setting there are fine specimen trees, mainly oak, but also including some superb examples of sycamore, larch, ash and beech, and further on a copse of tightly planted Scots pines and the occasional cypress and chestnut. Along here, the summits of the high-level Central Fells of Crinkle Crags, Bow Fell and the Langdale Pikes can be seen peeping through a gap in the screening trees over on your L to the W. Also the westerly peaks of the Fairfield Horseshoe appear ahead on the L (N). At Rydal Hall veer slightly uphill to your R obeying the footpath signs, walking NW, and ignoring the sharply inclined path off to your R. Walk between the outbuildings, and follow the main path round to the L. Avoid another path off uphill on your R and cross Rydal Beck.

At the end of the unmetalled lane turn R along the metalled road that leads uphill past Rydal Mount, William Wordsworth's home from 1813 to 1850, and then further up the fell to open country. Proceed through an opening in a stone wall. The lofty fell to your L (NW) is Nab Scar, up which you will shortly be climbing. Take the path diagonally ahead to your L signed 'Public Footpath', which leads uphill beyond a k-gate. The fells of High and Low Pikes appear to your R in the NNE, and these mark your return route down. The well-constructed stony path zigzags up the fellside at a steep angle, and after avoiding a path off through the profuse bracken on your L under an ash tree, and then proceeding further uphill, your way levels off temporarily as the path reaches a l-stile.

The clear, rocky path continues to climb up the steep fellside in a series of traverses and zigzags, and extra height is gained fairly quickly on this demanding section of the route. Higher up a succession of new sightings come into view including, in their order of appearance, Loughrigg Fell ssw, Wansfell Pike se, Windermere sse, Rydal Water and Grasmere Lake against a magnificent backcloth of high mountain fells, and Red Screes ene. Among the higher fells to the w the following peaks can be identified – the Coniston Fells sw, Pike of Blisco wsw, Crinkle Crags w and Bow Fell and the Langdale Pikes wnw. Also a more revealing view of the Fairfield Horseshoe opens up to your r (n) with Hart Crag dominating your return route. Next Sergeant Man appears, identified as a small cone above the surrounding landmass to the l in the wnw, as your path winds between hillocks n.

The route then climbs moderately to the summit of Heron Pike along a stretch where there is evidence of a limestone band of rock among the surface stones. The Pike standing at 612 m (2,003 ft) is a small rocky knoll uplifted slightly from the surrounding rounded, grassy slopes. Revealed for the first time from here are the steep, eroded e slopes of Erne Crag beyond Blind Cove to the ne, and the flatness, when viewed from this approach, of Fairfield ahead to the n with the rounded dome of Great Rigg leading up to it in the middle distance. Further to the l, on the far horizon, are the massive shapes of the southern peaks in the Helvellyn group, including Dollywaggon Pike, Nethermost Pike and Helvellyn.

The rocky spurs descending on your l are those of Stone Arthur, with Great Tongue behind to the nw, while more is revealed of the great wide U-shaped valley to your r, down which tiny Rydal Beck flows e. Finally, the additional revelations include an attractive panoramic view down on your l to the w of part of Grasmere village with the Heron Pike Ridge and the Easedale valleys stretching away from it westwards.

The way to Fairfield   *Allow 1½ hours*

A wide gravel and stone path descends from Heron Pike and then rises again along the broad, grass-covered ridge leading up to Great Rigg to the n. The way next leads to a serrated-edge outcrop of rocks with a cairn positioned on top, situated above Erne Crag.

Following minor undulations the route climbs relentlessly to the crest of Great Rigg to the n. The summit cairn of Greatrigg Man is reached at a height of 766 m (2,513 ft).Most of the extensive views to be seen from this peak are already positioned. In addition to your rear, Alcock Tarn, a narrow stretch of trapped water situated on a ledge below Heron Pike, may be observed in the ssw. The larger and lower situated profile of Elter Water lies beyond. To the n a more complete exposure of the Helvellyn group is obtained, with Grisedale Tarn just appearing down below. The e to w side elevation of Striding Edge, the famous knife-edged arête leading to the top of Helvellyn, comes into view, with the pointed summit of Catstye Cam just peeping out behind it.

Walk up the wide eroded path that drops down a modest intervening depression before rising up the ultimate sedate slopes to the vast, flat summit area of Fairfield. On your final approach the initial landmarks are a shelter and a large cairn, which you pass between to reach the highest point. Continue n and soon you will spot another shelter on your r, constructed in the form of a cross. Here you must be particularly careful of the dangerous sheer edge on your r, composed of crumbling, shattered rock.

Fairfield has a height of 873 m (2,863 ft) and to observe all the extensive and revealing views to be seen from its rounded summit you will need to spend time wandering round the top edge, descending slightly from time to time to gain access to the most revealing vantage points at this, the highest point of your walk. Varied panoramas can be seen from these viewing positions:

FROM THE (N) CAIRN
This marks the start of the path leading down over Cofa Pike, then along Deepdale Hause up to St Sunday Crag, following which, the long spur descends ne into Patterdale.

To the nw the great rocky slopes of Tarn Crag and Falcon Crag loom up from the deep recesses below and to the e of Dollywaggon Pike.

FROM THE WESTERLY EDGE

There are fine views from here over the nearer bulk of Seat Sandal towards the Central Massif of the Lakeland Fells far away in the w.

FROM THE CROSS SHELTER

An absorbing view is obtained from near here down into the U-shaped valley of remote Deepdale, with its extensive drumlins left by former glaciers.

Flanking the R (s) side of this impressive valley are a series of magnificent crags, their steep, eroded and irregular slopes plummeting down into the deep voids below. The continuous profile of these crags is broken by sharp arêtes formed by lingering corrie glaciers and ice action. Subsequent further erosion has produced the extensive scree slopes that are a feature of this spectacular mountain scenery.

Further away to the SE the distinctive profile of the ridge containing the peaks of Froswick, Ill Bell and Yoke stands out against the skyline, with Red Screes to their R.

The way back to Ambleside   *Allow 3 hours*

Retread your way back between the first shelter and cairn that you passed earlier, and within 200 paces of these features veer to your L along the cairned path leading down the wide band to the E. More views of the crags, screes, rock buttresses and ridges down the edge of your L now come into focus. In favourable weather conditions keep to the L flank of the band in order to peer over the impressive edge from time to time to extend your views. Hart Crag, your next main objective, rises ahead on your R (SE) beyond the hause immediately below. During this next descent there is a superb view on your L down into the dark combe

25:1 The snow covered Central Fells observed from the slopes of Heron Pike.

and near vertical rock wall of the NE face of Hart Crag. From these spectacular heights the more uniform band of rock, Hartsop above How, descends in a graceful curve to the NE into the wide U-shaped valley above Patterdale.

From the hause traverse to your R up the slope leading SE to the top of Hart Crag. The main path swings to the L of the summit and then starts to drop to the E along the Hartsop above How Ridge. Avoid descending, by veering to the R (SSE) along a path that is indistinct at first, but which soon asserts itself as it winds through the rocks up to the summit of Hart Crag along a cairned route. This peak rises to a height of 822 m (2,698 ft).

Continue your descent along the cairned path to the SSE. The E buttresses of the ridge are still craggy with their slopes dropping steeply to the valley below. The path descends through a tangle of rocks to another col before climbing the less severe slope over grass and more scattered rocks to reach the top of Dove Crag at 792 m (2,603 ft). A wall commences on your R from this fell and serves as a faithful guiding line for much of the remainder of your descent. From the summit cairn to your L there are pleasant views down over the High Hartsop Dodd Ridge to the E, with the fells of High Street providing a backdrop.

Continuing down the ridge to the S beside the dilapidated stone wall you will soon reach the first of numerous peaty, boggy patches. Further on, the remaining descent along the ridge down over High Pike and Low Pike is revealed. Eventually the path becomes better drained as it cuts across rocky outcrops and along inclined bedding planes. The way descends along an obvious route to a venerable l-stile over a stone wall. When you reach Low Pike you have the choice of taking the main path that bends round below the summit to the L or selecting the higher route over the top and re-joining the main path further on.

The ridge now descends less steeply among more rounded and lower grassy fells, and then the path ahead branches out in at least three directions. The recommended way here is the path that bends furthest to the L (ENE), and which descends closest to an attractive bluff of rock on your L, on which heather and other plants flourish. The way bends back to the R once this feature is passed and the stones give way to grass as further height is surrendered. The route is soon upgraded to a cart-track and several gaps, without gates, provide convenient access through drystone walls, as the rough fells give way to more lush pastures. The track finally bends down to Low Sweden Bridge over Scandale Beck. You then pass through Nook End Farm and walk along Nook Lane down into Ambleside. At the end of the lane turn R into the road down from Kirkstone Pass, which almost immediately finishes at the main road just below. The car-park is located across a footbridge over Stock Ghyll on your R.

Alternative routes

ESCAPES

From several places along the outwards ridge there are possibilities for shortening the route by descending to the SW back towards Grasmere. The preferred two lines of descent are either from Heron Pike via Alcock Tarn, or from Fairfield down either side of Tongue Gill. From the E of Grasmere there are paths above Rydal Water that will lead you to Rydal Hall, where part of the outwards route can be used to return to Ambleside.

EXTENSIONS

The Horseshoe, as the name suggests, is a complete route in itself and opportunities for extending the walk, without significant descents, followed by long additional climbs up again to the high ground, are limited. There are, however, several ways in which further modest exploration of the terrain adjacent to the ridges may be undertaken. Suggestions are to visit Alcock Tarn on the way up, and here it is possible to pioneer a route to and from Heron Pike across the open fellside; and from the summit of Fairfield to visit Cofa Pike, although here it will be prudent to use the same path both down and up.

25:2 A freezing descent southward from Dove Crag.

WANSFELL PIKE and TROUTBECK

Lower Level Route 26

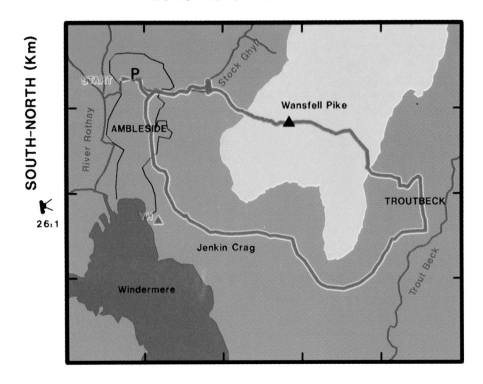

SOUTH-NORTH (Km)

P
START
26.1
River Rothay
AMBLESIDE
Stock Ghyll
Wansfell Pike
TROUTBECK
YH
Jenkin Crag
Trout Beck
Windermere

WEST-EAST (Km)

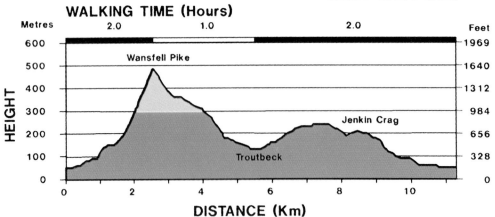

WALKING TIME (Hours)

Metres	2.0	1.0	2.0	Feet
600				1969
500	Wansfell Pike			1640
400				1312
300				984
200		Jenkin Crag		656
100		Troutbeck		328
0				0

HEIGHT

0   2   4   6   8   10

DISTANCE (Km)

STATISTICS

START and FINISH
- Ambleside Main Car Park - OLM 7 / MR 376047

WALKING DISTANCE	Km	Miles
- Excluding Height	11.3	7.0
- Including Height	11.4	7.1

TOTAL WALKING TIME : 5.0 Hours

TOTAL HEIGHT GAINED
- 560 Metres   1837 Feet

PRINCIPAL HEIGHTS	Metres	Feet
- Wansfell Pike	484	1581

OTHER FEATURES OF INTEREST
- Magnificent views of Ambleside and down Windermere; attractive village of   Troutbeck.

Route 26 · Wansfell Pike and Troutbeck

Allow 5 hours

STARTING LOCATION

Ambleside – Rydal Road car-park.

OLM 7/MR 376047.

Large-premium long-stay car-park.

CMS bus routes 505/506, 516, 518 and 555.

OVERVIEW/INTEREST

Immensely enjoyable short walk.

A steep climb to begin with.

Visit to Stockghyll Force.

Delightful church at Troutbeck.

Excellent views down over Windermere.

A walk for the entire family.

FOOTPATHS

Paths are very good.

No serious wet spots or erosion.

The way to Wansfell Pike   *Allow 2 hours*

Turn R from the car-park towards the centre of the village, passing the National Trust house bridging Stock Ghyll. Turn L immediately before the Market Hall and then L again along the road signed 'The Waterfalls' and then 'Stockghyll Wansfell Pike'. Continue uphill along the lane where soon Stock Ghyll comes within hearing distance, and then into sight on your L. This is followed by the first glimpse of Wansfell Pike to the SE, peeping up above the nearer screening trees. A little further on take the wide path off on your L, passing through a black iron gateway. The well-established, enclosed path then follows the course of the beck. At the division of the ways select the lower, L-hand path, go down the steps and cross the stream by the wooden footbridge.

Turn R and climb up the wooden steps, keeping to the main path and ignoring side turnings to both L and R. There are several revealing viewing positions for seeing the best of the cascades of Stockghyll Force, on the way up, from the top and as you descend. Continue up the L slope of the beck,

and at the top of the waterfalls where the path levels off re-cross the stream by another wooden footbridge. Descend down the opposite bank and turn down the L-hand path, which leads to an imposing black iron turnstile to exit from the enclosed area of the waterfalls.

Turn L at the place signed 'Public Footpath Kirkstone 3½'. This lane leads moderately uphill over a cattle-grid and then into the Grove Farm Private Road. Within 200 paces use the stile up on your R. A reassuring sign has been placed here that reads 'Footpath to Troutbeck via Wansfell'. The path up the grassy fell beyond is quite clear and Wansfell Pike can be seen on the horizon to your R (SE).

The path leads to a stile over a stone wall, but before you cross it pause and look back to observe the impressive view to your rear. Down below, the town of Ambleside is laid out, with the wide valley leading from it NW to Grasmere and beyond. Further R, and more to the E, the folds of the great mountain ridges constituting the Fairfield Horseshoe are revealed. Over the stile and across the walled lane, the path continues to rise ahead, first as a wide, grassy way and then increasingly over more rugged terrain as it winds through rocky outcrops up a demanding steep slope.

The views to your rear become more and more impressive as you gain additional height. The steeper top slopes are cairned, but the way up is so clear that here they are hardly necessary. Just below the summit the land flattens off momentarily and there is a large marker cairn on the L. The path now turns sharply to the L and climbs steeply in short zigzags up the last section to the summit. The top of Wansfell Pike consists of a series of interesting rock formations standing at a height of 484 m (1,581 ft), and the views from its commanding summit positions include:

S to SW   The lower fells of the Lake District plummeting southwards to embrace the placid waters of Windermere.

149

W	Great Langdale Valley snaking westwards into the heart of the high Central Fells, including Pike of Blisco, Crinkle Crags, Bow Fell and the Langdale Pikes.
NW	Part of the great geological fault line that contains Rydal Water, Grasmere, and much further to the N, Thirlmere.
N	The Fairfield Horseshoe and the rift leading up to the Kirkstone Pass, along which snakes a narrow road.
N to E	The High Street Fells and the many folds of the Easterly Fells.
SE	Your continuing route across the wide moorland down to Troutbeck.

The way to Troutbeck   *Allow 1 hour*

Descend to the SE following the direction 'Public Footpath to Troutbeck via Nanny Lane Follow Cairns'. After dropping quite steeply from the summit peak the terrain levels off to a more gradual rate of descent as the land rolls down in the form of open moorland. Looking back, Wansfell Pike does not appear nearly so impressive from this angle and elevation.

Pass through a narrow iron gateway breaching a stone wall as the path swings to the E across more placid terrain. A second wall is reached that demands either another tight squeeze or a climb over stepping-stones to cross. Turn R down the walled Nanny Lane on the far side and descend to the SE into Troutbeck.

A narrow road is reached by the side of Lanefoot Farm. Turn L here and proceed to the main cluster of buildings ahead, where you will find the Mortal Man Hotel situated down on your R. There is an amusing inn sign here with the following wording.

> *Oh mortal man that lives by bread*
> *What is it that makes they nose so red?*
> *Thou silly fool that lookst so pale*
> *Tis drinking Sally Birkett's ale!*

This seems the perfect place and note on which to end this section of the walk!

The way back to Ambleside   *Allow 2 hours*

Continue down the lane to your R and take the next lane off, also to your R just before Yew Tree Cottage is reached. This second lane bends behind the hotel on the far side of a small culvert. Cross another lane at right angles and continue along a cart-track. Your direction is now S, between a wall and a hedge. At the division ahead take the R fork, passing through a wooden gate to the R of a rusty iron one. The grassy track leads downhill to a copse ahead. Here pass through two gates, at which point a stream may be observed below to your R. At the next stile your continuation route is to the R uphill, but before you do this you may like to turn in the opposite direction and visit the well-cared-for church. This is Jesus Church, Troutbeck, and dates from 1736. Inside, the church is beautifully simple with attractive stained-glass windows.

Return to the point where you departed from the main route, cross the stream and at the branch of the paths go through the gate directly ahead, where your way is indicated by a blue arrow sign. Your path goes uphill, developing into a lane, before it connects with the road at High Fold Farm House. Turn L down this. Just past Troutbeck Post Office and General Stores proceed up the lane on your R signed 'Bridleway to Ambleside'. This is Robin Lane and at least two dwellings advise you this is the case. The lane swings round on a controlled sweep to the R as the rise becomes imperceptible. Continue along the bridleway, where soon you will pass a marker stone worded 'Ambleside via Jenkins Crag Skelghyll'. A little further on, branch L along a path signed as before but with a different spelling of 'Skellgill'. Pass through the gate and down the pleasant pathway through high pasture land.

Your path descends to a metalled farm road, at which you turn to the R and cross a stream. Proceed up the hill oppposite. Pass through the farmyard near the top of the brow and take the track off to the R just beyond the farmhouse. Keep to this main path, ignoring a side track uphill on your R. The way penetrates a wooded area and soon you will come to Jenkins Crag, a National Trust pro-

15
THE EASTERLY FELLS
Part 1

Route 27 · High Street and Red Screes

Allow 8 hours

STARTING LOCATION

Car-park at Hartsop village.

OLM 5/MR 410131.

Holds 25 to 30 cars.

CMS bus route 108.

OVERVIEW/INTEREST

An exciting and challenging route.

Plenty of ups and downs.

Close-up scenery is rugged and remote.

Magnificent distant views.

Some splendid ridge walking.

Moderate scrambling on Red Screes.

Save this walk for a fine day!

FOOTPATHS

Footpaths good with one notorious exception.

Badly eroded slope down from Thornthwaite Crag.

Red Screes provides interesting ascent up gullies.

Terrain along most of route is well drained.

The way to High Street   *Allow 3 hours*

Leave the car-park by the k-gate, and fork L along the way signed 'Public Bridleway Hayeswater'. Initially keep to the surfaced track, ignoring a grassy way down to the R. Soon on the skyline ahead, the slopes of The Knott appear to the ESE. Panning round to your R from here is the ridge of Grey Crag SE, then the remote intervening valley of Pasture Bottom, and finally the band of Hartsop Dodd to the S. A short distance further on, look around for a far-ranging view to your rear of the mountains to the W of Hartsop village. On the near horizon is the long, snaking Hartsop above How Ridge and beyond this craggy band lie higher fells, including the Fairfield Horseshoe and the Helvellyn group. The whole area is already remote and rugged with few trees to be seen.

After a gate, take the broad gravel path to the E, which crosses Hayeswater Gill. The path then climbs up the opposite fellside, skirting private land ahead by turning sharp L. From here a good route winds upwards through several gates. When you have gained more height, turn around again for a clearer view of the massive Fairfield and Helvellyn groupings to the W, and now the attractive tarn of Brothers Water can be observed below.

Further on, just before you lose the view round a bend to your R, take a final look to your rear where, in clear weather, you can identify the distinctive, rounded cone of Catstye Cam to the WNW, and the arêtes of Swirral Edge and Striding Edge leading the eyes along their narrow crests to the massive summit of Helvellyn.

Facing front again, the broad ridge leading from The Knott to High Street comes into view to the SE. Your path continues to climb to the SE to reach the tranquil, well-hidden tarn of Hayeswater. This lies in a glaciated basin and has been dammed at its NW tip in order to raise the level of this catchment of drinking water.

Follow the path round to your L, and having crossed the exit stream of Hayeswater Gill pass through a gap in the stone wall to continue up the steep path that rises to the ridge leading to The Knott. The way here is initially to the NE, but then it veers progressively to the ESE. There are several alternative routes up the steep fellside now, the longest but most comfortable gradient is along a series of traverses to your R, and this is the recommended way. When you reach the ridge, the going becomes easier for a time as you veer R along it, and then your path intersects with a better established route up from Angle Tarn. In the far distance, to the NW beyond Place Fell, lies the high mountain complex of Skiddaw and Blencathra.

The main path leads round and below The Knott; therefore to reach its summit turn to your R (SSE) up the fellside just beyond a dilapidated stone wall. Follow the line of this wall up the grassy fell along the indistinct footpath. You will soon gain the summit, on which there is a large, pyramid-shaped cairn marking the flattish, grassy and somewhat disappointing top. Your compensation is the superb 360° vista from a height of 739 m (2,423 ft). These views, starting from the N, include:

N   Martindale and Boredale, with the long, pointed ridges of Rest Dodd and the Nab, and Beda Fell interspersing the lower land.

E   The shattered rock formations of the steep, eroded slopes of Rampsgill Head and Kidsty Pike.

S   The wide, awesome expanse of the High Street Ridge leading to Mardale Ill Bell, Froswick and Thornthwaite Crag, the pronounced beacon of which can be seen from here on a clear day.

SW   Stony Cove Pike and further behind to the R the summit of Red Screes.

W   The Fairfield and Helvellyn groupings, and beyond these the higher peaks of the Central Fells.

NW   The faint outline of Skiddaw and Blencathra.

Descend to the ESE along the line of the fallen wall to regain the main path below, along which you turn R to the S towards High Street. Soon to your L the long, craggy ridge of Riggindale Crag comes into prominent view to the SSE, and beyond

it the massive outline of Harter Fell is also visible. Part of Haweswater reservoir can also be seen down below, nestling at the foot of these in a most irregular shape. Continue along the ridge S and when the paths divide keep to the L-hand one nearest to the E edge of the high ground, as this affords the better continuing views.

Next locate the cairn marking the top of Riggindale Crag. In clear weather, descend along the ridge for a few paces to witness the quite spectacular view down to your R over Blea Water towards Mardale Ill Bell, and in the far distance Harter Fell. The direction of these is from SE to SSE. Blea Water is a perfect example of a large gouged-out, glaciated combe with moraine deposits sealing off the exit stream to trap part of the catchment waters flowing down into it from the high rock-faces above. From your position it is possible to see the coastline to the S on particularly clear days beyond the much nearer outline of Ill Bell and Yoke.

Return uphill and traverse to your L round the wide grassy slope to reach the path again, and follow this S alongside the stone wall to the summit of High Street. The final approach slope is named Race-course Hill, and it is a paradox that sometimes you will see shaggy, ungainly wild ponies contentedly grazing up here. These animals are probably quite incapable of any sustained gallop! The summit stands at a height of 828 m (2,718 ft) and it is the highest point of the entire route. The top of High Street is as flat as a pancake, and its wide, rounded shoulders block most long-distance views, making the trig. point one of its most interesting features!

However, if you descend just a small distance down the grassy slope to the W, your persistence will be well rewarded with more fine views. In the near distance are the two grassy, rounded ridges descending to the N from Thornthwaite Crag and dramatically ending in the steep fells of Gray Crag and Hartsop Dodd. Beyond these are the now-familiar shapes of Fairfield and Helvellyn, while further W among the numerous peaks of the Central and Coniston Fells the shapes of Bow Fell, the Scafells, Pillar and the Gables may be identified. By contrast, part of Windermere comes into view down below to the SSW.

The way to Red Screes

Allow 3 hours

Leave High Street to the SSW alongside a dilapidated stone wall to your R. Follow this direction down to the shallow hause ahead and here avoid all forks leading off to the L, but instead work your way round to the R, veering SW to rejoin the main, badly eroded, wide path connecting High Street with Thornthwaite Crag. Turn L down this and follow its graceful curve to the R up to the summit of the Crag. Thornthwaite Crag has a most unusual, very large beacon and from the flat rocks below this landmark, there is a panorama of breathtaking mountain scenery. This viewing platform is the second highest point attained on the route, standing at a height of 784 m (2,569 ft). In favourable weather, you can see:

NE	High Street.
E	Mardale Ill Bell.
ESE	Harter Fell and Nan Bield Pass.
SE	Kentmere Pike.
S	Froswick, Ill Bell and Yoke.
SSW	Windermere.
SW	Wansfell Pike, Coniston Fells and Red Screes.
W	Langdale Pikes, Crinkle Crags, Bow Fell and Scafells.
WNW	Stony Cove Pike and Fairfield group.
NW	Helvellyn.
NNW	Skiddaw and Blencathra.
N	Place Fell.

Depart from the Crag by the path to the NW, following the course of a crumbling stone wall to your R. Along here a view of the southern end of Ullswater appears ahead to the NNW. To start with, a good stony path leads L to reach the top of the steeper, badly eroded slope falling to the hause at Threshthwaite Mouth. The worst of this ground needs to be descended with extreme caution. Eventually the steep, difficult slope gives way to a firm rock band, which marks the line of separation of two long-spent glaciers, one moving N to Ullswater and the other S towards Windermere.

The following scramble up the rocky terrain of Threshthwaite Crag is demanding, but immensely enjoyable. The steep climb over rocks finally gives

27:1 Walkers on the higher slopes of Riggindale Crag overlooking Haweswater Reservoir.

way to a more agreeable slope, and you continue up this along a pleasant, peaty path. Keep to the R when the tracks divide ahead, then walking WNW. When flatter ground is reached take the next L fork in the path, and as your route veers away from the line of the wall SSW, make for the large cairn ahead, which marks the summit of Stony Cove Pike. All the views from here should be fixed in your mind by now. Leave the summit on the same compass bearing as your approach, SSW, and locate a further cairn positioned near to an inevitable wall, which you cross, thereby changing your direction to W.

Soon a small tarn is passed to your R, and further along your path veers to the L as the terrain begins

155

to sweep down to the sw. During this part of the descent, a magnificent view opens up of Windermere to the s and sw, your sighting of it from here split in two by the nearer summit of Wansfell Pike to the ssw. The bulk of Red Screes dominate the view to the w. Craggy outcrops together with one or two areas of boggy ground have to be crossed as the terrain becomes wilder, with the scraggy grassland now interspersed with knolls of exposed rock.

The path sweeps round to the R, and then back again L, as it mounts small rocky outcrops along St Raven's Edge, which overlooks the Kirkstone Pass down below to your R,. Along here the southern part of Ullswater can again be sighted to your rear, as too can Brothers Water, both lying to the N. Continue for a short distance s along the ridge path, and then descend down the steepish path that falls sharply to your R. Follow the rough way down through the stony gully, and then walk along the established path at the bottom, which leads across the sloping fellside to the Kirkstone Pass inn. This hostelry was built in 1496 and stands at 1,500 ft above sea level, and is claimed to be the highest Inn in Lakeland!

Cross the A592 road, and turn R through the large car-park. At the far end pass through a k-gate, and take the path to your L (wNw), which, after a short distance, zigzags steeply up the lower slopes of Red Screes. Large erratic boulders and smaller rock fragments are scattered all over the fellside here, and your path delicately threads a way through these. After swinging to the L the path establishes a line to the NW, by bending back R, and as you climb higher many familiar landmarks, including the beacon of Thornthwaite Crag, reappear to the NE. Nearing the final, extensive scree slopes below the summit edge you have a close-up view of the massive ice-shattered, concave combe to your L, with its eroded slopes intensifying in steepness as it climbs almost vertically to the long summit ridge above.

Then follows some excitement in scrambling up one of the steep scree gullies, which will bring you to the final easy slopes above leading to the summit cairn. Although there are plenty of loose stones and the slopes look terrifyingly steep, these

are not particularly difficult to scale. You emerge from the screes onto a grassy slope and paths from here lead to the summit cairn and trig. point a short distance further on. Red Screes is 776 m (2,541 ft) high, and on a clear day the commanding views from its summit are incredible. The fells to the E, several of which you have already walked over today, have already been positioned, and the following summary lists only the new mountain scenery to the w:

sw	Coniston Water, with the Coniston Fells behind on the skyline; Coniston Old Man and Wetherlam can clearly be identified.
wsw	Harter Fell in Eskdale; this is a pointed peak standing out separately from the other fells.
w	Pike of Blisco, Crinkle Crags, Bow Fell, Esk Pike, Langdale Pikes, Scafells and Great End.
wnw	The Gables. Pillar group and High Stile Ridge.
nnw	Fairfield Horseshoe, Helvellyn and Catstye Cam.

The way back to Hartsop   *Allow 2 hours*

Head off to the sw, and walk along the edge of the fell to a large cairn to your L. At this cairn turn through 90° R, and proceed NW over the brow of the fell to locate a good clear path descending beside a stone wall. Follow this down, without deviating, to the hause below at Scandale Pass. Turn R at the col and descend ENE along the narrow path that traverses the flank of the steep slope to the L of the emergent watercourse of Caiston Beck.

Following a long, gradual descent the white-painted Brothers Water Hotel comes into view across the intervening valley to the NNE with the tarn appearing to the L of this prominent building. A k-gate marks your return to more populated regions. You next enter an area of relatively fertile meadows as you pass through another k-gate, then between a gap in a stone wall with a barn beyond. Here you turn to the R, and then proceed through a further k-gate signed 'High Hartsop Dodd'. Next

27:2 Looking northward down across Hayeswater.

cross a field that contains some enormous, erratic boulders, then a stream and continue along a diaognal towards farm buildings, which you pass to your L. Locate a k-gate in the stone wall, turn R down the path beyond, and the veer L round Hartsop Hall.

More gates follow before you pass above Brothers Water, a lovely reeded tarn postioned in a quite delightful setting. Then another k-gate provides entry to parking facilities at Cow Bridge. Turn R and cross the attractive stone bridge, then turn R again along the A592 road, and at the telephone kiosk ahead branch off L down the lane back into the village of Hartsop.

Alternative routes

ESCAPES

At the hause of Threshthwaite Mouth the walk can be drastically curtailed by turning R and descending along Pasture Beck back to Hartsop.

A further opportunity for shortening the walk and avoiding the severe climb up Red Screes is at the Kirkstone Pass, by descending northwards along the road for just over 1 km (¼ mile) before taking the footpath off to the L signed 'Permitted Path', and following this down to link up with the main route descending along Caiston Glen.

EXTENSIONS

The described route is strenuous and in bad weather quite a challenge, with route-finding far from straightforward. In such conditions no extensions are recommended! In good weather, the very fittest walkers could consider extending the route at Scandale Pass by continuing to climb to the NW to scale first Dove Crag and then Hart Crag. From here there is a choice of return routes, either along the Harstop above How Spur, or down the exacting path between Dove and Hart Crags into Dovedale. You will need extended hours of daylight to accomplish this formidable mission!

BOREDALE and ULLSWATER
Lower Level Route 28

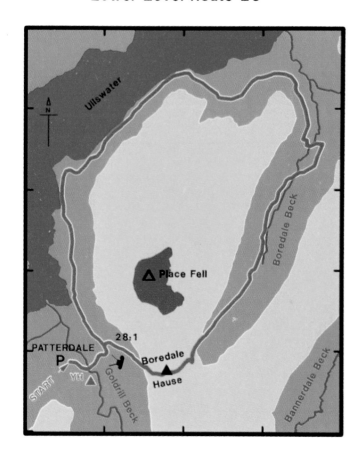

SOUTH-NORTH (Km)

Ullswater

△ Place Fell

28:1

PATTERDALE

P

START   YH △   Goldrill Beck

Boredale
Hause

Boredale Beck

Bannerdale Beck

WEST-EAST (Km)

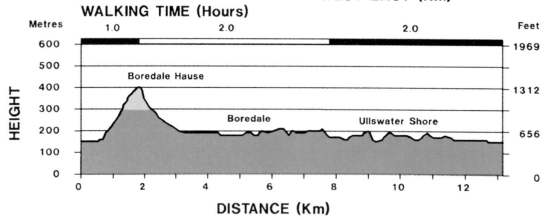

WALKING TIME (Hours)

| Metres | 1.0 | 2.0 | 2.0 | Feet |

Boredale Hause

Boredale   Ullswater Shore

HEIGHT

DISTANCE (Km)

STATISTICS

START and FINISH
- Patterdale - OLM 5 / MR 396158

WALKING DISTANCE	Km	Miles
- Excluding Height	13.2	8.2
- Including Height	13.3	8.2

TOTAL WALKING TIME : 5.0 Hours

TOTAL HEIGHT GAINED
- 460 Metres   1509 Feet

PRINCIPAL HEIGHTS	Metres	Feet
- Boredale Hause	400	1310

OTHER FEATURES OF INTEREST
- Remote Boredale; attractive SE shore-line of Ullswater.

Route 28 · Boredale and Ullswater

Allow 5 hours

STARTING LOCATION

Patterdale – car-park opposite the Patterdale Hotel.
OLM 5/MR 396158
Holds over 30 cars.
CMS bus route 108.

OVERVIEW/INTEREST

Delightful shorter walk eminently suitable for
children.
Serious climbing soon over.
Remoteness of inhospitable upper Boredale.
Tranquillity of Ullswater's (SE) shore-line.
Enjoyable route in all kinds of weather.
Good views.

FOOTPATHS

Clearly marked footpaths are always good and at
times superb.
No significant boggy areas.
One relatively rough section at the start of the
descent from Boredale Hause.

The way to Boredale Hause   *Allow 1 hour*

From the car-park turn L down the A592. Pass the
White Lion Hotel, and take the next turning on
your L, signed 'Boredale Hause Angle Tarn Side
Farm'. Cross Goldrill Beck by the stone bridge,
continuing down the lane to Side Farm. Veer L at
the end of this lane and then proceed through the
gate on your R, signed 'Angle Tarn Boredale
Hause'. Cross the small culvert, and turn uphill to
your R (ESE). After about 50 paces this path reaches
the main route traversing the fellside, which you
join by veering R. The path leads uphill SE. Extensive views now open up above the tree-line on your
R as you gain further height. These include Oxford
Crag, and looming up behind it the long ridge of
Birks and St Sunday Crag SW. To the L of these, the
spurs descending towards Brothers Water can be
observed in the shapes of Hartsop Dodd SSE,
Middle Dodd S and High Hartsop Dodd to the SSW.
Turning round more to the rear the fells leading up

to Helvellyn come into prominence, including
Birkhouse Moor WNW, to the R of Grisedale.

At the division of the paths, select the higher
one to your L, and repeat this manoeuvre again further up. Then Brothers Water appears to the S, with
Kirkstone Pass further away on the horizon. There
is also a more revealing exposure of Grisedale to
the W, and far away in this direction the distinctive
cone-shaped peak of Catstye Cam can be made out
at the E end of the Swirral Edge Ridge on Helvellyn.

After the second L fork, a grassy path twists up
the fellside towards a large cairn ahead to the E.
Near here another path comes in acutely from the
R; this is from Hartsop. The top of Boredale Hause
is soon reached and at 400 m (1,310 ft) this is the
highest point of your route. The hause is a major
junction, for apart from your path up from Patterdale, your descent into Boredale and the path
previously mentioned from Hartsop, there are also
paths leading up to Place Fell to the N, down into
Martindale to the NE and to Angle Tarn to the SSE.

The way to Ullswater   *Allow 2 hours*

Continue E through the hause as your way curves
to the L and becomes better defined. Then Boredale
comes into view, with the path along this secluded
and enclosed valley visible for much of its length.
The plug of high ground straddling its mouth is
Hallin Fell NE. Your path initially descends
through a steep, rocky gully where for a short distance the going is relatively rough. Before long a
gentle downhill gradient is reached and fast time
can be made along this section. The path descends
to a stone wall, and after passing through a
wooden gate, you continue NE along the wide
grassy way. Before you reach Boredale Head Farm
there is a narrow permissive path off to the L across
the fellside, which skirts above the farm, and
which you are requested to use when the farm yard
is filled with animals. The public right-of-way
nevertheless remains through the farm!

159

28:1 Autumn tints around Patterdale.

Beyond the farm a metalled lane is reached. Continue along this, crossing Boredale Beck about 1½ km (1 mile) further on. The lane then winds uphill to reach Garth Head Farm. Turn L immediately after you have passed the buildings on your L and walk downhill along the way signed 'Public Footpath'. After a stile the path leads to a quaint improvised stone bridge across the beck, and on the other side, where the ground can be somewhat wet, you have a choice of ways. You can continue to your L uphill along the permissive path to reach a stile in the far L corner of the field, after which you turn R along the established path that runs NNE by a stone wall. Alternatively you can join this path a little further on, by first veering to the R after crossing the beck and climbing to the R-hand corner of the field, above a barn, where access to the path running NNE is obtained at two recently positioned stiles.

Before long a section of Ullswater comes into view ahead. When the stone wall turns downhill, continue ahead along the path, which maintains a constant height, due N. Your way next enters an area of bracken as it descends slightly, before rising round the brow of the fellside to your L. For a time the path is less distinct, until a more estab-

and your path bear round to the L, a rocky promontory comes into view to your R, this is Silver Point and the small island just to the W of it is Norfolk Island. This area is well worth exploring for the views alone, but added attraction is Silver Bay, a visit to which should be to the liking of any children in your party. Beyond this feature as you continue along the shore-line, a really impressive view of the head of the lake is revealed, and the long ridge leading up to Fairfield in the form of St Sunday Crag can be observed across the water to the SW.

At a clump of trees your path veers to the L away from the lake and winds round the open fellside above a retaining wall on your R. The path then descends gradually to bring you down to Side Farm, an establishment that very enterprisingly caters for horse riders and provides refreshments. Turn R here along the path signed to Patterdale and Glenridding, and cross Goldrill Beck to reach the main A592 road. Turn L up the road to the car-park.

Alternative routes

ESCAPES

This is a relatively short and undemanding walk, and once you have descended into Borrowdale it is not possible to condense the route described. At the top of Borrowdale Hause you can walk down, using part of the path leading S towards Hartsop, and then back-track along the valley and return to Side Farm. From here it is only a short distance back to the car-park at Patterdale.

EXTENSIONS

The walk only takes a good morning or afternoon, and therefore it is feasible to walk round it in both directions in the same day! Probably a more attractive proposition for extending the route will be to explore Place Fell by climbing to the summit of this impressive large mountain area from the top of Boredale Hause. From the summit there are paths that lead you first N, and then NE to the end of Boredale near Beckside, where you may rejoin the main route to the SW round Ullswater.

lished path comes in from your R and down which you turn L. Locate a narrow path threading down towards the lake on your R, and take it to join the main gravel pathway that leads round the SE shore of Ullswater. Turn L along this wide path, now heading W.

The way back to Patterdale   *Allow 2 hours*

The path winds round the fellside above the lake, climbing up and down several rocky spurs that fall steeply into the deep waters below. Blue way-marker signs now indicate the way. When the lake

KENTMERE HORSESHOE
High Level Route 29

SOUTH-NORTH (Km)

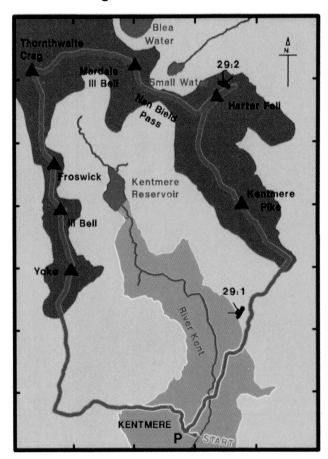

WEST-EAST (Km)

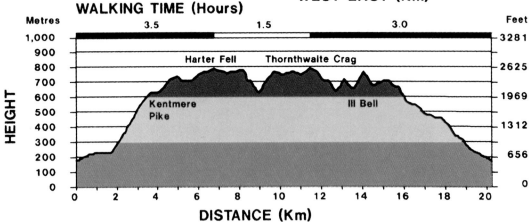

STATISTICS

START and FINISH			TOTAL HEIGHT GAINED		
- Kentmere (Nr Church) - OLM 7 / MR 456042			- 1080 Metres 3543 Feet		
WALKING DISTANCE	Km	Miles	PRINCIPAL HEIGHTS	Metres	Feet
- Excluding Height	20.2	12.6	- Kentmere Pike	730	2397
- Including Height	20.4	12.7	- Harter Fell	778	2539
			- Thornthwaite Crag	784	2569
TOTAL WALKING TIME : 8.0 Hours			- Ill Bell	757	2476

OTHER FEATURES OF INTEREST
- Upper Kentmere Valley and Reservoir, Haweswater and High Street (Roman Road).

16
THE EASTERLY FELLS
Part 2

HIGH-LEVEL ROUTE

Route 29 · Kentmere Horseshoe

Allow 8 hours

STARTING LOCATION
Car-park at Kentmere Church.
OLM 7/MR 456042.
Tiny car-parking facilities – holds up to 10 cars.
Some extended arrangements at 'The Nook' further on.
Not on a bus route!

OVERVIEW/INTEREST
Splendid ridge walk with open aspects.
Wild and remote area of high crags.
After initial climb not unduly strenuous.
Fine hause at Nan Bield Pass.
Extensive views down over Haweswater and Windermere.
Suitable for most grades of walkers including sturdy children.

FOOTPATHS
With few exceptions the paths are good, definite and pleasant to walk along.
Some wet, peaty ground to cross.
Part of descent route a little less obvious.
No real problems though.

The way to Harter Fell
Allow 3½ hours

Leave the car-parking facilities along the approach lane passing St Cuthbert's Church to your L. Take the first footpath on your L after the church, signed 'Public Footpath to Upper Kentmere Kentmere Reservoir'. To your rear there is a revealing view down the Kentmere Valley to the S, with the orderly landscape highlighted by Kentmore Tarn and several attractive wooded areas, providing a soothing setting in contrast to the more rugged ground visible ahead.

At the division in the path, fork R, and after this, your way leads through three gateways, during the course of which Rawe Cottage is passed to your R, before you reach an imposing farm building to your L. Large erratic boulders sited by retreating glaciers abound in this area. Beyond the buildings keep to the main path NNE, and at the top of the next incline the slopes of Kentmere Pike come prominently into view ahead.

Now locate an important gap in the stone wall on your R, positioned about 25 paces before the next gate. Pass through this, down to the River Kent, and cross the river, by a footbridge, which is due for replacement. Then proceed along the path leading off to the L over a hillock, to reach a wall, which you climb by a stone stile. Turn L up the lane, continuing to walk towards the head of the valley. There are now good views over the L-hand wall, where in clear weather, beyond Upper Kentmere, the peaks of Ill Bell, Froswick, Thornthwaite Crag and part of the High Street group are visible between NW and NNW.

After negotiating more gates, a tributary stream is crossed by a stone footbridge and the uphill path is signed 'Public Bridleway Mardale' as you continue NNE. Follow the pathway round to the R to reach the farm of Pout Howe, which you pass to your L. Your way is through the second gateway on the L, marked 'Bridleway' and then you swing immediately to your R up the grassy bank to con-

163

29:1 Upper Kentmere protected by Froswick, Ill Bell and Yoke.

nect with a metalled path, along which you turn R. Continue uphill through the gateway, and having passed between the first buildings situated here, turn sharp L uphill round a large boulder, which marks the end of a stone wall. Pass 'Style Howe' residence to your L and a short distance further on a gate provides access to the open fells.

Now work your way diagonally uphill to the NNW, following an intermittent grassy path across the broad, sloping fellside. The path becomes better established as a rocky route threads through the surrounding bracken. Near a prominent outcrop of rocks to your L, cairn markers appear to guide your way. Towards the top of the diagonal

section of the route turn around to see the snaking outline of part of Windermere below to the SW. The route leads NNE to an extensive stone wall and this is crossed by a stile. Continue up the fell on a similar diagonal, which now veers NNW, and soon the main ridge path is reached, the intersection of which is marked by a cairn.

The route is still NNW up a shallower gradient by the side of an iron fence. Attractive views now open up into Longsleddale through which the River Sprint flows in the ESE, and beyond, in clear weather, the lower foothills of the Pennines can be observed. The railings on your R give way to a stone wall as a guiding trig. point appears on the horizon. This marks the summit of Kentmere Pike. When you reach this point you will find it lies just to your R over the dividing stone wall. You are now standing at a height of 730 m (2,397 ft). Over on your L, between Ill Bell and Froswick, the massive outline of Red Screes comes into view to the WNW, with part of the magnificently shaped Fairfield Horseshoe also showing more to the R in the NW.

Walk NW, first downhill across the connecting hause, and then uphill once more, across the long, shallow final moorland slopes that lead to the summit area of Harter Fell. Some boggy peat hags will be encountered along here, but these can easily be avoided. Towards the top, the challenging outline of Nan Bield Pass comes into focus down to your L to the NW. In this direction, in favourable weather, Helvellyn can be picked out, with its satellite peak Catstye Cam also prominent. In such conditions the Central Fells of Lakeland are also visible from here, appearing between Ill Bell and Froswick. Down below, if you are prepared to make a slight diversion to your L, you will spot Kentmere reservoir, in wild inhospitable surroundings.

A large cairn with intermingled ironwork marks the summit of Harter Fell. This peak commands a height of 778 m (2,539 ft), and this is marginally below the highest point of the route at Thornthwaite Crag ahead. Walk just a little further NNE to obtain a stunning view down over Haweswater, with the tell-tale, unnatural-looking water-level band revealing it to be a huge reservoir. Of the fells not previously mentioned the Kidsty Pike Ridge and Riggindale Crag snaking down into Haweswater are most impressive from this viewpoint.

The way to Thornthwaite Crag   *Allow 1½ hours*

From the prominent summit cairn head off W and descend down the steep, narrow corridor of Nan Bield Pass to reach the rocky col at its base. During the twisting way down, impressive views appear to your R NNW of the tarns of Small Water and Blea Water, and the massive combes that house them. Climb out of the hause up the rocky path to the

WNW to regain most of the height just surrendered.

Then follow the cairned path to the NNW, to gain first the rocky summit of Mardale Ill Bell, and afterwards NW to reach the clearly defined routes coming down SSE from High Street. Allow your direction of travel to swing from NW to SW as you round the wide, now almost level slopes of the fell, to join the wide path from High Street leading to the distinctive beaconed summit of Thornthwaite Crag. When you reach this path, it is leading SW, but the final approach to the towering beacon ahead is to the E as your path swings upwards in a broad semi-circle. This distinctive landmark stands at 784 m (2,569 ft), and the impressive lakes and mountains visible from the vicinity of its peak include:

SSW	Windermere.
W	Red Screes.
NW	Helvellyn.
N	Hayeswater.
NNE	High Street.
ENE	Mardale Ill Bell.
ESE	Harter Fell.
SSE	Froswick and Ill Bell.
SW	Coniston Fells on distant horizon.

The way back to Kentmere   *Allow 3 hours*

The following, long undulating descent to the Garburn Pass is predominantly S over the intervening pointed peaks of Froswick and Ill Bell. Commence your descent initially SSE, keeping to the edge of the ridge to your L as you walk down to and across the expansive band linking Thornthwaite Crag to Froswick. At the intervening hause select the L-hand zigzag path that leads to the summit of Froswick. There is then a repeat up and down, this time to the summit of Ill Bell, which is a higher and more exacting peak to scale than Froswick. The path leads across a morass of tangled rocks to no less than three summit cairns! Along this section a pronounced lower-level peak rises from the surrounding landmass to the WSW, and this can be identified as Wansfell Pike, overlooking Ambleside. Descend along the now-familiar direc-

tion of travel s, and then veer sse away from the branch path to your R, which descends towards Windermere. Further down make for the rocky outcrop that is marked with a cairn and as the fall-line steepens cross a wall by a l-stile. From here the way continues to descend with the stone wall now a permanent guiding feature to your L.

Some wet areas are reached next and there are several alternative ways through this badly drained land, none of which are continuously well defined. However, keep walking to the s, and within sight of the reassuring stone wall on your L. Your path eventually veers away from the wall, but within a relatively short distance of this, it connects with the broad and well-defined Garburn Pass Bridleway. Turn L along this for the final moderate descent over rough stony ground back into Kentmere. This lies to the ese. Several gates are passed before the path leads into a surfaced lane, with Kentmere Hall visible to the s. Follow this lane down, passing Hartrigg Farm on your L, and 'The Nook' on your R, to arrive back at the church.

Alternative routes

ESCAPES

The route may be shortened and any further climbing avoided by turning s at the bottom of the Nan Bield Pass and returning to Kentmere via the lower level pathways that descend to the e of Kentmere reservoir.

EXTENSIONS

The obvious extension is to visit the summit of High Street and perhaps even continue further N to the top of either The Knott or even Kidsty Pike. The only snag is that much of your return walk to rejoin the main route southwards to Thornthwaite Crag will necessitate retracing your outward steps.

29:2 Haweswater Reservoir revealed from Harter Fell.

LOWER KENTMERE
Lower Level Route 30

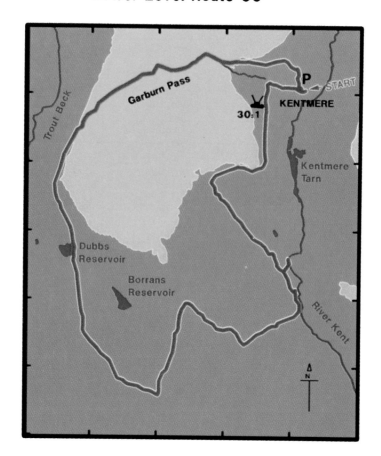

SOUTH-NORTH (Km)

WEST-EAST (Km)

WALKING TIME (Hours)

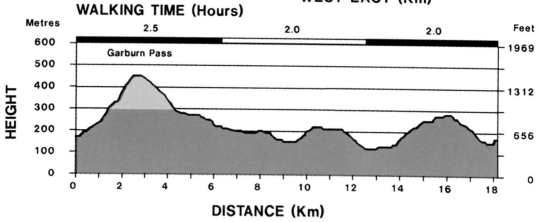

STATISTICS

START and FINISH
- Kentmere (Nr Church) - OLM 7 / MR 456042

WALKING DISTANCE	Km	Miles
- Excluding Height	18.0	11.2
- Including Height	18.1	11.2

TOTAL WALKING TIME : 6.5 Hours

TOTAL HEIGHT GAINED
- 540 Metres   1772 Feet

PRINCIPAL HEIGHTS	Metres	Feet
- Garburn Pass	440	1440

OTHER FEATURES OF INTEREST
- Lower Kentmere Valley and Tarn, rural scenery; views of Kentmere Horseshoe.

Route 30 · Lower Kentmere

Allow 6½ hours

The way to Dubbs Reservoir   *Allow 2½ hours*

Walk along the lane to the NW away from the church. This twists uphill past the entrance to Hartrigg Farm off to the R. Then the beautifully situated cottage named 'The Nook' is passed on your L, where you can simultaneously park and contribute a small donation to cancer research. A branch path leads off to Kentmere Hall, but instead you turn R, following the way signed 'Public Bridleway to Troutbeck via Garburn Pass'. A wide gravel path leads uphill, first NNW, and then veering W. On the L, as you gain height, there is a splendid view to the S down the lush, flat Kentmere Valley, and the long strip of water which is Kentmere Tarn can be spotted on the R-hand side of this lower land. In contrast, to your rear R the peak of Kentmere Pike rises on the far horizon to the ENE. Straddling these two contrasting landscapes, the gentle, green, grassy contours of Sallows appear to the L of a gate ahead.

After passing through the gate an ascent of some 2 km (1¼ miles) rises ahead to the top of the Garburn Pass. The way is clear, up the wide bridleway and the gradient varies from comfortable to moderate over rough stony ground. Then round a bend in the track the craggy dome of Castle Crag with its satellite outcrops comes prominently into view on your R to the NNW. Towards the top of the pass look around for a fine view back down onto Kentmere village with its attractively irregular setting of dwellings clustered round the focal point of the stark-looking church. These are to the ESE. Another gate is reached and at the top of the brow there is a path leading off up the fells to your R, which winds N to Yoke, Ill Bell and Froswick, in that order, along the Kentmere Horseshoe. However, your lower route is down to the L, still along the Garburn Pass Bridleway, which starts to descend in a wide sweep to your L (SW).

Over to your R, across the intervening valley, the peak of Wansfell Pike comes into view to the W, and the path leading down from its mantled summit into the attractive, elongated village of Troutbeck may be clearly observed. Further to the R the massive shape of Red Screes dominates the horizon to the NW. Soon, through a gap in the wall to your R, the green and pleasant flat valley of upper Troutbeck Park may be observed to the NNW with the Hall nestling unobtrusively among attractively wooded slopes. The long spur of rock splitting the lower ground into two here is aptly named The Tongue. Gates, big and small, are encountered next. Then, round a bend, the shimmering top end of Windermere is revealed way down to the SW, as much nearer, over the brow of the fell ahead, the orderly, white-painted buildings of Troutbeck peep out, tenaciously hugging the line of the road through the village.

Turn to your R now to observe the fine ascending

Overleaf

30:1 Approaching Kentmere Hall from the South.

169

ridge of Yoke, Ill Bell and Froswick leading up to Thornthwaite Crag NNE, and then let your eyes wander to the L to pick up, first the col of Threshthwaite Mouth, and then the outline of Stony Cove Pike to the N. Below these impressive features Hagg Gill leads the eyes down into the more restful setting of the flat valley of Troutbeck. In virtually the opposite direction, as you face front again, the distant outline of the Coniston Fells is seen rising to the WSW.

A small concentrated plantation of mixed conifers, mainly larch, pine and spruce are passed to your L, and along here side turnings to the L into disused quarries and R down into the valley should be ignored. You are confronted with more gates before a division of the ways is reached. Here take the higher route to your L along Dubbs Road. The path now leads gradually down through pleasant rolling pastures to Dubbs reservoir, which is positioned behind protective stone walling to the R of your path. The reservoir is owned by North West Water and fly-fishing is allowed on it.

The way to Browfoot *Allow 2 hours*

Continue S along the bridleway down to Moorhowe Road and turn L along this quiet back road. Continue SE along the road for about 1½ km (1 mile) until you reach a track off on your L through a gate signed 'HIgh House Farm'. Turn L here. Continue along the excellent path/driveway winding gently uphill through attractive rural scenery and agricultural land to High House Farm. Pass between the farm buildings to your R, and having turned L, continue uphill and proceed through the central one of three gates. At the top of the next rise the profiles of Kentmere Pike and Harter Fell become visible ahead to the NNE.

You next approach a gate barring your way. This has a helpful directional sign on it reading 'Footpath and Bridleway Turn R'. Do so, along a grassy raised terrace, at the end of which a further gate provides entrance to an enclosed walled track, which leads off to the SE. Continue along this track, and further on take the L-hand fork ESE. Your route now leads to a narrow, metalled lane, down which

you turn L. Walking down the road, extensive views open up ahead, in the far-off distance the splendour of the high craggy fells comprising the Kentmere Horseshoe are revealed in the NNE, while the nearer, wooded, more rounded and lower slopes of the Kentmere Valley complete a perfect composition. Pass a footpath leading off to the R, and just before the lane bends downhill sharp R, take the concessionary route off to your L signed 'Foot and Bridle Path Alternative Short Cut Avoiding Farmyard'.

The way is round Browfoot Farm, down to your R and the route is extremely well indicated by blue waymarker signs. In circling the farm, your path leads awkwardly through a k-gate, across a stream, turns to the R downhill beside a wire fence, before reaching a gate; then through another gate to the L, a further L turn through a gap in a stone wall, and a final descent to pass through a k-gate onto a tree-lined lane alongside the River Kent! Turn L up the lane that leads N by the side the river.

The way back to Kentmere *Allow 2 hours*

More gates follow, straddling a turning uphill to your L. Next the way passes between two very attractive dwellings. Your track continues to rise modestly to the NNW between enclosing stone walls. Now for a small diversion to visit the pottery showroom at Sawmill Cottage. Take the next turning to the R and follow the way through a gate signed 'Sawmill Cottage' and along a narrow path adjacent to the river on your R. Then cross a side stream to reach the superbly situated and tastefully developed buildings that comprise the establishment named Sawmill Cottage. The attraction is the studio and showroom, in which is displayed a collection of fine and exclusive ceramics shaped by Gordon Fox. The showroom has a colourful history, being previously a sawmill, the last commission of which was railway sleepers for the Kendal to Windermere Railway Line constructed in 1860.

After your visit to the showroom, retrace your steps back to the point where you departed from the through route, and turn R at the T-junction, resuming your previous direction of travel to the

NW. The way leads slightly uphill along a wide, grassy cart-track that leads through a gate. Continue to climb to the NW, passing an abandoned building on your L, and a watercourse immediately afterwards. Then through another gate you reach the wilder and more open fellside. The rounded fells rising ahead are Sour Howes NW and Sallows NNW. When you reach a boggy patch, continue uphill along the grassy path NNW walking through the bracken to a gap in the wall. Your path now narrows to that of a sheep track and drops to cross Park Beck near to a large larch tree. The path then veers to the R and it converges with the stream descending to your L. Follow this further uphill, pass through the gateway ahead, and continue to climb along the faint track beside a stone wall on your R.

The direction of the route now gradually changes as your path swings round and becomes better established in a new ENE direction. You are now passing through expansive, gently sloping, grassy fells and further gates are passed as the well-established track meanders gradually further uphill. Now select the wide grassy cart-track to your L, which leads more steeply up the fellside N towards a grouping of craggy bluffs on the near skyline above you. Make for the one to your R, which provides another excellent viewing point into the now familiar upper Kentmere reaches to the NE. Ewe Crags and Goat House Scar are the crags along the rocky ridge to the L. These fall steeply and dramatically towards Kentmere village below, and which they appear about to engulf at any moment!

Then descend to your R down the grassy slope to rejoin the path which you left a short distance further back. Turn L towards Kentmere village. A good wide track descends, alongside Hall Wood on your R, to Kentmere Hall. Before the trees block

your view there is a sighting of the narrow stretch of water of the irregularly shaped Kentmere Tarn down below to your R. More gates follow prior to crossing the small stream of Hall Gill by an arched concrete bridge. A gate gives entry to the surrounds of Kentmere Hall, which is now a farm. From here turn to the R down the gravel lane that leads E back to Kentmere Church.

Alternative routes

ESCAPES

Once you have climbed to the top of Garburn Pass all the hard work has been done, and having reached an effective 'Point of no return', possibilities for curtailing the prescribed route are limited, and more importantly, almost certainly not required. One option is when you reach Sawmill Cottage, instead of retracing your steps to regain the main route continue N down the valley to rejoin the main route at Kentmere Hall. You do, however, have to walk through the grounds of a chemicals factory and this alternative is less attractive than the higher way with its more open aspect.

EXTENSIONS

The most rewarding extension is from the top of Garburn Pass. Instead of descending down the continuation of the bridleway, make a detour up the narrow footpath that leads off to the L at Garburn Nook to explore the higher ground around Sour Howes. To regain the Dubbs/Garburn Road below to the W, in order to continue along the main route, you will need to descend carefully down the open fellside as distinct paths do not provide the necessary connection. Fortunately, however, there are access points to the walled lane by means of stiles. Then turn L down the lane to continue along the main route.

DOW CRAG, CONISTON OLD MAN and WETHERLAM
High Level Route 31

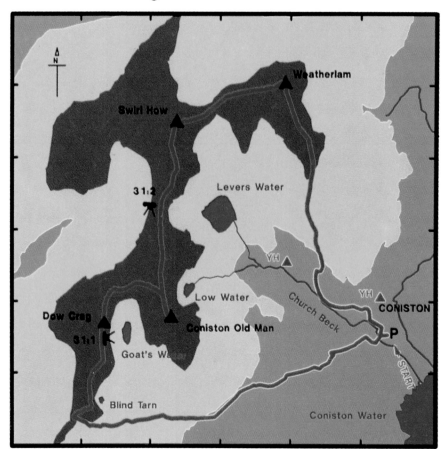

SOUTH-NORTH (Km)

WEST-EAST (Km)

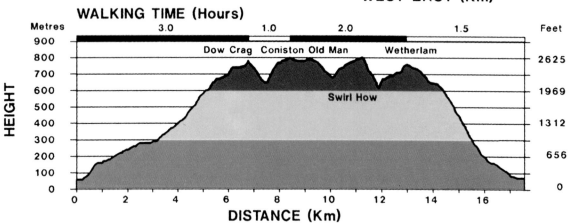

STATISTICS

START and FINISH
- Main Car Park, Coniston - OLM 6 / MR 304975

WALKING DISTANCE	Km	Miles
- Excluding Height	17.5	10.9
- Including Height	17.8	11.1

TOTAL WALKING TIME : 7.5 Hours

TOTAL HEIGHT GAINED
- 1140 Metres   3740 Feet

PRINCIPAL HEIGHTS	Metres	Feet
- Dow Crag	779	2555
- Coniston Old Man	803	2635
- Swirl How	802	2630
- Wetherlam	762	2502

OTHER FEATURES OF INTEREST
- Walna Scar Road, high level tarns and disused mineral mines.

17
THE CONISTON FELLS

Route 31 · Dow Crag, Coniston Old Man and Wetherlam

Allow 7½ hours

STARTING LOCATION
Coniston main car-park.
OLM 6/MR 304975.
Large car-park and coach park.
CMS bus route 505/506 – 'Coniston Rambler'.

OVERVIEW/INTEREST
Splendid high-level ridge walk.
Climbs 4 major peaks in the Coniston Fells.
Ascents well spaced out.
Vast mountain terrain with superb views.
Several entrapped corrie tarns.
Route particularly varied with some scrambling.

FOOTPATHS
Paths exceptionally good and obvious.
No appreciable erosion.
Rocky top soil well drained.
No significant wet or boggy patches.

The way to Dow Crag

Allow 3 hours

Turn L from the car-park past St Andrews Church. Cross the bridge and veer L along the A593, signed to 'Broughton and Ulverston'. Branch up the next lane on your R, signed 'Footpath to Old Man Walna Scar & Seathwaite'. You climb quite steeply, passing a footpath to the Miners' Bridge and Coppermines Valley. Then the lane bends first sharp L and then R, before it snakes up the more open fellside at a less demanding gradient. Along here views open up of the slopes leading up to Coniston Old Man, and the other high fells in this grouping to the NW. Look back over your R shoulder to see the high mountains to the NE, including Fairfield. On your L there is a glimpse of part of Coniston Water in the SE. Keep on gaining height along the Walna Scar road as gates, paths off, helpful signposts and old mine and quarry danger warnings come and go in rapid succession.

Pass the private road off to Bursting Stone Quarry on your R as the track reaches high moorland terrain down to the S. The irregular outline of Brown Pike lies ahead to the R in the WNW. This impressive fell marks the start of the ridge leading to Dow Crag. When further height is gained the high cove below Goat's Water comes into view on your R with a spectacular sighting of the high rocky crags, including Dow Crag, which cradle it with their steep, sheer, slopes to the W. Your path now veers NW as a massive cairn is reached to your L. At the junction of the ways take the lower L path, which leads off to the WSW.

Cross Cove Bridge, sometimes known as Torver Bridge, and continue W along the track. The slopes leading up to Coniston Old Man are revealed to the N as more of the high level cove comes into view. Looking back from here Ruskins' former home, the imposing white building of Brantwood, may be clearly identified standing on the slopes above the E shore of Coniston Water. Your path climbs, twisting up the steeper and more rocky ground of Goatfoot Crags, as the coastline appears down to your L in the SSW. At the top of the next shallower rise the top of the pass across the Walna Scar Ridge is reached. This is somewhat disappointingly marked by a pathetic, flattened cairn that you might be tempted to contribute to rebuilding. Continue over the crest of the brow for a short distance to observe the revealing views into the beautiful Duddon Valley to the W. The valley is protected by the mountains of Ulpha Fell WNW and the higher more pointed Harter Fell NW.

Turn uphill again and climb first NE to reach Brown Pike, and then NNE to scale the rocky slopes of Dow Crag. The views from the top of Brown Pike are impressive and the following features may be observed from here in clear weather:

SSE	Coniston Water and Morecambe Bay.
SSW	Duddon estuary.
WSW	The lower part of the Walna Scar Ridge.
W	Duddon Valley and Devoke Water.
WNW	Ulpha Fell.
NW	Harter Fell.
NNW	The Scafell Massif.
NNE	Buck Pike.
NE	Coniston Old Man.
E	Windermere.

From Brown Pike the cairned and well-trodden path descends NNE to the shallow hause before climbing to the next rocky pinnacle, that of Buck Pike. From here there is one final relentless climb and scramble over rocky ground, and then up between large volcanic boulders to reach the erratic summit of Dow Crag. Along this part of the route there are some magnificent views down over the dangerous R edge of the ridge to the dark, spectacularly deep gullies and plunging eroded rock faces that line the E flank of the spur. The tiny Blind Tarn may be spotted, so named because it has no visible exit stream. Further on, the much larger Goat's Water is visible in a really barren setting with large boulders randomly scattered near its outlet stream, which runs into Torver Beck.

The exciting scrambling on the summit of Dow Crag is carried out at 779 m (2,555 ft). You will recognize many of the impressive sightings from the summit, the new horizons and extended exposures are those of:

W	The Isle of Man (on exceptionally clear days).

31:1 Peering down at Goat's Water from the rocks of Dow Crag.

NNW	Bow Fell, Crinkle Crags and Glaramara.
N	Skiddaw.
NNE	Blencathra.
NE	Helvellyn group and Fairfield.
E	Coniston Old Man.
SW	Black Combe.

The way to Coniston Old Man   *Allow 1 hour*

Descend through the jumble of rocks to the NNE, following the line of the higher ground along the connecting ridge. Do not surrender height to your L (W to NW) but continue along the crest of the spur. Over on your R (ESE) you will observe a number of massive scree slopes, while ahead the profiles of Grey Friar NNW and Swirl How NNE loom up among lower outlines. In the far distance to the NNE the distinctive conical peaks of Pike of Blisco and to its R the Langdale Pikes are visible on a clear day.

The height of the band of rock diminishes as it bends to the R (NE), and then progressively further to the E as you reach Goat's Hawes. From here your way rises again in a broad sweep to attain the summit of Coniston Old Man. Be careful on the first part of the ascent from the col to keep to the L-hand main path, and on no account be tempted to strike off to the R too soon along the minor branch paths. Further up take the clear R fork ESE, which continues to climb through intermingled fixed boulders and looser stones to the band beyond.

This leads into a good, red, gravel path that traverses to the SE on an upwards diagonal at a reduced rate of climb. Your path converges on the main ridge route from the N, coming in above on your L. Turn R along this and walk southward to reach the summit of Coniston Old Man, a short distance above. This mountain stands at 803 m (2,635 ft) and is, by a couple of metres, the highest point of your route. It has a comfortable summit area centred on a large square of elevated stones. There is also a tall marker cairn, and on occasions, also meteorological measuring devices.

You will be familiar with most of the views to be seen from its commanding peak and these are therefore not recorded again in complete detail here. Suffice to mention that there are basically two types of panorama to be enjoyed from this lofty fell: in the S 180° segment, the mountains fall to the lower foothills that embrace Coniston Water, and beyond this the flatter lands of the Duddon Estuary; by contrast to the N, the encircling vast array of competing high peaks of every conceivable height, shape, form and colouring. Some features that are visible for the first time are Low Water, down below to the NE with copper sulphate deposits giving it a blue tinge, the peaks of High Raise NNE, the Fairfield Horseshoe NE and High Street and the associated eastern fells further away, also in the NE.

The way to Wetherlam   *Allow 2 hours*

Retrace your final approach steps along the ridge, this time to the NW. Do not, however, descend to Goat's Hawse, but continue along the broad, well-used, rock-strewn path that descends marginally in a wide curve to the N and your R. Further to your R, Windermere can be seen far away to the E. Nearer to, the mammoth ridges of Black Sails and Lad Stones, which lead to the summit of Wetherlam, come into view to the NE. Ahead of you lie the bulks of Little and Great How Crags a little to the R of the main spur along which you are walking. Below to the E, over the shoulder of the band, Levers Water shyly reveals itself.

A narrow col named Levers Hawse is next reached, and as you descend down to it, Seathwaite Tarn, comes into view to the W. Then the massive bulk of Grey Friar looms up in the NW, dominating and blocking all further sightings in that direction. The ground then rises again to Little How Crags to the NNE. When the higher Great How Crags are scaled, there is a revealing exposure of the narrow ridge, called Prison Band, leading down from Swirl How to connect with the route up to Wetherlam via Keld Gill Head to the NNE. Your path continues along Swirl Band, falling and rising over protruding hillocks as net height is gained, to reach the summit of Swirl How.

There is a large, distinctive, conical-shaped cairn on the top of Swirl How, which reaches a height of 802 m (2,630 ft). From this summit in the foreground the eroded rocky crag of Great Carrs can be seen NNW, and to the R of this, the sweeping great grassy band of Wet Side Edge takes the eye as it descends uniformly to Little Langdale Valley to the ENE. However, it is beyond these immediate features that the gaze must be focused N to take in the most magnificent array of high mountain peaks imaginable. The main summits in this extensive panorama are listed below, from L to R.

WNW	Hard Knott Crags.
NW	Scafell Range.
NNW	Crinkle Crags and Bow Fell.
N	Glaramara.
NNE	Pike of Blisco, with Skiddaw beyond; the Langdale Pikes; and High Raise and Sergeant Man, with Blencathra beyond.
NE	The Helvellyn and Fairfield ranges.

If this is not sufficient, the diminishing remains of a crashed aeroplane can be seen on the barren, inhospitable slopes to the NNW.

Leave Swirl How by Prison Band, a narrow, adventurous, rocky ridge that descends steeply to the E, following a phoney start ESE along a gently sloping, curving path. The descent is well cairned and the route follows the pinnacle ridge with several different ways down most of the short pitches. Some 200 m (yd) of height is surrendered in descending to Swirl Hawse at the bottom. The climb from this col starts with another steep rocky slope, now to the ENE, but this soon gives way to a traverse to the L along a comfortable gradient. Your way turns E along a narrow but well-defined stony path.

More agreeable traverses follow as height is gradually gained, before the summit of Wetherlam is reached. On the final approach Blea Tarn may be observed in the complicated valley system below to the NNE, with the crag of Side Pike strutting up behind the tarn.

Wetherlam has a height of 762 m (2,502 ft), but it does not have a really imposing summit area. The views from this peak are similar to those seen from the top of Swirl How, but with more extensive perspectives into the northerly and easterly fells. It must, however, be recorded that there are first sightings of Stickle Tarn N, and Elter Water ENE and of Ambleside protected by Wansfell Pike towering above it in the E. Also, significant mountain peaks to be observed for the first time include Grasmoor and Robinson NW.

The way back to Coniston   *Allow 1½ hours*

Leave the summit along the fairly level path to the SSE, making for a cairn ahead on the edge of the ridge towards Hen Crag. The established stone and grassy path then descends down a gradual gradient across the broad fellside, still maintaining a SSE direction. The path is dry to start with as height is lost at a comfortable rate along the broad grassy band. For the first time on the walk you will now have a clear view along the whole length of Coniston Water.

The path eventually turns to the L at a place marked by cairns, and for a time it then drops rapidly to the ENE, down terrain that does hold water. After this, your route swings back to the R, and it then descends by means of a number of tight zigzags, also marked by guiding cairns. A short traverse follows across the grassy fellside before the way turns down once more, bending to the SSE. Next there is another twist to the L down through the bracken as a small reeded tarn appears below to your L (ENE).

The narrow path then converges on a superior track, Hole Rake, coming over from Tilberthwaite. Turn R down this wider path and continue your descent to Church Beck below. There is a maze of alternatives awaiting your selection here. Keep descending in line with a row of dark slate cottages, and pass above these. The pathway leads down to the valley containing Church Beck and a pot-holed cart track. Turn L along this.

Follow the uneven cart track down into Coniston, ignoring a path off to the R crossing the beck at Miners' Bridge. The continuation of the track will lead you downhill to the main street of the village, opposite the post office and with the Black Bull Hotel to your R. Turn R along this shopping street and then L onto the B5285 back to the car-park.

Alternative routes

31:2 On the band to Swirl How from Coniston Old Man and Dow Crag.

ESCAPES

The two most convenient places to shorten the route are at either Goat's Hawse or Swirl Hawse. At Goat's Hawse, situated between Dow Crag and Coniston Old Man, turn R to the S and descend down the path that leads round the E side of Goat's Water back to the Walna Scar road. Turn L down this and retrace your outward route back into Coniston. From Swirl Hawse, the col situated between Swirl How and Wetherlam, take the path descending to the R, first SE and then S. This drops gradually past Levers Water and then continues on a SE diagonal to join up with the main route near to the row of cottages at Church Beck.

EXTENSIONS

Along the ridges there are several opportunities for further quick up and downs, e.g., from Goat's Hawse descend and have a closer look at Goat's Water; and from Swirl How continue along the ridge to the NW and take in Great Carrs.

One significant addition to this walk is from the summit of Wetherlam to descend to the NE along Wetherlam Edge, working to the R (E) in a semi-circle to Tilberthwaite. From here walk up by the gorge and take the Hole Rake route, which winds to the S, then SW to meet up with the main way coming down from Wetherlam at MR 293991.

TARN HOWS and TILBERTHWAITE
Lower Level Route 32

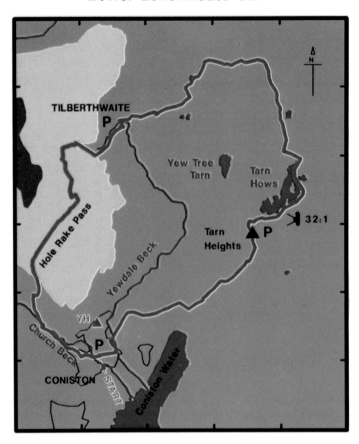

SOUTH-NORTH (Km)

TILBERTHWAITE
P

Yew Tree Tarn

Tarn Hows

Hole Rake Pass

Yewdale Beck

Tarn Heights
P
32:1

Church Beck

YH
P
START

CONISTON

Coniston Water

WEST-EAST (Km)

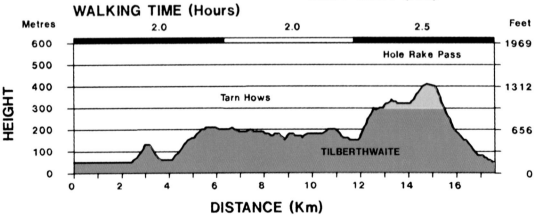

WALKING TIME (Hours)

| | 2.0 | | 2.0 | | 2.5 | |

Metres — Feet

Hole Rake Pass

Tarn Hows

TILBERTHWAITE

HEIGHT

DISTANCE (Km)

STATISTICS

START and FINISH
- Main Car Park, Coniston - OLM 6 / MR 304975

WALKING DISTANCE	Km	Miles
- Excluding Height	17.5	10.9
- Including Height	17.6	10.9

TOTAL WALKING TIME : 6.5 Hours

TOTAL HEIGHT GAINED
- 620 Metres   2034 Feet

PRINCIPAL HEIGHTS	Metres	Feet
- Tarn Heights	210	690
- Hole Rake Pass	410	1350

OTHER FEATURES OF INTEREST
- Tarn Hows, Hodge Close Quarries, gorge at Tilberthwaite, views of Wetherlam.

Route 32 · Tarn Hows and Tilberthwaite

Allow 6½ hours

STARTING LOCATION

Coniston main car-park.

OLM 6/MR 304975.

Large car and coach park.

CMS bus route 505/506 – 'Coniston Rambler'

OVERVIEW/INTEREST

Splendid walk with plenty of interesting sights.

Lush meadows, woodlands and farmsteads.

Contrasting high moorland area.

Tarn Hows, disused quarries at Hodge Close and Tilberthwaite Gorge.

Perfect route for family groups.

FOOTPATHS

Very good and supportive.

A virtual absence of boggy ground.

Clearly defined paths a joy to walk along.

No significant erosion.

The way to Tarn Hows

Allow 2 hours

From the car-park turn R along the B5285 away from the village centre. Turn L down the road signed 'Ambleside 7½'. There is already a prominent view of the Coniston Fells dominated by the Old Man up to your L, in the WNW. Opposite the school, turn R up the way signed 'Public Footpath'. Cross Yewdale Beck by Shepherd's Bridge and then turn sharp L over a stone stile.

Proceed along the narrow footpath leading imperceptibly uphill along the course of the stream. Cross a stile and make for the R of a gate and a stone wall ahead, walking at this stage NNE. Pass through a k-gate and continue along the now well-defined path leading uphill. A stone wall is breached next at a gateway where the route is marked with a white arrowhead. Look around here to observe Coniston Water down below to the S.

Walk uphill towards the extensive gorse thicket and then locate an indistinct path off to your R, which you need to follow. This is just before a faded marker post with a white-painted top. Pass

to the R of this. A narrow path is soon re-established and this tracks diagonally across the field to the E to reach a wooden stile in the stone wall to your R, which you climb over. A well-defined path, accompanied with white-topped marker posts, now ascends through Guards Wood.

The path then drops down a wide grassy way leading to Boon Crag Farm. Cross the p-stile and turn R along the gravel farm track, passing the farm buildings to your L. Then continue through the timber yard to reach, and turn L at the Coniston-to-Hawkshead road. Take the newly constructed footpath on your L which leads, after crossing a small culvert, to the single track road from Tarn Hows. Cross this road and proceed along a well-defined gravel path opposite that leads uphill into a forest area alongside a watercourse. The next part of the walk through the forest is delightful, and in this mixed woodland you will be able to identify many species of tree including larch, spruce, Scots pine, yew, beech, birch, hawthorn, hazel, oak and sycamore.

Follow this path for some distance as it ascends to cross the main stream on your R at a point where the ground levels off momentarily. Here veer to the L along a narrower and more attractive path, which traverses between trees up a grassy bank. This path leads to a wider forestry track, near the confluence of no less than three choices of ways uphill ahead to your L. Select the one furthest to the R, direction NNE. Some distance ahead pass a locked gate on your L and proceed further uphill to the N along a grassy path. Cross the wire fence on your L at the fast disappearing remains of a stile, which provides an exit from the enclosed forest area.

Make directly for the highest ridge ground on the R, and proceed along this, locating a grassy path that leads NNE. Go to the higher rocky outcrops in this area, which provide splendid viewing

Overleaf   *32:1 Tarn Hows bathed in early morning sunshine – Wetherlam in the background.*

platforms, particularly back down along Coniston Water to the SW, and of the massive easterly slopes of the Coniston Fells. The single track road bordering Tarn Hows to the S comes into view ahead on your R, make for this and then turn R along it.

The views of Tarn Hows from the heights above are very agreeable, and the combination of the shape of the tarn with its inlets and islands, surrounded by and infested with tall coniferous trees, against the more distant mountain background, makes an irresistibly photogenic setting. These relatively low crags above Tarn Hows also provide revealing views of more distant mountains and the following peaks and features may be identified:

SW	Coniston Water.
WSW	Coniston Old Man.
NW	Wetherlam.
NNW	Langdale Pikes and Sergeant Man.
NNE	Helvellyn group and Fairfield.
NE	Red Screes.
ENE	High Street, Froswick, Ill Bell and Wansfell Pike

Go down to the tarn to your R, to gain access to the pathways that circumnavigate the water. After passing through a k-gate with an unnecessarily powerful spring, at a fork ahead take the L, lower path, which follows more closely the E shore-line of the tarn. Your narrowing path continues along the water's edge and eventually rejoins the main wider path you recently left. At this point turn L and cross the wooden footbridge round the N shore of the tarn. Pass through a further k-gate and as the path swings progressively to the L take the second gravel track off on your R to the N.

The way to Tilberthwaite   *Allow 2 hours*

You are now walking along part of the Cumbria Way, and here the route is to the N and then NNE. The path leads to a gate and l-stile, which gives entry to a broad, walled track down which you turn L. After some distance a metalled lane is reached, turn L downhill to reach the A593 Coniston-to-Ambleside road below at Arnside Cottage. Cross the main road on a diagonal and select the narrow,

metalled track leading uphill and signed 'High Oxen Fell' NNW.

On reaching the top of the brow, more fine sights are revealed, down into Little Langdale Valley to the W, including Lingmoor Fell NW, Pike of Blisco WNW, and to the R majestic Bow Fell appears NW. The peaks of Rossett Pike and Glaramara to the NNW and Sergeant Man to the N complete this fine picture. The track continues in the direction of Wetherlam to the WSW. Pass through High Oxen Fell Farm, and after several gates continue along the main path that winds uphill to the W.

Your way undulates for some distance, but just before a second small reeded tarn is reached by the R side of the track, and with the buildings of Hodge Close visible through the trees ahead, turn L through a gate and proceed along a broad grassy pathway SSW. There are slate spoils here on your L and a wire fence to your R. Soon, glimpses of the spectacular remains of disused quarries can be observed to your R, near Hodge Close. These abandoned workings contain deep holes with interconnecting tunnels that are now submerged. This provides a mecca for experienced divers, however these black waters are exceedingly dangerous and unfortunately contain the remains of at least one female diver who met with an accident there and whose body has never been recovered.

Your route continues S, but first make a short detour by passing through a gate in the fence to your R, to obtain an unrestricted view into the disused quarry to your R. Retrace your footsteps to the track leading off S, and after going through two gates veer to the R along the main path adjacent to a wall. Ignore several branch paths leading uphill to your L. At the end of the pleasant descent traverse, with an extensive view of the E flank of Wetherlam in view across the valley to the W, turn sharply to the R to reach the road at Holme Ground, down which you turn L.

Select the next track off on your R, signed 'Public Footpath High Tilberthwaite'. Prior to reaching the farm gate, take the rocky path off L signed 'The National Trust Path to Tilberthwaite Car Park'. After crossing rough, wooded fellside, pass through a k-gate and follow the stony bank of Yewdale Beck to the road ahead WNW. Turn L along the road and cross the stream by the imposing bridge to arrive at Tilberthwaite car-park on your R.

The way back to Coniston

Allow 2½ hours

Climb the steps at the lower end of the car-park and turn R along the footpath that winds up the fellside quite steeply through slate spoils. The way soon opens out into more agreeable landscapes and a typical hill climb follows along a path that snakes up the fellside to the SE. Just beyond the opening to a disused quarry situated further up the hillside, at a point where the main path levels off, take the higher narrower path to the L that climbs S up the fell. There is a most impressive deep gorge in the recesses to your R with a small stream, Yewdale Beck, flowing down over boulders at the bottom of its deep void. Above on the R and to the W is the north aspect of Wetherlam, its huge bulk obliterating any further views in that direction.

A short scramble across a narrow gully follows, and beyond this continue along the main stony path to your L, but which then veers R. The track edges round the slope of the fell, and at the division of the ways ahead take the L fork. Your path climbs gradually to the L (S) and a small meandering stream cuts a depression below to your R. Make for the higher ground here by bearing further to your L up the grassy slope. A good path then traverses the fellside at a fairly constant height. The way winds round the fellside in a long, sweeping curve to the R as it rises to reach the pass between Furnace Fells and Yewdale Fells.

At the top there is a good view of Coniston Old Man to the SW. A narrow, reeded tarn is passed down on your R as you walk along Hole Rake. Your final descent starts here, as the distant coastline comes into view in the SSW.

A row of dark, slate-clad cottages appear below as your path loses its separate identity in a maze of alternative ways down. Descend along those of your own choosing, but pass above the cottages to reach the valley track below, and turn L.

The wide, rutted track follows the course of Church Beck. Cross the stream at the arched Miners' Bridge, and then turn L, following the established pathways down into Coniston. Pass the Sun Hotel and then follow the lane down into the village and the car-park situated off the B5285 road.

Alternative routes

ESCAPES

You can spend a lazy day in the vicinity of Tarn Hows if you like. A pleasant alternative return route from the tarn is to descend along the path at the side of the outlet stream, situated at the SW corner of the tarn, to the A593 road below at MR 322998. Turn L there and walk along the road the short distance to High Yewdale. Then turn L along the footpath to Low Yewdale. At this location you can use part of the Cumbria Way Footpath to reach Coniston.

EXTENSIONS

The described route does not lend itself to major additions unless you are prepared to resort to significant further strenuous climbing. Should this appeal to you, the obvious extension is to climb to the summit of Wetherlam. This is best achieved at MR 300006 by selecting the path off to the R, crossing the beck, and climbing by way of Birk Fell Man and Wetherlam Edge along the circuitous paths that lead to the top of this fine mountain. Return to the prescribed route at MR 293991 by descending along the spur of Hen Crag and Lad Stones, to the S from the summit of Wetherlam.

Appendix 1: Relevant Addresses

Introduction

There are many reference books that provide comprehensive facts and general information about the English Lake District. This Appendix is therefore confined to presenting a list of relevant contact addresses and telephone numbers.

It is perhaps worth mentioning that the Lake District National Park publish a comprehensive series of Information Fact Sheets, which are issued free of charge. These cover such subjects as The National Parks, Tourism, Land Use, Conservation, Design, Climate, Geology, Mining and Quarrying, Hill Farming, Employment and data on several of the larger towns and villages. Copies of these fact sheets may be obtained from either Blencathra Centre or Brockhole.

Relevant contact addresses and telephone numbers

Address	Telephone number
BROWNS COACHES Market Place Ambleside Cumbria LA22 9BU	05394 2205
CUMBERLAND MOTOR SERVICES LTD (CMS) Tangier Street Whitehaven Cumbria CA28 7XF	0946 63222 and 0539 733221
CUMBRIA TOURIST BOARD Ashleigh Holly Road Windermere Cumbria LA23 2AQ	05394 44444

ENGLISH HERITAGE North Office Carlisle Castle Carlisle CA3 8UR	0228 31777
FELL BUS 25 Manor Park Keswick Cumbria CA12 4AB	07687 72403

FORESTRY COMMISSION

GRISEDALE VISITOR CENTRE South Lakes Forest District Grisedale Ambleside Cumbria LA22 0QJ	0229 860373
WHINLATTER VISITOR CENTRE Braithwaite Keswick Cumbria CA12 5TW	07687 78469

LAKE DISTRICT NATIONAL PARK

BLENCATHRA CENTRE Threlkeld Keswick Cumbria (Park management and visitor services)	07687 79601
BROCKHOLE VISITOR CENTRE Windermere Cumbria LA23 1JL (Park management and visitor services)	05394 46601
LAKE DISTRICT SPECIAL PLAN- NING BOARD Busher Walk Kendal Cumbria LA9 4RH (Administration and planning)	0539 724555

Right: *Buttermere, Crummock Water and the surrounding fells.*

TOURIST INFORMATION CENTRES	
Bowness Bay	05394 42895
Coniston	05394 41533
Grasmere	05394 35245
Hawkshead	05394 86525
Keswick	07687 72803
Pooley Bridge	07684 86530
Seatoller Barn	07687 77294
Ullswater	07684 82414
Waterhead	05394 32729
WEATHER LINE	05394 45151
	(24-hour)

MOUNTAIN GOAT   05394 45161
Victoria Street
Windermere
Cumbria LA23 1AD

MOUNTAIN RESCUE SERVICE
999 EMERGENCY

NATIONAL TRUST   05394 35599
The Hollens
Grasmere
Ambleside
Cumbria LA22 9QZ

NORTH WEST WATER AUTHORITY   0539 740066
Mintsfeet Road South
Kendal
Cumbria
LA9 4BY

TELETOURIST EVENT LINE   05394 46363

YMCA   05395 31758
National Centre
Lakeside
Ulverston LA1Z 8BD

YOUTH HOSTELS ASSOCIATION   091 221 2101
D Floor
Milburn House
Dean Street
Newcastle-upon-Tyne NE1 1LF

Appendix 2: Statistical Summary

This appendix comprises a statistical summary with the routes listed
in numerical sequence within high and lower categorizations.

HIGH-LEVEL ROUTES

Route	Description	Walking time	Walking distance (excluding height)		Total height gained		Highest peak	
		hours	km	miles	metres	feet	metres	feet
1	Skiddaw	7.0	14.5	9.0	980	3215	931	3053
3	Blencathra	5.5	12.9	8.0	900	2953	868	2847
5	Grasmoor and Grisedale Pike	7.0	17.1	10.6	1270	4167	852	2791
7	Dale Head, Hindscarth and Robinson	7.0	18.7	11.6	1190	3904	753	2473
9	Hay Stacks and High Stile Group	7.5	17.8	11.0	1020	3346	806	2644
11	Pillar and Red Pike	9.0	21.1	13.1	1650	5413	892	2927
13	Burnmoor Tarn and Sca Fell	7.0	18.0	11.2	940	3084	964	3162
15	Scafell Pike and Bow Fell	8.0	18.6	11.5	1290	4232	978	3210
17	Great Gable and Glaramara	8.0	17.7	11.0	1380	4528	899	2949
19	Crinkle Crags and Bow Fell	7.0	16.0	9.9	1290	4232	902	2960
21	Sergeant Man and the Langdale Pikes	7.0	16.0	9.9	1090	3576	736	2414
23	Helvellyn	7.0	16.1	10.0	1230	4035	950	3118
25	Fairfield Horseshoe	6.5	16.9	10.5	940	3084	873	2863
27	High Street and Red Screes	8.0	19.1	11.9	1260	4134	828	2718
29	Kentmere Horseshoe	8.0	20.2	12.6	1080	3543	784	2569
31	Dow Crag, Coniston OM and Wetherlam	7.5	17.5	10.9	1140	3740	803	2635
		117.0	278.2	172.7	18650	61186	13819	45333

LOWER-LEVEL ROUTES

Route	Description	Walking time	Walking distance (excluding height)		Total height gained		Highest peak	
		hours	km	miles	metres	feet	metres	feet
2	Bleaberry Fell and High Seat	6.5	14.7	9.2	700	2300	608	1995
4	High Rigg and St John's	5.5	15.3	9.5	510	1673	357	1163
6	Thornthwaite Forest and Lord's Seat	5.5	13.5	8.4	700	2297	552	1811
8	Hause Gate and Grange Crags	5.0	13.3	8.3	430	1411	365	1198
10	Mosedale and Crummock Water	5.5	15.2	9.5	440	1444	305	1000
12	Ennerdale	5.0	15.3	9.5	240	787	270	885
14	Eskdale and Harter Fell	7.0	17.7	11.0	750	2461	653	2140
16	Pike of Blisco and Blea Tarn	5.0	10.2	6.3	690	2264	705	2304
18	Watendlath and Lodore	5.5	15.1	9.4	510	1673	330	1080
20	Lingmoor Fell and Side Pike	4.5	11.5	7.2	570	1870	469	1530
22	Silver How and Rydal	5.0	12.5	7.8	540	1770	394	1292
24	Ullscarth and Dead Pike	6.0	13.1	8.2	700	2297	726	2370
26	Wansfell Pike and Troutbeck	5.0	11.3	7.0	560	1837	484	1581
28	Boredale and Ullswater	5.0	13.2	8.2	460	1509	400	1310
30	Lower Kentmere	6.5	18.0	11.2	540	1772	440	1440
32	Tarn Hows and Tilberthwaite	6.5	17.5	10.9	620	2034	410	1350
		89.0	227.4	141.6	8960	29399	7468	24449

OVERALL SUMMARY OF BOTH HIGH-LEVEL AND LOWER-LEVEL ROUTES

Description	Walking time	Walking distance (excluding height)		Total height gained		Highest peak	
	hours	km	miles	metres	feet	metres	feet
16 High-Level Walks	117.0	278.2	172.7	18650	61186	13819	45333
16 Lower-Level Walks	89.0	227.4	141.6	8960	29399	7468	24449
	206.0	505.6	314.3	27610	90585	21287	69782

	%	%	%	%	%	%	%
16 High-Level Walks	57	55	55	68	68	65	65
16 Lower-Level Walks	43	45	45	32	32	35	35
	100	100	100	100	100	100	100

Publisher's Acknowledgements

The publishers are grateful to the author for granting permission to reproduce all the colour photographs.

The plans included in the route diagrams are based upon information extracted from Ordnance Survey Outdoor Leisure Maps of The English Lakes, scale 1 : 25000, with the permission of Her Majesty's Stationery Office © Crown copyright. The route diagrams themselves were made by the author in collaboration with Dr. William Rouse.

INDEX

Page numbers in *italic* refer to the illustrations

Aaron Slack, 101, 103
Alcock Tarn, 144, 147
Allen Crags, 90, 91, 95, 101, 102
Ambleside, 147, 149, 151, 167,
    178
Angle Tarn, 90, 92, 102, 114, 115,
    154, 159
Anglers Crag, 75, 76
Applethwaite, 16
Ashness Bridge, 22, 23

Band, The, 111, 115, 118
Barf, 40, *44–5*, 46, 47
Bassenthwaite Lake, 20, 37, 43,
    44–5, 46, 49, 55, 138
Beckstones, 43
Bell Crags, 63
Binka Stone, 137
Black Sail Pass, 51, 70, 177
Blea Crags, 51
Blea Rigg, 121, 124, 125
Blea Tarn, 95–7, *97*, 111, 118, 119,
    123, 138, 178
Blea Water, 154, 165
Bleaberry Fell, 19–21, 22, 25
Bleaberry Tarn, 63, 67, 73
Blease Fell, 17, 31
Blencathra, 14, 17, 20, 25–31, *26–7*,
    30–1, 33, 37, 38, 49, *52–3*, 55,
    62, 90, 91, 100, 138, 154
Boredale, 159–61
Borrowdale, *15*, 50, 55–6, 101, 102,
    105, 109, 138, 161
Bow Fell, 20, 39, 46, 50, 83, 89–93,
    90, 95, 102, 111–15, *115*, 118,
    118, 122, 143, 144, 154, 184
Bowness Knott, 76, 77
Braithwaite, 37
Broad Crag, 91, 93
Broom Fell, 46
Brothers Water, 153, 156, 157, 159
Browfoot, 172
Brown Pike, 175, 176
Browncove Crags, 135
Brownrigg Moss, 140, 141
Brund Fell, 109
Burnmoor Tarn, 70, 79–81
Buttermere, 39, 51, 59, 60, *60–1*,
    61, 62, *62*, 63, 65, 67, 69, *70*,
    73, 100
Buttermere Lake, 39, 40, 59–60, 63,
    65, 100

Capell Crag, 102

Carl Side, 16
Castlehead Crag, 19
Castlerigg Stone Circle, *34*, 35
Cat Bells, 20, 38, 49, *50*, 55
Catstye Cam, 132, 144, 153, 159,
    165
Causey Pike, 20, 25, 33, 37, 38–9,
    46, 49, 55, 57, 62
Cockley Beck Bridge, *86–7*
Cofa Pike, 144, 147
Coledale Hause, 39, 40, 41
Combe Head, 102
Coniston, 178, 181, 185
Coniston Fells, 81, 91, 95, 96, 113,
    122, 123, 131, 140, 144, 154,
    172, 175–85
Coniston Old Man, 81, 96, 122,
    175–9, *179*, 181, 185
Coniston Water, 122, 175, 177,
    178, 181, 184
Crag Fell, 71, 75
Crag Hill, 20, 25, 39, 40, 41, *41*, 62,
    90
Crinkle Crags, 83, 89, 91, *93*, 95,
    111–15, *112–13*, *115*, 118, 122,
    143, 144
Crummock Water, 39, 51, 59, 60,
    63, 65–7, 69, 100
Cumbria Way, 53, 57, 119, 184,
    185

Dale Head, 25, 38, 49–51, 65, 70,
    90–1, 100, 102, 105, 108
Dalegarth, 79, 81
Dead Pike, 137–41
Deepdale, 145
Deepdale Hause, 144
Derwent Water, 19, 20, *20–1*, 22,
    23, 38, 39, 43, 46, 49, *52–3*,
    55, 56, *56*, 57, 91, 102, 108,
    138
Dock Tarn, 109, 138
Dove Crag (Fairfield), *146*, 147, 157
Dove Crags (Grasmoor), 40
Dovedale, 157
Dow Crag, 81, 84, 113, 122, 175–9,
    176, *179*
Dubbs Reservoir, 151, 169–72
Duddon Valley, 84, 176
Dunnerdale Forest, 84, 87

Eagle Crag, 138
Easedale, 121, 124, 144
Eel Crags, 39, 41, 50

Elter Water, 122, 127, 178
Elterwater, 117, 119, 128, 144
Ennerdale, 62, 63, 70, 71, 72, 73,
    73, 75–7, *76–7*, 100
Esk Hause, 90, 92, *100*, 101–2, 103,
    114, 115
Esk Pike, 39, 90, 91, 102, 114, 115,
    122
Eskdale, 79, 81, 83–7, *85*

Fairfield, 117, 121, 124, 127, 132,
    138, 154, 161, 175
Fairfield Horseshoe, 122, 143–7,
    149, 153, 165, 177
Falcon Crag, 22, 23
Fleetwith Pike, 51, 59, 60, *62*, 63,
    65, 70
Friar's Crag, 23
Froswick, 145, 163, *164*, 165, 169

Garburn Pass, 165, 167, 169, 173
Gasgale Crags, 40, 41
Gibson Knott, 141
Gillercomb Head, 100
Gimmer Crag, 125
Glaramara, 49, 50, 90, 95, 99–103,
    103, 105, 109, 123, 184
Goat's Hawse, 177, 179
Goat's Water, 175, 176, *176*, 179
Grange Crags, 55–7
Grange Fell, 57
Grange-in-Borrowdale, 56–7
Grasmere, 121, 124, 127, 128–9,
    129, 140, 144, 147
Grasmoor, 37–41, *41*, 60, 65, 66,
    69, 90, 123, 178
Great Borne, 71, 75, 76
Great Carrs, 178, 179
Great End, 71, 90, 91, 93, 101, 105,
    109, 115 122
Great Gable, 50, 70, 80, 90,
    99–103, *100*, 105, 122, 138,
    154
Great Knott, 89, *93*, 95, 111, 113,
    115
Great Langdale Valley, 95, *97*, 111,
    115, 117, 118, 119, 122, 124,
    128, *151*
Great Rigg, 144
Green Gable, 70, 90, 100, *100*, 101,
    154
Greenup, *106–7*, 138, 140
Grey Friar, 81, 84, 177

Grisedale, 121, 132, 159
Grisedale Pike, 20, *20–1*, 33, 37–41, *41*, 43, 46, 47, 49, 90, 102, 123
Gutherscale, 51, 55, 57

Hall's Fell Ridge, 25, 29, *30–1*, 31
Harrison Stickle, 90, 95, 96, 122–4, 125, 131
Harrop Tarn, 137, *139*
Hart Crag, 144, 145–7, 157
Harter Fell, 71, 79, 83–7, *86–7*, 91, 154, 165, *166–7*, 172, 176
Hartsop, 153, 157, 159, 161
Hartsop above How, 147, 153, 157
Hause Gate, 53, 55–7
Haweswater, 154, *155*, 165, *166–7*
Hay Stacks, 51, 59–63, *60–1*, 65, 70, 100
Hayeswater, 153, *157*
Helm Crag, 121, 124, 127, 128, 140, 141
Helvellyn, 20, 28, 33, *24*, 38, 43, 46, 49–50, 91, 102, 117, 121, 124, 131–5, *133*, *134*, 138, 144, 153, 154, 159, 165
Heron Pike, 127, 143–4, *145*, 147
High Crag, 59, 61–2, 65, 70, 80, 138
High Gillerthwaite, 75, 77
High Rigg, 25, 33–5, *34*
High Seat, 21–2, 56
High Snab Bank, 51
High Spy, 49, 50, 53, 57, 105
High Stile, 39, 49, 59–63, *62*, 65, 70, 73, 75, 76, 80, 91, 100
High Street, 29, 117, 132, 147, 153–7, 163, 165, 167, 177
Hindscarth, 20, 25, 39, 49–53, 55, 60, 70, 100
Honister, *62*, 63
Hopegill Head, 40, 41, 46, 47
Horn Crag, 81

Ill Bell, 145, 163, *164*, 165, 169
Ill Crag, 91, 93

Jack's Rake, 122–3, *123*, 124, 125, *125*
Jenkins Crag, 150–1

Kentmere, 169–73, *170–1*
Kentmere Horseshoe, 163–7, *164*, 169, 172
Keswick, 13, 19, 20, 46
Kidsty Pike, 165, 167
Kirkstone Pass, 147, 156, 157, 159
The Knott, 153, 154, 167

Langdale Pikes, 49, 89, 90, 95, 96, 102, *103*, 111, 114, 117, 118, *118*, 121–5, 131, 143, 144, 177
Lingmell, 101

Lingmoor Fell, 89, 97, 111, 117–19, 122, *125*, 184
Lingmoor Tarn, 119
Little Dodd, 77
Little Langdale Valley, 96, 97, 111, 117, 178, 184
Little Man, 14, 17
Lodore Falls, 105–9
Longside Edge, 14, 16, 17, *17*
Lord's Rake, 80, 81, 93
Lord's Seat, 40, 43–7
Loughrigg Fell, 129, 140, 144
Loughrigg Terrace, 128, 129
Low Birker Tarn, 83–4
Lower Kentmere, 169–73, *170–1*
Lower Man, 135
Loweswater, 40, 51, 63, 66, 67

Maiden Moor, 25, 39, *41*, 49–50, 55, 57, 105
Mardale Ill Bell, 154, 165
Mediobogdum, 81, 85
Mellbreak, 51, 59, 65, 66, 67
Mickleden, 89, 92, 111, 114, 118
Millbeck, 14–16
Mosedale, 65–7, 79
Mosedale Horseshoe, 70, 80, 83, 91

Nab Scar, 143
Nan Bield Pass, 165, 167
Nethermost Cove, 132
Newlands Valley, 37–8, 39, 49, 55, 62, 90
Nitting Haws, 53

Old Dungeon Ghyll Hotel, 89, 95, 96–7, 111, 115
Ore Gap, 90, 92, 114
Oxendale, 95, 111, 115, 118

Patterdale, 134, 144, 147, 159, *160–1*, 161
Pavey Ark, 90, 96, 122, 123, 124, 125, *125*
Piers Gill, 101
Pike of Blisco, 89, 95–7, 111–13, 114, 115, 118, 123, 144, 177, 184
Pike of Stickle, 49, 89, 90, 95, 122, 123, 125
Pillar, 51, 60, 69–73, *73*, 75, 76, 79, 83, 90, 91, 100, 154
Place Fell, 159, 161
Prison Band, 177, 178

Rannerdale Knotts, 67
Raven Crag, 102
Red Bank, 127–8, 129
Red Pike, 25, 59, 63, 65, 66, 67, 69–73, 75, 76, 77, 79
Red Screes, 144, 145, 153–7, 165, 169
Red Tarn, 95, 113, 115, 132

Riggindale Crag, 154, *155*, 165
Robinson, 20, 25, 39, 49–53, 55, 60, 65, 70, 100, 178
Rosthwaite, 105, 109
Rowling End, 38, 39, 49, 55
Rydal, 127–9, 143, 147
Rydal Water, 122, 124, 128, 144

Sail, *38*, 39, *41*, 62, 123
St John's, 33–5
St Raven's Edge, 156
St Sunday Crag, 132, 144, 159, 161
Sand Hill, 40, 41
Sca Fell, 70, 79–81, *80*, 83, *85*, 93
Scafell Crag, 80
Scafell Group, 46, 50, 71, 83, 100, 102, 115, 154
Scafell Pike, 71, 81, 89–93, *90*, 103, 109, 115
Scafell Ridge, 101, 102, 109, 122
Scale Force, 63, 65, 67, *67*
Scales Fell, 28, 29, 31
Scales Tarn, *26–7*, 28, 29, 31
Scandale Pass, 156, 157
Scarth Gap, 60, 61, 63, 70, 73
Seathwaite, 103, 105
Seatoller, 99, 102, 103, 105, 109
Sergeant Man, 90, 117, 121–2, 128, 144, 184
Sharp Edge, *26–7*, 28, 29, 31
Side Pike, 89, 95, 97, 111, 117–19, *118*, 122, 178
Silver Bay, 161
Silver How, 117, 124, 127–9
Skelgill Bank, 49
Skiddaw, 13–17, *15*, *17*, 19, 20, 29, 31, 33, 37, 43, 46, 49, *52–3*, 55, 62, 70, 91, 100, 154
Sleet How, 40
Slight Side, 81, 83, *85*
Sour Howes, 173
Sourmilk Gill, 65, 67, 69, 73, 121
Sprinkling Tarn, 101
Standing Crag, 131, 137, 138, 140
Starling Dodd, 76, 77
Steel Fell, 131, 137, 140, 141
Steeple, 71, 73, 75, 76
Stickle Tarn, 122, *123*, 124–5, *125*, 178
Stockghyll Force, 149
Stonethwaite, *106–7*, 138
Stony Cove Pike, 155, 172
Striding Edge, 28, 131–2, 134–5, *134*, 144, 153
Sty Head, 103
Styhead Tarn, 101, 103
Swirl Hawse, 178, 179
Swirl How, 81, 96, 122, 177–8, 179, *179*
Swirral Edge, 132, 135, 153, 159
Symonds Knott, 80

Tarn Hows, 181–5, *182–3*
Thirlmere, 22, 29, 34, 56, 131, *133*,
    137, 138, *139*, 140
Thirlspot, 135
Thornthwaite Crag, 154, 155, 156,
    163, 165, 167, 172
Thornthwaite Forest, 43–7
Thornythwaite Fell, 102
Three Tarns, 92, 114
Threlkeld, 25, 33
Threshthwaite Mouth and Crag,
    155, 157
Tilberthwaite, 179, 181–5
Troutbeck, 149–51, 169, 172

Ullock Pike, 14, 17, *17*
Ullscarf, 131, 137–41
Ullswater, 132, 155, 156, 159–61
Ulpha Fell, 71, 79, 84, 176

Walna Scar, 84, 175–6, 179
Wansfell Pike, 144, 149–51, *151*,
    156, 167, 169, 178
Wasdale, 79, 80, 101
Wast Water, 70, 80
Watendlath, 23, 105–9
Wetherlam, *93*, 96, 117, 122, 127,
    175–9, *182–3*, 184, 185
Whinlatter Pass, 37, 43, 47
Whiteless Pike, 65, 67, 70

Windermere, Lake, 96, 117, 122,
    128, 140, 144, 151, 154, 155,
    156, 164, 167, 169, 177
Windy Gap, 101, 103
Wordsworth, William, 128, 129,
    143
Wrynose Bridge, 96
Wythburn, 131, 135, 137

Yewbarrow, 70, 79
Yewdale, 185
Yoke, 145, 154, *164*, 169